*UFOs, Aliens and M[ysteries]
Incredible Truth B[ehind UFOs]
and Strange Events:*

Author: Michael Arrow

Foreword

Welcome to a fascinating journey through the world of curious facts and astonishing stories! In this book, we take you on an exploration of the strangest, most surprising, and most unbelievable occurrences from history, science, nature, and culture. Whether they are historical curiosities, mystical events, lucky coincidences, or simply amazing, useless knowledge, this book is designed to quench your thirst for knowledge and awaken your curiosity.

In a world constantly striving forward and making new discoveries, it's sometimes worthwhile to take a step back and be inspired by the curious and often unbelievable stories of our past. The collection before you is a mix of humorous, educational, and sometimes downright quirky facts and stories that are intended not only to bring a smile to your face but also to broaden your horizons.

From historical coincidences that changed the world, to incredible scientific discoveries that are hard to believe, to mystical events that remain mystifying to this day, this book has something for everyone. Sit back, relax, and be amazed by the diversity and wonder of the world.

Note: This book was also created with the help of modern artificial intelligence (AI), which specializes in compiling and processing information from a variety of freely accessible sources.

Therefore, it's possible that the grammar and writing style may take a back seat to the engaging content. The goal was to provide an entertaining and educational read that quenches your thirst for knowledge and piques your curiosity.

Enjoy reading.

Michael Arrow

Contents

UFOs, Aliens and Mysteries - The Incredible Truth Behind UFOs and Strange Events: ___1

Chapter 1: Historical Curiosities ___9

    1.1. The Apple That Changed the World: Isaac Newton and Gravity ___9

    1.2. The man who died several times: The mystery of Grigori Rasputin ___13

    1.3. The assassination attempt that triggered the First World War ___16

    1.4. The Incredible Escape from Alcatraz ___19

    1.5. The secret codes of the Navajo Indians in World War II ___22

    1.6 The Dance Plague of 1518 ___25

    1.7 The Vanished Colony of Roanoke ___27

    1.8. The Rain of Blood of 1916 in India ___30

    1.9. The London Coach Dispute ___32

    1.10 The Boston Molasses Disaster ___34

    1.11 The Stockholm Massacre ___36

    1.12 The Augsburg Calendar Dispute ___39

    1.13 The Artichoke War ___41

    1.14. The Dutch Tulip Mania ___43

    1.15. The counterfeit fraudster Alves dos Reis ___46

    1.16. The Soldier Bear Wojtek ___48

Chapter 2: Scientific Wonders ___50

    2.1. The discovery of DNA by a lucky coincidence ___50

    2.2. The mystery of dark matter ___53

    2.3. The incredible abilities of tardigrades ___55

    2.4. The infinite number: The paradox of Pi ___57

2.5. The Placebo Effect: How Faith Can Move Mountains ___ 59

2.6. The mysterious "Wow!" signal ___ 61

2.7. The formation of jellyfish inside icebergs ___ 63

2.8 The discovery of water on Mars ___ 65

2.9. CRISPR-Cas9 genetic engineering / molecular scissors ___ 67

2.10 The Brain – A Miracle of Nature ___ 69

2.11. The Antikythera Mechanism: A Mystery from Antiquity ___ 73

2.12. The Pavlov Experiment: The Discovery of Conditioning by a Drooling Dog ___ 75

2.13 The iron lung – a breathing device between fear and hope 79

Chapter 3: Mystical Events ___ *81*

3.1. The Bermuda Triangle: Myths and Facts ___ 81

3.2. The eerie ghost ships of the seas ___ 85
    Die „Carroll A. Deering" ___ 88
    The "Tai Ching 2" ___ 91
    Die „Baychimo" ___ 94

3.3. The Mystery of Loch Ness: Does the Monster Really Exist? ___ 96

3.4. The Prophecies of Nostradamus ___ 99

3.5. The mysterious crop circles: Messages from space? ___ 102

3.6 The Dyatlov Pass Incident ___ 104

3.7 The Tunguska Event ___ 108

3.8. The mystery of the ship "SS Ourang Medan" ___ 110

3.9 The Philadelphia Experiment ___ 111

3.10. El Dorado: The Lost City of Gold ___ 113

3.11. Encounters with unknown underwater objects ___ 115
    The K-222 Encounter ___ 115
    The Lake Baikal Encounters ___ 117
    The Shag Harbour Sightings ___ 119

Chapter 4: Incredible Coincidences ___ *121*

4.1. The Titanic and the fictional ship Titan: An eerie prediction ___ 121

4.2. The story of the two Kennedys: coincidence or fate? ___ 124

    The man who was struck by lightning seven times _____126

    4.4. The Incredible Coincidence by Edgar Allan Poe _____128

    4.5 The two hurricanes that hit the same village – exactly 100 years apart_____128

    4.6. The twin brothers and their parallel lives_____129

    4.7 The Incredible Survival of Violet Jessop _____131

    4.8. The incredible survival story of Juliane Koepcke _____133

    4.9. The lottery winner: Bill Morgan_____135

    4.10 The Savior in Need_____136

Chapter 5: Curiosities from Nature_____137

    5.1. The strangest animals in the world: From the axolotl to the naked mole rat _____137

    5.2. The tree that bears 40 fruits _____139

    5.3. The mysterious singing sand dunes _____142

    5.4. The Wandering Rocks in Death Valley _____143

    5.5. The immortal jellyfish organism_____145

    5.6. The case of the "pig cloud" in Australia _____147

    5.7. The "Zone of Silence" in Mexico _____148

    5.8. The Taos Hum _____150

    5.9. frozen birds_____152

    5.10 The phenomenon of "green flashes" _____153

    5.11 The Legend of the Kraken _____154

    5.12 The Bombardier Beetle: A Walking Flamethrower _____156

    5.13. The Secret of Carmine – Red from a Louse _____157

Chapter 6: Myths, Monsters, Cryptozoology _____159

    6.1. The Yeti – The Snowman of the Himalayas _____159

    6.2. The Best of Gévaudan _____162

    6.3. The Legend of the Living Dinosaur in the Congo: Mokele-Mbembe _____165

    6.4 The Legend of the Dogman in Michigan _____167

6.5 Discovery of Denisovans _____ 169

6.6. Bigfoot _____ 171

6.7. The legends of the Mongolian death worm _____ 174

6.8. The Legend of the Mothman _____ 176

6.9 The Legend of the Goatman _____ 179

6.10. Sightings of humanoids in Brazil _____ 181

6.11 The Lizard Man _____ 183

6.12 The Green Children of Woolpit _____ 186

Chapter 7: Happy coincidences and inventions _____ 188

7.1 The discovery of penicillin _____ 188

7.2. How Velcro was invented by a dog _____ 191

7.3. The origins of Coca-Cola _____ 193

7.4 The coincidence that led to Post-it Notes _____ 195

7.5. The history of potato chips _____ 195

7.6 The discovery of vulcanized rubber _____ 197

7.8 The discovery of the microwave _____ 198

7.9. The discovery of the color Prussian Blue _____ 200

7.10 The invention of cornflakes _____ 201

7.11 The invention of the tea bag _____ 204

Chapter 8: Aliens, UFOs, Extraterrestrial? _____ 206

8.1 The Roswell Incident _____ 206

8.2 The balloons in the sky of Los Angeles 1942 _____ 209

8.3 The "Foo Fighters" sightings during World War II _____ 211

8.4 The "Black Knight" satellites _____ 213

8.5 The unidentified flying objects over Belgium _____ 214

8.6 The unidentified flying objects over Phoenix _____ 216

8.7. The unidentified flying objects over Nellis Air Force Base _ 218

8.8. The mysterious "Starchild Skull" _____ 220

8.9 The strange stories of alien abductions _____ 222

8.10 Japan Airlines Flight 1628 _____ 224

8.11. The Encounter at Ariel School _____ 226

8.12. The USS Nimitz Encounter (2004) / Tic-Tac Event _____ 228

8.13 The USS Omaha Encounter (2019) _____ 230

8.14 The Rendlesham Forest Event: the British Roswell _____ 232

Chapter 9: Other Curiosities _____ *235*

9.1 The Voynich Manuscript _____ 235

9.2. The "Kryptos" artwork at CIA headquarters _____ 237

9.3 The Lost City of Atlantis _____ 240

9.4 The Story of the Flying Dutchman _____ 242

9.5 The Nazca Lines _____ 244

9.6. The unidentified flares of Marfa _____ 246

9.7. The metallic spheres of Klerksdorp _____ 248

9.8. The Treasure of Oak Island _____ 250

9.9 The Secret of the Crystal Skulls _____ 252

9.10. The strange noises in the catacombs of Paris _____ 254

9.11 The enigmatic faces of Belmez _____ 256

9.12. The Marree Man-Geoglyph in Australia _____ 258

9.13 The mysterious underwater "pyramids" _____ 259
- The Pyramids of Yonaguni, Japan _____ 259
- Die „Bimini Road", Bahamas _____ 261
- The Pyramids of Cuba _____ 262

9.14 The Bat Bomb _____ 265

The Gate to Hell _____ 266

9.15 The Turkish Chess Automaton _____ 268

Closing words _____ *270*

imprint _____ *271*

Chapter 1: Historical Curiosities

This chapter gives you a glimpse into some of the most fascinating historical curiosities. Each of these stories demonstrates how small events can have major impacts and how the unexpected has often changed the world. Stay tuned, as the coming chapters offer many more amazing insights into the wonders of our history and culture.

1.1. The Apple That Changed the World: Isaac Newton and Gravity

The scene is legendary: A young scholar sits beneath a tree, an apple falls, and suddenly the secret of the universe is revealed to him. At least, that's how popular tradition tells it, which paints an almost fairytale-like picture of Sir Isaac Newton's discovery of gravity. Whether this event actually happened is a matter of debate among historians to this day. It's more likely that Newton himself liked to tell this anecdote in conversations with friends and students to make his ideas more vivid. But regardless of whether the apple really hit him on the head or whether it merely served as a convenient metaphor, the image is so powerful that it is still considered a symbol of the birth of modern science.
Newton was a child of the 17th century, an era of upheaval. Born in 1643, he experienced an England in political and religious flux, scarred by civil war and revolution. During this uncertain time, he withdrew early into the world of thought. Even as a student at Cambridge, he demonstrated an unusual aptitude for mathematics and natural philosophy, as science was then known. His "apple moment" is said to have come during the years of the great plague of 1665/66, when the university was closed and Newton returned to his parents' home in Woolsthorpe. Isolated from academia, he occupied himself with questions that others might have considered trivial: Why does an apple fall straight down and not diagonally to the side? What force ensures that celestial bodies like the moon do not escape into the vastness of space?

This is where Newton's true genius begins. He connected everyday observations—like the apple on the tree—with the movements of celestial bodies. Before him, thinkers like Galileo Galilei and Johannes Kepler had already laid important foundations: Galileo explored the laws of falling bodies, Kepler described the orbits of the planets around the sun. But it was Newton who put the pieces of the puzzle together and dared to propose that one and the same force both pulls the apple to the ground and keeps the planets in their orbits. This universality of gravity was revolutionary.
In 1687 he published his main work, the *Mathematical Principles of Natural Philosophy* In this monumental book, he formulated not only the law of gravity, but also the famous three laws of motion, which still fill every physics textbook today. In doing so, he laid the foundation for classical mechanics – a worldview that shaped humanity for over two centuries until Albert Einstein opened up new dimensions with his theory of relativity.

But back to the apple. The popularity of this story is not only due to Newton's scientific genius, but also because it translates a complex idea into a simple, tangible scene. Everyone knows an apple tree; everyone has seen fruit fall from a branch. Suddenly, an insight that changed humanity's worldview seems very close. It's as if the great secrets of the universe lie dormant in one's own garden – one simply has to recognize them.
Interestingly, there is actually still a "Newton's Apple Tree" today. The famous tree is said to have stood in the garden of his parents' house in Woolsthorpe, and descendants of this tree are now growing at universities and research institutions around the world—from Cambridge to Canada and even at NASA. Science is thus literally cultivating the roots of its own history.
The technology company Apple also adopted this image when it was founded in 1976. The first company logo depicted not the now iconic bitten apple, but Newton himself, sitting under an apple tree, holding a book. Above him hangs an apple, ready to fall—a clear allusion to the origin of great ideas. The scene was framed by a banner bearing the words: *„Newton… A Mind Forever Voyaging Through Strange Seas of Thought… Alone.*"In English: "Newton... a mind forever sailing alone through strange seas of thought." This first logo already made it clear: Apple wanted to be seen as a symbol of creative genius and groundbreaking innovation. The fact that the logo was later simplified had more to do with marketing appeal than with any lack of respect for Newton.
Newton himself was a curious character, as were his discoveries. He was considered a loner, often withdrawn, and could be extremely suspicious. In his final years, he immersed himself more in alchemy and theology than in natural science—interests that seem eccentric to us today, but at the time were part of the repertoire of many scholars. That this man, of all people, discovered the laws of the universe seems almost ironic in retrospect: someone who spent his life searching for hidden meanings stumbled upon the most universal and rational of all forces.

There are also voices that say: Without the "apple myth," Newton's discovery would have been much more difficult to communicate to the general public. One must not forget that science was not yet a mass movement in the 17th century. Universities were places for a small elite, and complicated mathematics was incomprehensible to most people. The anecdote of the apple translated the abstraction into an image that everyone could understand. In a sense, it was the first major scientific communication of the modern era.

Incidentally, the apple has a surprisingly long tradition as a symbol of knowledge. Even in the biblical creation story, it represents knowledge and temptation—even though the Bible itself never explicitly mentions the apple. In Greek mythology, it is an apple that triggers the Trojan War. And in Newton's story, it once again represents the beginning of a new era. No other fruit has had such a lasting impact on human history—from Eve to Apple Inc.
Today, of course, we know that gravity isn't just a simple "pull" of the Earth on the apple, but a fundamental property of spacetime itself, as Einstein demonstrated. Yet Newton's law is still astonishingly precise and useful. Every rocket trajectory, every satellite calculation, and even the simple throw of a football can be explained by it. So, one could say: The apple that supposedly fell on Newton's head still rolls through our everyday lives today.

When the Apollo astronauts first set foot on the moon, Newton's theory was still the basis of all calculations. Without his theory of gravity, no human being would ever have been able to leave Earth's orbit. In this sense, Newton's "apple tree" now sits on a completely different pedestal—that of space history.
So perhaps it wasn't so crucial whether Newton actually landed the apple on his head or not. What matters is that he had the ability to develop a universal question from a banal event. That is the true secret of genius: not seeing the things everyone else sees—but asking the questions no one else dares to ask. Newton's apple thus became a symbol of the power of curiosity, which continually drives people to push the boundaries of the known.

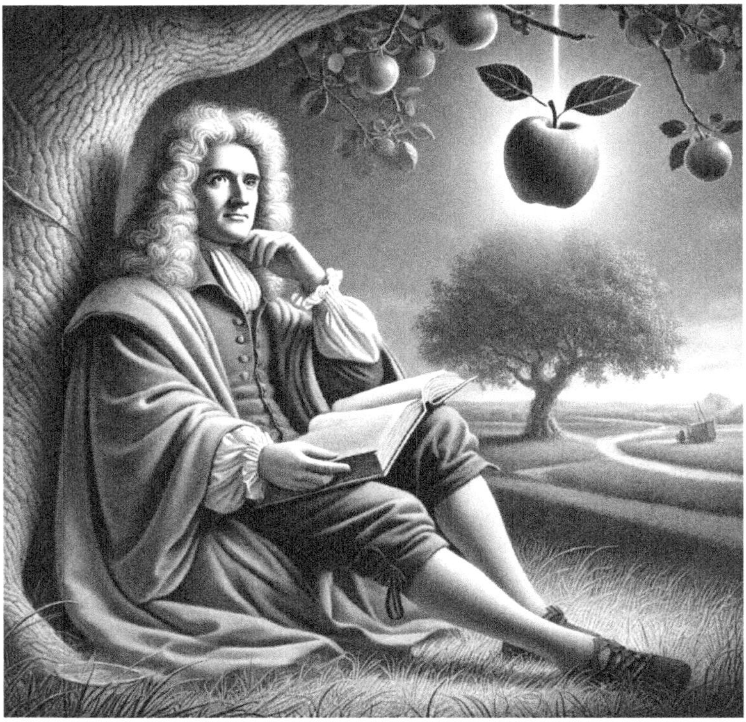

1.2. The man who died several times: The mystery of Grigori Rasputin

When one hears the name Grigory Yefimovich Rasputin, one immediately thinks of dark cellars, poisoned wine goblets, deadly conspiracies, and a man who simply refused to die. He was a monk and a charlatan, a faith healer and political schemer, a mystical advisor to the royal family—and simultaneously its downfall. Hardly any figure in Russian history is as shrouded in legend as this bearded itinerant preacher from Siberia, who managed to rise to become the most powerful man at the court of St. Petersburg.

Rasputin was born in 1869 in the small village of Pokrovskoye in the Urals. Even as a young man, he was an outsider who allegedly had visions, performed miracles, and attracted attention with his hypnotic charisma. Contemporaries described his eyes as "penetrating" and "almost uncanny" – a gaze that captivated friends and foes alike. On his pilgrimages through Russia, he earned the reputation of a "staretz," a spiritual itinerant healer. His reputation as a man with special powers spread like wildfire – in a country that had always been receptive to mysticism, belief in miracles, and the veneration of saints.
His path eventually led him to the court of the royal family. Tsar Nicholas II and, above all, Tsarina Alexandra met Rasputin around 1905. Their son Alexei suffered from hemophilia, an incurable blood disorder. Even minor injuries could trigger fatal bleeding, and doctors were powerless. Rasputin, however, seemed able to calm the boy, stop his bleeding, or at least alleviate it. To this day, historians puzzle over how he did it. Was it simply hypnosis? Was it because Rasputin instructed doctors to stop administering certain medications—including aspirin, which impairs blood clotting? Or was it a combination of emotional comfort and psychological influence?
Whatever the cause, it was clear to the tsarina: this man was sent by God. In her desperation, Alexandra clung to Rasputin, and thus the Siberian peasant gained unparalleled influence at court. As Europe lurched into World War I, nobles and ministers whispered that, in truth, it was Rasputin, not the tsar, who ruled Russia.
His influence was indeed considerable. It is said that Rasputin awarded positions and offices to his confidants and even intervened in military matters. Whether he truly controlled all politics is disputed – but the mere suspicion was enough to make him a hate figure. For many, he embodied the entire evil of Tsarist rule: corruption, incompetence, and mysterious backroom decisions. And Rasputin did little to dispel this image. He enjoyed his power, he provoked, he lived dissolutely. In St. Petersburg, the wildest rumors of orgies, feasts, and womanizing circulated. His opponents called him a "demonic seducer," while his supporters saw him as the only man who could still save the empire. This contrast made him a legend—and a man who urgently needed to be removed.

His death in December 1916 became one of the most famous murder stories in world history. Prince Felix Yusupov, Grand Duke Dmitri Pavlovich, and the politician Vladimir Purishkevich hatched a plan to finally get rid of the "Holy Devil," as he was called. On the night of December 29, they lured him to the basement of the Yusupov Palace—ostensibly under the pretext of meeting the beautiful Irina, Yusupov's wife. Instead, they served him wine and cakes poisoned with cyanide.

But then the unexpected happened: Rasputin showed no signs of poisoning. He calmly drank the wine, ate the cakes, and continued to chat. The conspirators became nervous. Finally, Yusupov pulled out a pistol and shot Rasputin. The man fell and stayed there—but a short time later, he got up again and staggered out into the snow-covered courtyard. There, the conspirators shot again, beat him, and finally threw his body into the icy Neva River.

The next morning, his body was pulled from the river. Reports claimed that water was found in his lungs—an indication that he was still alive when he fell into the icy water. Whether this is true is uncertain. But the legend was born: Rasputin, the man who survived poison, bullets, and blows, and seemed invincible even in death.

Even today, the phrase "harder to kill than Rasputin" is still circulating in Russia when someone is exceptionally tough.

The story of his death made Rasputin immortal. Depending on the source, he was killed three, four, or even five times before his final death. These exaggerations show how much people viewed him as a supernatural being—half demon, half saint. Some believed he had the ability to foresee his own death. Indeed, shortly before his death, he wrote a letter warning that if he were killed by common people, the Tsar would have nothing to fear. But if nobles laid hands on him, it would bring about the downfall of the Romanovs. A few months later, the February Revolution of 1917 overthrew the Tsar—and in 1918, Nicholas II and his family were executed. For many, this was proof that Rasputin's curse had come true.

His figure has since moved between myth and history. Was he a brilliant psychologist, a charlatan, or truly a man with extraordinary powers? Was he the tool of a desperate tsarina or the mastermind of an entire political system? The only thing that is certain is that hardly anyone has divided the Russian court as much, captivated it as much, and terrified it as much as he did.

After his death, Rasputin became the subject of countless books, films, and conspiracy theories. Sometimes he appears as a demonic sorcerer, sometimes as a tragic prophet, sometimes as the victim of a decadent aristocracy. His name is inextricably linked to the downfall of the Romanovs, as if it were the last dark omen of a dying monarchy.

In the 1920s, bizarre stories circulated in Paris that Rasputin's severed limb was venerated as a relic – another example of the almost grotesque myth-making surrounding his person.

Whether you consider him a miracle worker or a charlatan, whether you take his prophecies seriously or consider them cleverly fabricated legends – Rasputin remains the symbol of how a single, charismatic personality can influence history at the right moment. And he remains the man who had to die several times before he was truly dead.

1.3. The assassination attempt that triggered the First World War

On the morning of June 28, 1914, a tense but festive atmosphere prevailed in Sarajevo. Archduke Franz Ferdinand, heir to the Austro-Hungarian throne, was on a state visit to the Bosnian capital with his wife, Sophie. What was intended as a demonstration of power and a political stunt turned into a catastrophe within hours, the reverberations of which continue to shape the world today. Franz Ferdinand was not a popular heir to the throne. His rigid seriousness, conservative views, and lack of diplomacy made him suspicious to many politicians. But on this day, he appeared unusually approachable. At his side was Sophie, the woman he had married for love against all odds. Their marriage was considered unsuitable at the court in Vienna, as Sophie "only" came from a Bohemian aristocratic family. The fact that she was now even allowed to appear beside him at official events was a personal triumph for Franz Ferdinand—and, tragically, would also be her death sentence.

Security measures that day were, to say the least, inadequate. The heir to the throne's motorcade traveled in open cars, the route was public knowledge, and Sarajevo was a powder keg. Several young men were waiting in the city for their opportunity. They belonged to the Serbian nationalist secret organization "Black Hand," which had set itself the goal of "liberating" Bosnia from Habsburg rule. Among them: Gavrilo Princip, a 19-year-old student from a poor background, sickly and unprepossessing—and yet destined to upend an entire era.

At first, the assassination attempt appeared to be a miserable failure. One of the conspirators, Nedeljko Cabrinović, threw a hand grenade at the Archduke's car. But the driver noticed the movement, accelerated, and the grenade exploded beneath the car behind him. Several officers were injured, but Franz Ferdinand himself remained unharmed. Cabrinović attempted to take his own life by swallowing a poison capsule, but the poison was old and ineffective. He finally jumped into the Miljacka, the river that flows through Sarajevo—although on that hot June day, it was only knee-deep. The would-be assassin was promptly pulled out by police and arrested.

Cabrinović's failed suicide attempt is a symbol of the assassins' almost grotesque unprofessionalism. History books portray it as if fate itself had orchestrated the attack—it was only through the many coincidences and mishaps that the assassination attempt was even possible.

After the attack, Franz Ferdinand initially continued his journey. He angrily complained about the "ridiculous security measures," but insisted on visiting the injured officers in the hospital that afternoon. A fatal decision.

On the way there, a coincidence occurred that went down in history. The Archduke's driver accidentally took the wrong route. When he realized his mistake, he stopped the car to turn around – right in front of the Café Schiller, where, of all people, Gavrilo Princip happened to be. Princip, who had already given up in frustration after the failed attack, could hardly believe his luck: The heir to the throne's car was parked just a few meters away, practically motionless. He drew his pistol and fired two shots – one hitting Sophie in the abdomen, the other Franz Ferdinand in the neck.

The scene that followed was shocking. "Sopherl, don't die! Stay alive for our children!" Franz Ferdinand is said to have cried before collapsing. Minutes later, both were dead.

The impact of these two shots was devastating. Within a few weeks, a regional assassination transformed into a global crisis. Austria-Hungary issued Serbia an ultimatum worded in such a way that it was almost impossible to accept. Germany demonstratively backed Vienna, Russia backed Serbia. France, in turn, stood by Russia, and Great Britain followed. An assassination in a provincial town became a global conflagration.

People speak of the "July Crisis"—those weeks in which diplomacy still attempted to halt the escalation. But Europe's alliance system was so rigid and so fraught with mistrust that every step made war more inevitable. On August 1, 1914, Germany declared war on Russia, two days later on France, and soon afterward the invasion of Belgium began. Thus, the First World War was unleashed—a war that would claim the lives of over 17 million people.

Gavrilo Princip himself survived the assassination attempt for only a few years. Since he was under 20 at the time of the attack, he could not be sentenced to death under Austrian law. Instead, he received a 20-year prison sentence. However, his health was poor, and he died of tuberculosis and malnutrition in 1918, the last year of the war—half-starved, half-forgotten, while millions of soldiers outside paid for his work with their blood.

The irony of history is hard to miss. Had Cabrinović's bomb detonated, the war might have broken out sooner—or been prevented by the shock. If the Archduke's driver hadn't taken the wrong road, Princip would never have been in a position to shoot. If Franz Ferdinand hadn't insisted on the hospital visit, the assassination attempt might have failed completely that day. But history knows no subjunctives. In the end, a small coincidence was enough to plunge the world into ruin.

Even today, speculation rages about whether it was truly just a "coincidence." Conspiracy theories claim that secret services, major powers, or dark forces in the background had a hand in it. But the sober documents paint a picture of amateur assassins, unfortunate coincidences, and a political situation so explosive that a single spark was enough. Gavrilo Princip was that spark.

And so the First World War began—not on a battlefield, not with a bombing, but with two shots in a small town on the edge of Europe. Two bullets that swept away an entire world order.

1.4. The Incredible Escape from Alcatraz

There are prisons whose very name evokes dread. Alcatraz – "The Rock" – is undoubtedly one of them. The small island in the middle of San Francisco Bay seemed like a fortress of hopelessness. America's most dangerous and incorrigible criminals were imprisoned here: bank robbers, murderers, and even the infamous Al Capone. Surrounded by icy water, dangerous currents, and constant guard, Alcatraz was long considered absolutely escape-proof. Anyone who dared to brave the rock was considered as good as dead.
But on the night of June 11-12, 1962, the unimaginable happened: three men disappeared without a trace from the high-security prison – and to this day no one knows for sure whether they met their end in the water or landed as free men.
The main protagonists of this legendary escape were Frank Morris and the brothers John and Clarence Anglin. Morris was known as an extremely intelligent but equally petty criminal who had previously escaped from prison several times. The Anglin brothers came from a poor farming family in Florida. They specialized in bank robberies – but with one curious quirk: They always wore suits and ties, as if they were trying to play gentleman crooks. These three men, brought together by chance in Alcatraz, decided to attempt the impossible. They meticulously prepared their escape for months. Their cells were located directly against a poorly ventilated wall. Using homemade tools—including spoons they converted into chisels in the prison workshop—they dug small holes into the crumbling masonry night after night. They cleverly disguised the noise with music from a chess radio station. Every morning, they covered the openings with painted pieces of cardboard that looked deceptively like the wall.

As a substitute for pillows, they constructed realistic dummy heads—molded from soap, painted with skin dye from prison materials, and adorned with real hair collected from the prison's barbershop. When the guards looked into the cells that night, they saw nothing but men seemingly sleeping peacefully. Behind the cells, an unused service corridor led to the roof of the building. Here, the prisoners secretly gathered supplies: raincoats, which they sewed into a kind of raft, and improvised oars made of planks. They worked in shifts, always at the extreme risk of discovery.
On the night of their escape, Morris and the Anglins slipped through the holes, climbed up the service shaft, squeezed through narrow grates, and finally reached the roof. From there, they descended to the water. Then they set out into the bay on their raft—and disappeared forever.

In the morning, chaos reigned in the prison. As the guards checked the cells, they came across the elaborately crafted doll heads – and froze. A full-scale alarm was sounded, and boats and helicopters combed the bay. But there was no sign of the escapees. Only a paddle and a torn raincoat were found.

The authorities' official version remains: The men drowned in the icy water. The currents in the bay are treacherous, temperatures often drop below 12 degrees Celsius, and the distance from the mainland is several kilometers. A skilled swimmer might have a chance—but three prisoners on a makeshift raft? From the FBI's perspective, the situation was clear.

But this is precisely where the legend begins. There are numerous indications that the escape may have been successful. Rumors repeatedly surfaced that the Anglin brothers had been sighted in South America. In 2013, the San Francisco police received a letter, allegedly from John Anglin himself, in which he declared that he was still alive—seriously ill, but free. Whether this letter was genuine remained unclear.

As early as 1962, just months after the escape, it became clear that the "impossible" swim across the bay was indeed feasible. In an annual swimming competition from Alcatraz to the mainland, participants completed the distance without a raft, using muscle power alone. The official claim that the current was "insurmountable" was thus refuted.

Hollywood finally immortalized the case. In 1979, the film *Escape from Alcatraz* starring Clint Eastwood. Millions of viewers watched with excitement as the men dug the holes, crafted the doll heads, and finally disappeared into the night. The film deliberately ended open-ended: We see the empty cells—but no corpses. The audience was left to decide for themselves whether they had made it.

US authorities never completely gave up the search either. For decades, the FBI sifted through clues and alleged sightings. But definitive proof of life or death was never found. The myth lives on.

Today, Alcatraz is a tourist attraction. Over a million people visit the former prison island, now a museum, every year. And hardly a visitor leaves the cells without standing at the Anglin brothers' wall and asking the question: Did they make it?

The story has something almost fairytale-like about it. Three men against a system deemed insurmountable. A prison deemed "escape impossible." And yet a trail leading into the darkness. Whether Morris and the Anglins truly survived or whether they found their grave in the icy bay remains a mystery to this day. But perhaps it is precisely this unsolved mystery that makes the story so immortal.

The legend took a bizarre twist in 2016, when Dutch researchers used modern computer simulations to reconstruct the currents in the bay on the day of the escape. Their conclusion: If the men had set sail shortly after midnight and headed northeast, they would have actually had a good chance of reaching the shore near the Golden Gate Bridge. However, if they had set sail an hour later, the raft would inevitably have drifted out to sea. A tiny difference in departure time could therefore mean the difference between freedom and death.

1.5. The secret codes of the Navajo Indians in World War II

War is not only fought with guns, tanks, and aircraft, but also with words—more precisely, with information. Those who can communicate faster than their opponents, who can transmit encrypted orders without the enemy decrypting them, have a decisive advantage. Especially in World War II, where battles were often decided within hours, secure communication literally meant the life and death of entire divisions.

But while the Axis powers deployed their best cryptologists to intercept radio messages, the US military developed a method that was as ingenious as it was unexpected: they resorted to a language that hardly anyone outside a specific community spoke – the Navajo language.

The Navajo are among the indigenous peoples of North America, whose habitat lies primarily in the deserts and canyons of the Southwest. Their language is one of the most complex in the world. It has numerous unusual sounds, an extremely complicated grammar, and—crucially—it was transmitted almost exclusively orally in the 1940s. Written dictionaries practically existed. For outsiders, Navajo was virtually unlearnable, especially since there were no direct equivalents for many modern terms.

This, some Marine Corps officers saw as an invaluable opportunity. In 1942, the first Navajo Code Talker program was launched. Around 30 Navajo men were recruited to develop a completely new communications system. They had to transliterate military terms unfamiliar to their language using Navajo words. For example, a tank was called a "turtle" because it was heavily armored and moved slowly. A battleship was called an "iron fish." And the word "hummingbird" stood for a fighter plane.

The system was astonishingly effective. A Navajo code talker could transmit an encrypted message in 20 seconds, something that conventional cryptographic machines would have taken around 30 minutes to complete. The code was never static, but flexible, with more than 400 developed terms and additional encryption mechanisms. For the Japanese and Germans, it was a closed book.

Japanese cryptologists later explained that while they were able to crack countless American codes, as soon as they intercepted a message in Navajo, they were puzzled. Even if they once thought they understood the pattern, the code talkers changed their terminology.

The Navajo code talkers became especially famous during the Pacific War. During the Battle of Iwo Jima in the spring of 1945, they transmitted more than 800 messages within a few days – without error. An American commander later declared: "Without the Navajo, we would not have won Iwo Jima." For the Marines, the code talkers were literally life-saving.

Their recruitment was anything but a given. Many of the Navajo came from families that had been discriminated against and disenfranchised by the United States for decades. In residential schools, they were even forbidden to speak their native language – they were supposed to be "Americanized." That this very language, which was previously intended to be eradicated, now became a secret weapon is one of the bitterest ironies in history.

The Navajo soldiers themselves, however, viewed their task with pride. They knew they possessed a unique skill that no one else possessed. Some later recounted that they spoke to each other in Navajo in the trenches—not only as a code, but also as a reminder of their homeland, far from the battlefields of the Pacific.

The existence of the code remained top secret for a long time. Only decades after the war were the former code talkers allowed to speak publicly about their role. In 1968, the program was officially declassified, and recognition slowly began to emerge. Many of them received high honors, even the United States Congressional Gold Medal of Honor in 2001.

Hollywood picked up the story – the film became famous *Windtalkers* (2002) starring Nicolas Cage, which is loosely based on the experiences of the Navajo. Although the film was heavily dramatized, it brought the heroic role of the code talkers to the attention of a wider public for the first time.

Today, the Navajo Code Talkers are considered a symbol of the ingenious combination of tradition and modernity. Their language, passed on only within their community for centuries, decided global battles in the 20th century.

Legends still persist that the Axis powers attempted to crack the code—Japan is even said to have trained linguists to learn Navajo. But even if there is some truth to this, without a deep cultural understanding, the language remained opaque. A single word could have a completely different meaning depending on the accentuation. For outsiders, it was simply a linguistic labyrinth.

When you watch veterans' reunions of Navajo code talkers today, one thing stands out: Many of them view their role not only in military terms, but also in spiritual terms. They were the guardians of a language that brought light in the darkest hours of war. One veteran once said, "Our words were our weapons. And no bullet could destroy them."

Perhaps the real point of this story is that a language that was suppressed and banned for decades suddenly contributed to the salvation of an entire country. What was once considered "backward" became a state-of-the-art secret weapon. And while generals were still tinkering with complicated encryption machines, in the Pacific, it was sometimes enough for two Navajo soldiers to exchange a few sentences in the trenches – and the enemy didn't understand a word.

Today, you can take language courses in Navajo – even via an app. So anyone who wants to learn one of the "most uncrackable languages in the world" can do so from the comfort of their couch. Whether that would save an army, however, is questionable.

1.6 The Dance Plague of 1518

Imagine the scene: A summery Strasbourg street in July 1518. Between half-timbered houses, market stalls, and the smells of bread, meat, and beer, a woman suddenly begins to dance. There's no boisterous celebration, no music, no merry company—just Mrs. Troffea, frantically moving her feet, flinging her arms, and never stopping. Initially amused, then increasingly irritated, the neighbors observe the strange spectacle. But what began as an isolated incident developed within days into mass hysteria that held all of Strasbourg in suspense: the so-called "dancing plague."

Ms. Troffea allegedly danced for days, without a break, without visible joy. Eyewitnesses reported that she wore a tortured expression, as if she could no longer control her own body. Soon, other people joined her—at first a few, then dozens, and finally hundreds. Men, women, children: they all danced as if driven, until they trembled, sweated, and fought for their lives. Some collapsed from exhaustion, others continued dancing as if an invisible force were at work. The city administration initially reacted as was typical in the early 16th century: with pragmatism, but also with a touch of superstition. They assumed that those affected simply needed to "dance it out" until the disease subsided. So they organized public dance floors and hired musicians and violinists—and thus inadvertently exacerbated the disaster. Instead of providing relief, the number of dancers swelled even further. Strasbourg became the involuntary scene of a grotesque, nonstop party where no one could laugh.

The reports from that time are dramatic: people are said to have collapsed from exhaustion, others suffered heart attacks or strokes. Chroniclers described a city literally trembling to the rhythm of madness. For weeks, the streets echoed with the muffled footsteps of the exhausted, the wailing of those who could no longer bear it, and the tireless playing of the musicians tasked with keeping the spectacle "under control."

How can this bizarre phenomenon be explained? Modern historians have developed various hypotheses. One of the most popular is mass hysteria. Strasbourg suffered from famine, disease, and religious pressure at that time. The population was physically and mentally at its limit. In such a situation, psychogenic epidemics can occur – known today from cases in which entire school classes suddenly faint or people collectively develop tics. The dance plague could have been an extreme example: an entire city that plunged itself into the abyss while dancing.

Another theory is far more material: ergot poisoning. The fungal grain, which grows on damp rye, contains hallucinogenic substances—precursors to LSD. Those who unknowingly consumed it in bread could suffer from cramps, hallucinations, and an urge to move. Perhaps the Strasbourg residents simply danced because they were in a trance. However, this explanation is controversial, as not all symptoms fit, and because the poisoning is more likely to cause paralysis than a dance frenzy.

Religious interpretations were also not lacking. Some chroniclers saw the plague as a punishment from God, others believed that Saint Vitus had cursed the people. Even today, similar phenomena are called "Chorea sancti Viti" – St. Vitus's dance. Pilgrimage sites in the region experienced a sudden influx of visitors, as desperate people hoped to be freed from their oppression through prayers or offerings.

The dance plague of 1518 is by no means the only event of its kind. Similar "dancing mania epidemics" were already described in Aachen and Cologne in the 14th and 15th centuries. Strasbourg was merely the most well-known example—probably because the chroniclers there reported in particularly detailed detail and the number of dancers was supposedly particularly high.

The authorities' reaction also seems bizarre from today's perspective. After music and dance floors exacerbated the problem, the city council issued an abrupt ban: no more music, no more dancing. At the same time, many of those affected were locked in a special house so they could "let off steam." One could say: a medieval quarantine, but against dancing.

As abruptly as the dance plague had begun, it ended. After a few weeks, the phenomenon subsided, people returned to their daily lives, and Strasbourg sank back into its usual worries of hunger, disease, and politics. The chronicles, however, recorded the event, and so it continues to haunt the history books as one of the most bizarre mass phenomena.

The idea that an entire neighborhood staggered toward death while dancing sounds almost like morbid satire today. Yet the story demonstrates something fundamental: how deeply human behavior can be influenced by collective stress, beliefs, and external circumstances. A society on the brink of collapse can produce things that defy all logic.

Today, Strasbourg hosts music and dance festivals every year—voluntary, joyful, and without fatalities. One could say that the city has transformed the dark episode of its past into a joyful tradition.

Perhaps the greatest lesson of the Dancing Plague of 1518 remains that humans, collectively, are capable of the most absurd things—whether because they have to or because they believe they can. And who knows: Perhaps we still occasionally dance to the brink of madness today—only then our "dancing plagues" are called stock market bubbles, mass hype, or internet trends.

1.7 The Vanished Colony of Roanoke

In the late 16th century, England gazed longingly across the Atlantic. Spain had already built an empire that shook the world with the conquest of South America and the exploitation of gold and silver. England, on the other hand, was still an outsider in the race for colonies and wealth. Sir Walter Raleigh, a favorite courtier of Queen Elizabeth I, wanted to change that – and so the plan to establish an English colony in the "New World" was born.

They chose Roanoke Island, a small island off the coast of present-day North Carolina. It was strategically located and promised a good starting point for further ventures. In 1585, the first group of about 100 men landed. But it quickly became clear that the New World was no paradise. Food was scarce, the climate unfamiliar, and conflicts with the native Algonquian tribes exacerbated the situation. After less than a year, the settlers gave up and sailed back to England.

But the vision of an English colony persisted. Two years later, in 1587, a second expedition set out—this time with 115 men, women, and children, led by John White. It was an ambitious plan: instead of being just an outpost for soldiers, Roanoke was to become a real settlement, with families, fields, and a future.

John White, an experienced cartographer, hoped to establish a thriving little England on American soil. His daughter Eleanor was even heavily pregnant—and in August 1587, their child was born: Virginia Dare, the first English child born in the New World. The colony seemed to be in good hands.

But it soon became apparent that supplies were running low. White decided to return to England himself to seek support. He promised to return quickly—but history had other plans. England was at war with Spain, the Armada threatened the homeland, and all ships were needed for the fight. Thus, not months, but a full three years passed before White was finally able to land in Roanoke again in 1590.

The scene that unfolded before him is one of the greatest mysteries in American history. The settlement was deserted. No bodies, no battlefield, no trace of violence. The houses had been neatly dismantled, as if they had been deliberately dismantled. Not a single boat lay on the beach. There was no trace of the 115 colonists—including his daughter and granddaughter.

Only a single clue remained: the word "CROATOAN" was carved into a post of the fort, along with the letters "CRO" on a nearby tree. Croatoan was the name of an island south of Roanoke—now Hatteras Island—and also the name of a tribe living there. White interpreted this as a hint that the settlers had moved there. But a storm prevented him from sailing to Croatoan. He returned to England—and never saw the colony again.

Since then, countless theories have surrounded the fate of the "Lost Colony." One possibility is that the colonists actually stayed with the Croatoans and became integrated into their society. Later accounts from settlers in the 17th century mention "white Indians" with strikingly light skin and gray eyes—perhaps descendants of the Roanoke colonists.

Others speculate that starvation or disease decimated the settlers, and that the survivors either died in the forests or were killed by hostile tribes. Some researchers also consider it possible that the colony simply moved on—in search of a better location, perhaps inland, where archaeological finds later indicated European tools in Native American settlements.

The legend of Virginia Dare, the first English child in America, became a veritable myth in the 19th and 20th centuries. Her name appeared in poems, plays, and even advertisements—as a symbol of innocence, new beginnings, and the mystery of Roanoke. Today, wineries, streets, and schools in North Carolina bear her name.

Of course, there are also more adventurous speculations. Some 19th-century historians viewed the Roanoke settlers as victims of Spanish raids, while others added conspiracies of witchcraft and cannibalism. Modern conspiracy theories even go so far as to link the "Lost Colony" to aliens or secret cults – although there is no evidence for this.

What remains is the sobering realization: 115 people disappeared from view without any clear documentation of their fate. No graves, no letters, no survivor accounts. Only a word carved into the wood.

Archaeologists are still digging for clues. In recent decades, artifacts have indeed been discovered—pottery, metal fragments, musket balls—that indicate that some of the colonists settled further inland. But definitive proof remains lacking.

"CROATOAN" later became a pop-cultural buzzword. The writer Edgar Allan Poe is said to have whispered this word shortly before his mysterious death in 1849. And even in modern series like *American Horror Story* it appears again – as a symbol of unexplained secrets.

The Lost Colony of Roanoke is thus not only a historical mystery, but also a cultural phenomenon. It represents the dangers and hardships of early colonization—hunger, isolation, conflict—but also the insatiable human need to find answers to the unexplainable.

Perhaps the settlers actually joined the Croatoan, perhaps they died in the forest—or perhaps the truth lies somewhere in between. The only thing that is certain is that until conclusive evidence emerges, Roanoke will remain a mystery.

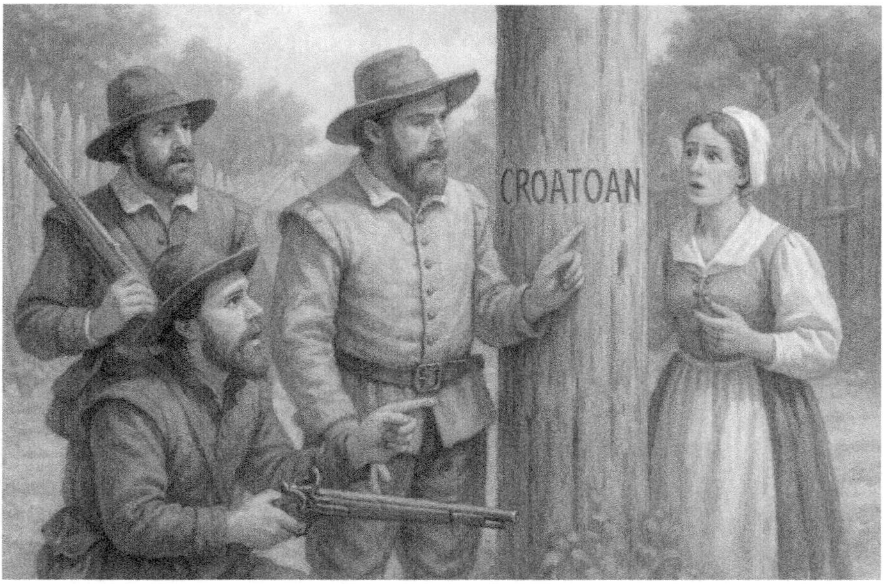
CROATOAN

1.8. The Rain of Blood of 1916 in India

In 1916, the Kerala region of southern India witnessed an unusual and eerie phenomenon that became known as the "rain of blood."

This strange rain, in which red, blood-like drops fell from the sky, sparked widespread concern and curiosity. The events of 1916 are not the only ones of their kind; similar phenomena were observed in Kerala in later years, leading to numerous speculations and scientific investigations.

It is reported that in July 1916, the inhabitants of Kerala were struck by a strange rain, in which the raindrops were a deep red color reminiscent of blood. The red rain left traces on clothing, buildings, and streets, spreading incredible wonder and horror in equal measure.

This unusual coloration lasted for several days and was observed in various parts of the region.

Both the local population and scientists were perplexed about the cause of the phenomenon. Some saw the event as a bad omen or a sign of divine wrath. Others suspected it was some kind of environmental pollution or that the rain had been discolored by unusual atmospheric conditions.

Scientists soon began collecting and analyzing samples of the red rain to determine the cause of the coloration. Various theories were proposed:
*Microorganisms*One of the leading theories is that the red rain was caused by microorganisms such as algae or fungal spores that entered the atmosphere in large numbers. These microorganisms may have been transported from distant regions by strong winds or hurricanes and then precipitated with the rain.

*Mineral dust:*Another theory proposes that the red rain was caused by mineral dust or sand particles carried into the atmosphere by wind from desert areas or other arid regions. These particles may have colored the raindrops as they fell through the atmosphere.
*Pollen grains:*Some scientists suggested that the red rain was caused by a high concentration of pollen grains from certain plant species. This pollen may have risen into the atmosphere and returned to Earth with the rain.

The 1916 blood rain was not the only time this phenomenon occurred in Kerala. In 2001, the region was hit again by red rain, prompting renewed scientific investigations. Analyses of the 2001 samples supported the theory that microorganisms could be responsible for the coloring.

A team of researchers from Mahatma Gandhi University in Kerala found that the red particles in the rain contained cells without DNA. These findings led to further speculation and discussion about the nature and origin of the particles, including the hypothesis that they might be of extraterrestrial origin.

However, this theory was largely viewed with skepticism by the scientific community and was not confirmed.

1.9. The London Coach Dispute

In the early 19th century, London was a rapidly growing metropolis with a steadily increasing population. The city was already a major commercial center, and the need for an efficient transportation system became increasingly urgent. At that time, carriages were the primary means of transporting people and goods.

The streets of London were full of private and commercial carriages, cabs and horse-drawn vehicles, crammed through narrow, often poorly paved streets.

The conflict began when the number of carriages on the roads increased exponentially, leading to significant traffic problems. Traffic jams were commonplace, and the roads were congested. Increasing competition between carriage companies further exacerbated the situation. Drivers fought for passengers and tried to outdo each other, often leading to dangerous maneuvers and arguments.

Another factor fueling the controversy was the introduction of new technologies. In the 1820s, the first omnibuses were introduced in London. These larger, horse-drawn vehicles could carry more passengers and quickly became popular.

The introduction of buses, and later steam and electric buses, threatened the livelihoods of many traditional carriage drivers. This economic uncertainty led to protests and resistance against the new means of transport.

The operators of traditional carriages and cabs saw the buses as a threat to their business.

The dispute reached its peak in the 1830s and 1840s. Tensions between the various transport providers escalated, and clashes regularly broke out in the streets. Coach and omnibus drivers accused each other of unfair practices.

Violent clashes between drivers occurred regularly. These included fights, sabotage, and road blocking. Reports of carriages deliberately colliding or buses being disabled were not uncommon.

The city administration introduced licenses for carriage drivers and omnibus operators to control the number of vehicles on the streets and increase safety. These measures helped reduce chaotic conditions and ensure that only qualified drivers and operators were involved in traffic. Regulation also included rules on speed, the use of certain roads, and the number of passengers.

The conflicts ultimately led to public debates about the need for a regulated transport system, the role of new technologies, and the social impacts of economic competition. These debates helped raise awareness of the need for reforms and innovations in urban transport.

1.10 The Boston Molasses Disaster

The Boston Molasses Disaster, also known as the "Great Molasses Flood," occurred on January 15, 1919, in the North End neighborhood of Boston, Massachusetts. This extraordinary disaster claimed numerous lives and caused significant damage. It remains one of the most bizarre and tragic events in the city's history.

The disaster began with a massive storage tank operated by the United States Industrial Alcohol Company. The tank, approximately 15 meters high and 27 meters in diameter, contained more than 8.7 million liters of molasses. Molasses, a thick, syrupy residue from sugar production, was stored in large quantities for use in the production of rum and industrial alcohol.

The United States Industrial Alcohol Company built the tank in 1915 to meet the growing demand for molasses, which was also used to make munitions during World War I. The tank was located in a densely populated area, surrounded by residential buildings, a fire station, a railroad depot, and a shipyard.

On January 15, 1919, an unusually warm winter day, the tank burst suddenly and without warning. Eyewitnesses reported a loud bang and a deep rumble, followed by a massive surge of brown liquid that rolled through the streets of Boston. A 4.5-meter-high tsunami of molasses moved at a speed of approximately 55 km/h, destroying everything in its path.
The enormous force of the wave tore buildings from their foundations, smashed railroad tracks, and overturned vehicles. The nearby Fire Station 31 was destroyed, and the molasses flood drowned people and animals alike.

A total of 21 people were killed and about 150 others were injured. The victims were often trapped in the thick molasses, making rescue attempts extremely difficult.

The rescue operation following the disaster was an enormous challenge. Firefighters, police officers, soldiers, and volunteers fought their way through the viscous mass to search for survivors. Horses trapped in the flood often had to be put down because they could not escape the sticky trap. The rescue effort lasted several days, and the cleanup spanned weeks and months.

Following the disaster, a comprehensive investigation followed to determine the causes of the accident. It was discovered that the storage tank had structural defects from the outset. The United States Industrial Alcohol Company had constructed the tank hastily and without proper safety testing. There were reports that the tank had been leaking since its construction, and that cracks and deformations had been ignored.

The investigation also revealed that the company was aware of the danger but took no action to correct the deficiencies. Witnesses from local residents confirmed that they often heard the sound of creaking metal and the hissing of escaping molasses, but their warnings were not taken seriously.

The disaster led to one of the most extensive and protracted legal battles in Boston's history. Over 125 lawsuits were filed against the United States Industrial Alcohol Company. The trials lasted several years and ultimately ended with a verdict declaring the company negligent. The injured parties and the victims' families received compensation payments totaling approximately $628,000, equivalent to several million dollars today.

The Boston Molasses Disaster had far-reaching effects on safety standards and building codes in the United States. The disaster led to stricter building codes and safety inspections, particularly for large industrial facilities. The need for careful review of construction projects and compliance with safety standards was emphatically emphasized.
Today, a memorial plaque in Boston commemorates the victims of the disaster.

1.11 The Stockholm Massacre

At the beginning of the 16th century, Scandinavia was a political powder keg. Denmark, Norway, and Sweden had been united in the so-called Kalmar Union since the end of the 14th century. On paper, this was an alliance of equal kingdoms under a common crown. In reality, however, it was a fragile construct in which the Danish kings sought to expand their power over Sweden – and the Swedish nobles tried by all means to break this dominance.

Tensions were immense: Sweden felt exploited by Denmark. Trade privileges went primarily to Danish merchants, high offices were held by Danish officials, and the Swedish upper class had to watch as their autonomy was gradually curtailed. Swedish nobles repeatedly rebelled against the union, and the Danish crown responded with violence. The conflict resembled a constant tug-of-war – sometimes Sweden gained more independence, sometimes the Danish side triumphed.

In this heated situation, Christian II, soon dubbed "Christian the Tyrant" in Sweden, ascended the Danish throne. His goal was clear: to definitively consolidate the union and subjugate the recalcitrant Swedes. In 1520, he marched into Sweden with an army, laid siege to Stockholm, and forced the city's surrender. Thus, Danish rule seemed to be secured.

On November 4, 1520, Christian was ceremoniously crowned King of Sweden in Stockholm. For many Swedish nobles, this was a bitter defeat, but they accepted his invitation to the coronation celebrations at the palace. They wanted to win the favor of the new ruler, perhaps even make a fresh start. For four days, the festive atmosphere prevailed: banquets, music, and flowing wine—a display of royal power and supposed reconciliation.

But the exuberant mood didn't last long. On November 7, the situation changed abruptly. The castle gates were locked, guards stormed the hall, and more than 100 guests—nobles, clergy, and leading citizens—were arrested. This came as a shock to the surprised Swedes: Hardly anyone had suspected that the celebration would turn into a trap.

The next day began what was known as **Stockholm Massacre** would go down in history. A hastily convened court, presided over by Bishop Gustav Trolle, raised serious charges: heresy and rebellion against the crown. The reason was that the Swedish nobles had curtailed the power of Trolle, a pro-Danish churchman, in the years prior. Christian II seized on this old conflict to eliminate his opponents in one fell swoop.

The trials lasted only minutes, and the verdicts had long been decided. Within a few hours, over 80 people were beheaded—including leading members of the Sture Party, who had fought for Swedish independence, as well as several bishops and noblemen. Executions were even carried out in the streets and market square of Stockholm. The victims' heads were displayed, their bodies left in public to intimidate the population.

The violence didn't end with the nobles. Ordinary citizens suspected of sympathizing with the Swedish cause were also imprisoned or executed. Contemporary accounts describe how the castle and the city were transformed into a single scene of horror.

The market square in Stockholm's Old Town, Stortorget, is still closely associated with the massacre. The windows of the surrounding houses are said to have been draped with cloths at the time so that residents wouldn't have to watch—or because they wanted to prevent them from seeing the sheer scale of the executions. Even today, city guides tell the story as if the screams of the victims could be heard between the old facades.

The political impact of the massacre was devastating—and ultimately self-destructive for Christian II. What was intended as a demonstration of power led not to respect, but to pure hatred. The bloodbath became a symbol of the cruelty of Danish rule and sparked a new wave of resistance. This resistance was led by a man who would soon become a central figure in Swedish history: Gustav Eriksson Vasa.

Vasa used the horror of the events to gain support throughout the country. Within a few years, he organized the uprising, which ended successfully in 1523: Gustav Vasa was elected King of Sweden, the Kalmar Union finally collapsed, and Sweden entered a new era of independence.

Ironically, with his brutality, Christian II achieved exactly the opposite of what he intended. Instead of strengthening the union, he destroyed it. And his own reign did not last long: in 1523, he lost the throne in Denmark as well and spent most of his later life in exile or imprisonment.

For Sweden, however, the Stockholm Massacre remained a trauma—and at the same time a warning sign. It marked the bloody birth of the modern Swedish nation. Even centuries later, poets, historians, and politicians remembered the victims who had given their lives for freedom.

In Sweden, Christian II is often called "Kristian Tyrann" – Christian the Tyrant – to this day. In Denmark, however, he is nicknamed "Christian the Good." This shows how much history depends on perspective: one person remembers banquets and wealth, another remembers blood and sword.

The Stockholm Bloodbath is thus more than just a medieval massacre. It demonstrates how political intrigue, religious conflict, and personal power struggles can shape entire nations. And it reminds us that even great empires can collapse from a single act of cruelty.

Anyone strolling through Stockholm's Old Town, Gamla Stan, today is truly still following the traces of the massacre. Stortorget, the large market square, is particularly closely linked to the events. Here, between the narrow, colorful townhouses, most of the victims were executed. Today, the square appears idyllic – cafés, tourists, and small shops dominate the scene. But if you look more closely, you'll find quiet reminders: 92 white stones are set into the facade windows of the red houses on the north side, symbolically commemorating the beheaded victims.

Stockholm Palace, which today serves as the royal residence, also stands on the foundations of the old castle where Christian II imprisoned the nobles. Of course, the walls have long since been renovated and are magnificent, but guided tours repeatedly recount the horrors of those November days.

At the Stockholm City Museum and the Medieval Museum below the Riksdag, you can also visit exhibitions that shed light on the bloody years of the Kalmar Union. There, you can view everyday objects, weapons, and contemporary chronicles – a direct link to the days when Stockholm teetered between coronation celebrations and massacres.

Guides in Gamla Stan often tell the story in a dramatic tone, pointing to the fountain at Stortorget. It supposedly overflowed with blood during the massacre—historically, this is more of a legend, but it still works as a goosebump-inducing moment today.

Anyone visiting Stockholm can still see the traces of the massacre today – albeit embedded in an old town that is now one of the most beautiful and peaceful in Europe. The contrast could hardly be greater.

1.12 The Augsburg Calendar Dispute

In 1582, Pope Gregory XIII introduced the Gregorian calendar to correct the inaccuracies of the Julian calendar. The Julian calendar, in use since the time of Julius Caesar, had an annual deviation of approximately 11 minutes. This seemingly small difference accumulated over the centuries to a significant discrepancy, causing the date of the beginning of spring to deviate increasingly from the actual astronomical beginning of spring.

The Gregorian calendar was intended to solve this problem by changing the rules for leap years and skipping the 10th day of October 1582, thus balancing the cumulative deviation.
While the Catholic countries of Europe quickly accepted the reform, it met with considerable resistance in Protestant and Orthodox regions.

Augsburg, an important trading and imperial city in the Holy Roman Empire, was a scene of this conflict.

The city was religiously divided: While part of the population remained Catholic, many citizens had converted to the Reformation and belonged to various Protestant denominations. This religious divide was also reflected in the city's political structures.

When the Gregorian calendar was introduced in the Catholic parts of the empire in 1583, the people of Augsburg faced the decision of whether or not to adopt the new calendar. This decision was not only a technical matter of timekeeping, but also a symbolic act of religious affiliation and loyalty.

The calendar dispute in Augsburg quickly escalated into a political and religious crisis. The Protestant majority of the city's population rejected the calendar reform, viewing it as a Catholic dictate. The Catholic authorities, however, pushed for the introduction of the new calendar in order to synchronize with the rest of the Catholic world and preserve the unity of the Church.

The Augsburg City Council was deeply divided on this issue. Discussions and debates dragged on for months without reaching an agreement.

There were public demonstrations and protests, and tensions between the denominations increased.

Some Protestant congregations refused to adopt the new calendar and retained the Julian calendar, leading to confusion and disagreement in the planning of religious and civil celebrations.

The calendar dispute in Augsburg was finally resolved through a compromise. The compromise allowed both the Gregorian and Julian calendars to be used in parallel. Catholic institutions and congregations followed the new calendar, while Protestant congregations continued to use the old one.

This pragmatic solution made it possible to defuse the immediate conflict, but it led to a long period of confusion and the coexistence of two different calendar systems in the city.

It took several decades for the Gregorian calendar to finally become widely accepted, as the political power of the Catholic Habsburgs grew and pressure on Protestant communities increased.

1.13 The Artichoke War

The Artichoke War, also known as "The Artichoke Wars," was an unusual and sometimes bizarre conflict that took place in the United States in the early 1930s.

In the 1920s and 1930s, artichoke production in California experienced a boom. The region around Castroville, which proclaimed itself the "Artichoke Capital of the World," was the center of the artichoke industry. The cultivation and sale of artichokes was a lucrative business, as demand for this exotic vegetable steadily increased. Artichokes were especially prized in Italian-American communities and were considered a delicacy.

The increasing demand and high price of artichokes led to intense competition among producers and traders. The market was increasingly dominated by powerful traders who sought to gain control over the entire production and distribution process.

This led to tensions between the farmers who grew artichokes and the traders who bought and resold the harvest.

One of the central figures in this conflict was Joe "Artichoke King" DiMaggio, a notorious New York gangster who played a significant role in the artichoke trade.

DiMaggio controlled large parts of the artichoke market and used his power to manipulate prices and eliminate competition.

The Artichoke War reached its peak as the traders' methods became increasingly ruthless. Rival gangs were reportedly destroying artichoke fields, hijacking truckloads of artichokes, and extorting farmers to control their production. These criminal activities led to significant violence and intimidation in the region.

New York City Mayor Fiorello LaGuardia decided to crack down on the criminal activities in the artichoke trade. LaGuardia, known for his fight against corruption and organized crime, issued a ban on the sale of artichokes in New York City. He declared the artichoke an illegal commodity, hoping to put an end to the illegal trade.

The artichoke ban in New York City had far-reaching effects on the market. It caused significant disruption and led to a collapse in prices. LaGuardia's actions forced many dealers to reduce or abandon their criminal activities altogether.

Pressure on farmers in California eased and violence decreased.

However, it wasn't long before the ban was lifted. Demand for artichokes was simply too high, and the ban proved economically unsustainable. Nevertheless, LaGuardia's intervention had a lasting impact on the trade. It led to increased efforts to regulate the market and drive criminal elements out of the business.

Measures were taken to better regulate trade and promote fairer business practices. The events also led to increased cooperation between farmers and legitimate traders to stabilize artichoke production and distribution.
Today, Castroville is still known as the "Artichoke Capital of the World" and celebrates an annual artichoke festival that commemorates the region's rich history.

1.14. The Dutch Tulip Mania

The Dutch Tulip Mania, also known as Tulip Fever, was an economic bubble in the 17th century that became one of the most famous speculative frenzy in history. This episode took place in the Netherlands between 1634 and 1637 and is considered one of the first documented speculative bubbles in the global economy.

The 17th-century Netherlands experienced an economic boom known as the "Golden Age." The nation was a center of trade, science, art, and economic innovation.

Tulips, originally from the Ottoman Empire, were introduced to the Netherlands in the late 16th century and quickly became a status symbol. The exotic and colorful flowers were particularly sought after by the wealthy upper classes.

Tulip bulbs were difficult to cultivate and thus became a valuable commodity because they were rare. The unusual and unique patterns and colors caused by a mosaic virus made some varieties highly sought after. This rarity and beauty of tulips led to a rapid increase in demand and, consequently, in prices.

Tulip mania began in the early 1630s, as more and more people entered the tulip bulb trade. The tulip market was not only dominated by wealthy collectors and gardeners, but also attracted speculators hoping for quick profits. Tulips became a speculative commodity, and prices for certain rare varieties soared.

Tulip bulbs were no longer viewed merely as plants, but as financial investments. Tulip bulb trading took place not only at flower markets, but also in taverns and on specially established exchanges. Contracts for the future purchase of tulip bulbs were traded, further fueling the speculative fever. These contracts were often purchased on credit, increasing the risks and potential losses for speculators.

The peak of tulip mania was reached in the winter of 1636/1637. Prices for tulip bulbs had reached astronomical heights.

One example of the extreme price increase is the "Semper Augustus" variety, whose bulbs sold for the equivalent of a luxurious Amsterdam canal house. Another case documents the sale of a single tulip bulb for 10,000 guilders, equivalent to the annual salary of a wealthy merchant.

High demand and extreme prices led more and more people to enter the market, hoping to profit from rising prices.
This led to a speculative price bubble in which prices far exceeded the actual value of the tulip bulbs.
In February 1637, the bubble burst suddenly and unexpectedly:

At an auction in Haarlem, buyers suddenly refused to purchase tulip bulbs at exorbitant prices. This led to a loss of confidence and a rapid price drop. Panic quickly spread, and prices plummeted.
Within a few days, tulip bulbs that were previously worth a fortune lost almost all of their value.
Many speculators who had bought tulip bulbs on credit faced financial ruin.

The banks and lenders who had financed these speculations faced a flood of defaults. The collapse of the tulip mania led to significant economic turmoil in the Netherlands, leaving many people impoverished and indebted.

However, it had surprisingly little long-term impact on the Dutch economy.
The Netherlands recovered quickly, and the tulip mania soon became a lesson in the dangers of speculation.

The tulip mania is often referred to as the first speculative bubble in history and has fascinated generations of economists and historians.

1.15. The counterfeit fraudster Alves dos Reis

The Alves dos Reis counterfeit money fraud was one of the largest and most sophisticated financial scandals of the 20th century. This fraud took place in Portugal in the 1920s and had significant repercussions for the Portuguese financial and economic system.

Alves dos Reis, a highly intelligent and charismatic fraudster, managed to deceive the Portuguese banking system and put an enormous amount of counterfeit money into circulation.

He began by creating forged documents claiming to be an official representative of the Banco de Portugal. Using these forgeries, he managed to convince Waterlow and Sons in London, a printing company that actually produced the genuine banknotes for the Banco de Portugal, to print additional 500-escudo notes.

These banknotes were of exceptionally high quality and were difficult to distinguish from the genuine ones.
Dos Reis convinced the printing company that the additional banknotes were intended for a secret transaction to support the Portuguese economy.

Through his charismatic and persuasive manner, he managed to convince the printing press's management of the authenticity of his story. In total, more than 100,000 additional banknotes worth approximately 500 million escudos were printed.

With the freshly printed banknotes, dos Reis began circulating his counterfeit money. He founded a series of shell companies and banks, including Banco Angola e Metrópole, to launder the money and integrate it into the Portuguese economy. Through this bank and other institutions, dos Reis was able to invest the counterfeit money and make it appear legitimate.
He invested in a wide variety of projects, including real estate, industrial facilities, and public works. Dos Reis quickly became one of the richest and most influential men in Portugal. His perceived financial successes earned him respect and admiration in Portuguese society.

Alves dos Reis lived a lavish lifestyle and made numerous large investments, which attracted attention. His sudden wealth and extensive investments aroused suspicion among various banks and business partners. The huge sums flowing through his bank, Banco Angola e Metrópole, were eventually noticed.

The Bank of Portugal began to notice irregularities in its financial system. There were more 500-escudo notes in circulation than had originally been issued. This discrepancy was a major warning sign that caught the attention of bank officials.

To find the source of the irregularities, the Banco de Portugal launched an internal investigation. They analyzed the serial numbers of the 500-escudo notes and discovered that some of the banknotes in circulation had duplicate serial numbers. This suggested that additional banknotes had been printed with the same serial numbers as the originals.

Some journalists covering financial topics also became aware of the irregularities and began investigating, uncovering the connection between Alves dos Reis and the large transactions that went through his bank.

In December 1925, Alves dos Reis was arrested. During interrogation and subsequent trial, he confessed to his role in the counterfeit money fraud. Alves dos Reis was sentenced to a long prison term in 1930.

The Bank of Portugal was forced to recall all 500-escudo notes in circulation and issue new ones. Portugal's economy experienced significant turmoil due to the loss of confidence in the financial system.

In 1955, Alves dos Reis died impoverished and forgotten after spending many years in prison.

1.16. The Soldier Bear Wojtek

Wars are full of suffering, death, and destruction – but sometimes, amidst the horror, stories emerge that sound so unbelievable they almost seem like fairy tales. One of these stories tells of a bear who became a soldier. His name: Wojtek.
It all began in 1942 in Iran, then Persia. Polish soldiers, who had been released from Soviet captivity under General Władysław Anders and were now fighting under British command, came across a small Syrian brown bear in the mountains. The animal was an orphaned cub, whose mother had fallen victim to hunters. A shepherd boy had found it and offered it for sale to the soldiers. The men, who had themselves lost their homes and families, took the little bear in. They named him Wojtek – which in Polish means something like "cheerful warrior" or "the one who brings joy in battle."
Wojtek quickly became a favorite of the unit. At first, he drank milk from old vodka bottles, later he ate bread, fruit, and, much to the soldiers' amusement, cigarettes—not for smoking, but chewing them like gum. Over time, he also developed a taste for beer, which he drank from pitchers or straight from the bottle, as if he were one of the men. Soon, the bear was no longer just a mascot, but a real member of the Polish 2nd Corps.
The soldiers raised him like a comrade. Wojtek learned to march upright, sometimes even saluting awkwardly with his paw, and slept among the men in the tent at night. He loved to wrestle with the soldiers—a kind of fun fight that he almost always won, even though he reportedly took care not to grab too hard. For the men fighting far from home, Wojtek was more than just an animal: he was a symbol of hope, normality, and a sense of home.
His fame reached its peak in 1944 at the Battle of Monte Cassino in Italy. There, the Polish 2nd Corps fought alongside the Allies against the German troops holding the Benedictine monastery on the mountain. To officially take Wojtek with them, the soldiers promptly registered him as a real soldier. He was enlisted in the 22nd Artillery Supply Company and even received a military rank: Corporal Wojtek.
During the battle, the bear helped transport ammunition crates – heavy wooden crates filled with grenades, which he carried back and forth between trucks and guns as if it were second nature. Eyewitnesses report that he did this calmly and with concentration, as if it were the most normal thing in the world. His performance was so impressive that Wojtek soon became the unit's official emblem. From then on, their vehicles bore the symbol of a bear carrying a mortar shell.
Wojtek's army file actually contains an entry with his name, rank, and position. This officially makes him the only bear in military history to have served in an army—complete with a salary (in the form of food) and his own "uniform number."

After the war, the Polish Corps never returned home—Poland had since been occupied by the Soviet Union and had become a different political state. Instead, the units were relocated to Great Britain. And, of course, Wojtek came along. The British press reported enthusiastically on the "Bear Soldier," and Wojtek became a minor celebrity.

But life in peacetime was more difficult for an adult bear. In 1947, after the demobilization of the Polish troops, it was decided to transfer Wojtek to Edinburgh Zoo. He lived there until his death in 1963. For the veterans, however, he remained a companion. Many visited him regularly, throwing cigarettes or chocolate bars over the fence to him and speaking to him in Polish. Visitors report that Wojtek often pricked up his ears when he heard Polish and immediately came curiously to the fence—as if recognizing his old comrades. Today, several memorials in Poland, Italy, and Scotland commemorate the most unusual soldier of World War II. In Edinburgh, Krakow, and even London, there are statues of Wojtek holding a grenade in his paws. His story has long been part of military folklore—but also an example of how a piece of humanity survived the darkest times of war.

Wojtek was so popular that he sometimes "marched" alongside the veterans at military parades in Scotland. He reportedly even attempted to march upright in step—much to the amusement of the spectators.

Chapter 2: Scientific Wonders

This chapter highlights some of the most astonishing scientific discoveries and phenomena that have expanded our understanding of the world. From the structure of DNA to the mysteries of dark matter, science continues to demonstrate how curiosity, chance, and persistence can lead to new discoveries. Stay tuned for the next chapters, where more fascinating stories and facts await you.

2.1. The discovery of DNA by a lucky coincidence

Sometimes a tiny moment changes world history—and sometimes even in the laboratory. The discovery of the structure of DNA in 1953 is a prime example. It was not only a milestone in biology, but also the result of a mixture of genius, rivalry, and a lucky coincidence.
DNA – deoxyribonucleic acid – had been known for decades, but for a long time, no one knew exactly how it was structured. It was suspected that it played a central role in inheritance, but the details remained mysterious. In the early 20th century, it was almost as if biologists were holding a mysterious book whose characters they couldn't decipher.
In the 1940s and 50s, the race to decipher DNA began. Several research teams in the US and the UK worked feverishly to decipher the structure of DNA. Among them were James Watson, a young, ambitious biologist from the US, and Francis Crick, a British physicist who had turned to biology late in life. They worked at the Cavendish Laboratory in Cambridge and formed an unlikely but brilliant duo.
Their competitors were just a few kilometers away at King's College in London: Rosalind Franklin, a highly gifted physicist specializing in X-ray crystallography, and Maurice Wilkins, also an experienced researcher. While Watson and Crick were more theorists who experimented with models, Franklin was the one who collected real data through precise laboratory work.

The decisive moment came in 1952. Franklin had taken an X-ray diffraction image of DNA, which would later become famous as "Photo 51." It revealed the characteristic pattern of a helix—a spiral structure. This image was the key. But whether by coincidence, misunderstanding, or questionable scientific ethics, Watson saw the photo through Wilkins without Franklin's knowledge. When he examined it, he immediately realized that it contained the answer to their questions.

From then on, things moved quickly. Watson and Crick combined the findings from Photo 51 with their own modeling ideas. In March 1953, they presented the famous double helix: two spirally wound strands connected by base pairs arranged like the rungs of a ladder. This model finally explained how genetic information can be stored and duplicated—the basis of all life.

After the discovery, Watson and Crick reportedly went to a pub to celebrate their success. There, Crick allegedly proclaimed: "We have discovered the secret of life!" – one of the most arrogant, yet at the same time most accurate, statements in the history of science.

On April 25, 1953, they published their results in *Nature*. The article was surprisingly short—barely more than a page—but its content changed biology forever. From that moment, modern genetics began: the study of genes, the genetic code, the possibility of understanding diseases, and eventually even the manipulation of DNA in genetic engineering.

But the story also had a tragic side. Rosalind Franklin, whose precise work provided the crucial clue, was long underappreciated. She died of cancer in 1958, at the age of just 37, presumably also exposed to radiation from her work. By the time Watson, Crick, and Wilkins received the Nobel Prize in Physiology or Medicine in 1962, Franklin was long dead—and the Nobel Prize is not awarded posthumously. Only decades later did her contribution begin to be truly recognized. Today, she is considered one of the most important, albeit underappreciated, scientists of the 20th century.

The role of chance in this story is remarkable. If Watson hadn't gotten his hands on the famous Photo 51—perhaps secretly, or at least without Franklin's consent—he and Crick might not have recognized the double helix so quickly. Other teams were also working on the structure, and it's conceivable that Franklin herself would have made the discovery, given the necessary time and recognition.

In the 1990s, when the structure of DNA was already known worldwide, British science journalists voted the double helix the "most beautiful scientific image of all time." An X-ray photograph that changed the world—and that actually only fell into the right hands by a lucky coincidence.

Today, the double helix is ubiquitous. It adorns the logos of research institutes, jewelry, advertising campaigns, and even tattoos. Hardly any other scientific discovery has become such a powerful symbol. The idea that our genome functions like a coiled rope ladder has not only revolutionized biology but also changed our self-image as humans.

Without Watson and Crick, without Franklin and Wilkins, without the famous Photo 51, there would be no genetic research, no DNA testing to establish paternity, no modern forensics, no genetic engineering, and probably no personalized medicine. And all of this began with a happy glance at an X-ray.

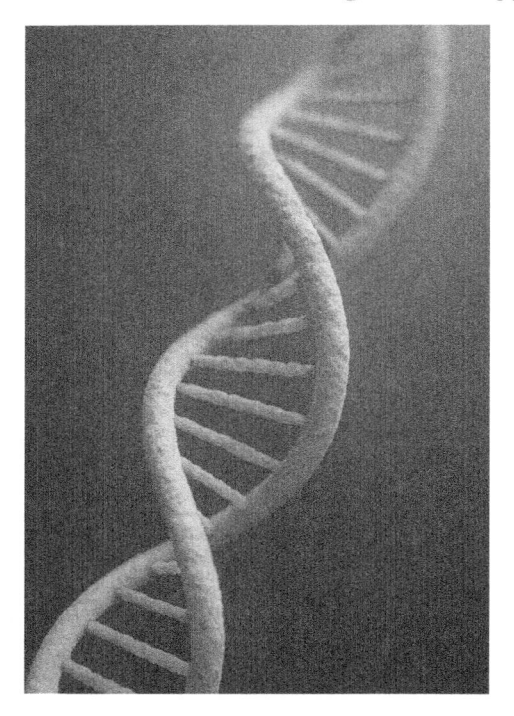

2.2. The mystery of dark matter

When we look up at the starry sky at night, it seems clear and transparent: twinkling stars, glowing galaxies, luminous nebulae. One might think the universe consists simply of what we see. But modern astronomy teaches us the opposite: Most of the cosmos is invisible. To be more precise, we cannot see almost 85 percent of the matter in the universe. Researchers call this invisible substance "dark matter."
The term sounds mysterious, almost fantasy-like. But in fact, it's a very sober, scientific mystery. Dark matter doesn't emit, reflect, or absorb light—it's invisible to telescopes. And yet we know it must exist. The reason: its gravity. As early as the 1930s, astronomers noticed something strange. The Swiss physicist Fritz Zwicky observed galaxy clusters and discovered that they were moving much faster than the known laws of gravity would allow. They should have been flying apart—and yet they stayed together. Zwicky concluded that there must be an invisible mass in space that creates additional gravity. He called it "dark matter."
At first, he was hardly taken seriously. But in the 1970s, astronomer Vera Rubin confirmed his hypothesis. She investigated the rotation speeds of galaxies and discovered that stars at the edge of a galaxy orbit at the same speed as stars near the center. This contradicted all expectations: Without additional invisible mass, the outer stars would have long since flown away. Only when galaxies are surrounded by a huge "halo" of invisible matter does the motion make sense. Since then, the existence of dark matter has been considered virtually certain. Today, astronomers assume that it makes up about 27 percent of the entire universe. By comparison, everything we see—stars, planets, gas clouds, people, books—is made of "normal" matter and makes up just about 5 percent of the universe. The rest? Unknown.
But what is dark matter? This is where the real mystery begins. So far, no one has been able to directly detect it. It emits no radiation, it doesn't react to electromagnetic forces, and it remains invisible. Researchers have developed a variety of theories. Perhaps it consists of as yet undiscovered particles, so-called WIMPs ("Weakly Interacting Massive Particles"), which interact only weakly with normal matter. Or perhaps it is axions, hypothetical particles that would be extremely light and almost intangible. Some even speculate that dark matter could consist of countless tiny black holes.
To find answers, physicists around the world have built huge detectors – deep underground, shielded from radiation and interference. In old mines in Italy, the USA, or beneath the Alps, they are searching for the rare collisions between dark matter and normal atoms. So far, however: nothing.
The experiments are so sensitive that they are sometimes disturbed by completely banal things—such as radon gas from the rocks or the tiny radioactive decay of dust grains. Dark matter, on the other hand, remains silent.

Some researchers are now drawing more radical conclusions: Perhaps dark matter doesn't exist at all. Perhaps our understanding of gravity is incorrect. Alternative theories such as "MOND" (Modified Newtonian Dynamics) propose that gravity works differently on large scales than we believe. But most astronomers continue to cling to dark matter – simply because it is the most elegant explanation for the observations.

And as if that weren't enough, there's a second great unknown: dark energy. While dark matter keeps galaxies from falling apart, dark energy appears to be doing the opposite—driving the universe's expansion ever faster. Together, dark matter and dark energy account for almost 95 percent of cosmic "mass-energy." In other words, we only truly understand about 5 percent of the universe.

A physicist once said, "It's as if we baked a cake, tasted it, and discovered that we only know the icing. The rest of the cake is invisible."

For the public, dark matter has long been a mythical entity. It appears in science fiction films, video games, even comics. It has become the modern "ether"—the invisible medium that was thought to be responsible for the propagation of light in the 19th century before it was refuted by Einstein's theory of relativity. Perhaps one day, dark matter, too, will be replaced by a radically new theory. But until then, it remains the greatest invisible mystery of natural science.

The interesting thing is: We feel its effects everywhere. Without dark matter, there would probably be no galaxies, no stars, no planets, no humans. It is the invisible glue of the cosmos—the invisible framework upon which the visible world rests.

2.3. The incredible abilities of tardigrades

When it comes to the question of which creature is the toughest on our planet, most people think of cockroaches. After all, they're said to be able to survive even a nuclear war. But in reality, there's an even tougher creature that breaks all records – and that hardly anyone knows about: the tardigrade, also affectionately called "water bear."

Tardigrades are tiny, eight-legged micro-animals, usually only 0.1 to 1 millimeter in size. Under the microscope, they look like miniature bears with round bodies and clumsy little feet—hence their name. But as cute as they may appear, their abilities are anything but harmless. Water bears are true survivors, braving conditions that would be fatal to almost any other living creature.

They can survive extreme temperatures: from almost -272 degrees Celsius, close to absolute zero, to over 150 degrees Celsius. They can withstand pressure thousands of times higher than normal atmospheric pressure on Earth—conditions found deep beneath the ocean. Tardigrades also survive lethal radiation, which would be devastating even to humans within seconds, almost unfazed. And as if that weren't enough, experiments have shown that they can even survive in the vacuum of space.

How do they do it? The secret lies in a process biologists call cryptobiosis. When conditions become hostile, tardigrades retreat into a kind of dry state. They curl up their bodies, retract their legs, and shrink into a tiny "barrel." In this state, they lose almost all their body water and reduce their metabolism to almost zero. This allows them to survive for years, some say even decades, in a kind of standby mode – and as soon as water and food become available again, they simply wake up again.

Researchers have "thawed" tardigrades that had been frozen for over 30 years. Some of them continued to live as if nothing had happened—a biological miracle that blurs the notion of life and death.

Tardigrades can be found almost everywhere: in moss, puddles, sand, sea floors, trees, and even glaciers. All you need is a microscope and a little patience to spot them. It's a strange idea that in almost every patch of moss live small creatures that are tougher than any other known animal.

Their abilities make them particularly exciting for science. Biologists and physicians hope to decipher the mechanisms of cryptobiosis. If we understand how tardigrades protect their cells, these findings could perhaps be applied to medicine—for example, in the preservation of organs or vaccines. They are also interesting for space travel: If tiny tardigrades can survive the vacuum and radiation of space, similar mechanisms might one day protect astronauts on long missions.

In 2007, tardigrades even officially became "astronauts." As part of the FOTON-M3 mission, European researchers sent them into Earth's orbit. There, they were directly exposed to the vacuum of space and cosmic radiation—conditions that would be fatal to humans within seconds. Upon their return, it was discovered that some of the animals had survived and were even able to reproduce. This makes tardigrades the first known animals to have survived a journey into open space.

Some scientists joke that if Earth were ever struck by a cosmic catastrophe—be it a meteorite, nuclear war, or radiation—tardigrades would likely be the last survivors. In this sense, one could say: The future belongs to tardigrades.

But as indestructible as they appear, tardigrades also have limitations. They cannot remain in cryptobiosis indefinitely, and not all survive extreme conditions equally well. Nevertheless, their abilities are unparalleled.

It's also remarkable that they've developed some genetic tricks that are rarely found elsewhere. Their genome contains genes that appear to originate from bacteria and fungi—so-called horizontal gene transfers. Tardigrades have likely absorbed pieces of foreign DNA over the course of evolution, which helped them survive.

Today, tardigrades are considered tiny superheroes of the microcosm. They remind us that nature often finds the most astonishing solutions where we least expect them. While we humans build gigantic machines and technologies to survive extremes, tardigrades need a tiny body and a bit of cryptobiosis to defy the conditions of space.

2.4. The infinite number: The paradox of Pi

There are numbers that seem inconspicuous, and those that become legends. One of the most well-known and fascinating numbers in mathematics Pi (π) clearly belongs to the latter category. Everyone learned in school that π is the ratio of the circumference of a circle to its diameter—a simple definition that anyone with a compass and ruler can understand. But behind this seemingly simple formula lies one of the greatest mysteries and, at the same time, one of the most beautiful symbols in mathematics.

The value of π begins with 3.14159... and never ends after that. π is an irrational number. This means its decimal places continue indefinitely without repeating a pattern. One could calculate millions of digits, and yet one would be no closer to capturing the "whole" number. Pi is infinite, chaotic—and yet precise enough to launch rockets into space.

Even ancient cultures were fascinated by this number. The Egyptians and Babylonians knew approximate values of π, which they used in the construction of pyramids and temples. Archimedes of Syracuse was one of the first to develop a systematic method for calculating π in the 3rd century BC: He approximated circles using polygons with increasingly more sides and thus estimated π to be between 3.1408 and 3.1429. For his time, this was an astonishingly accurate value.

With the development of new mathematics, the calculation of π also became more refined. In the Middle Ages, scholars used infinite series; later, mathematicians like Leibniz discovered that π appeared in all sorts of formulas and equations—far beyond geometry. The number became a symbol for the hidden connections of mathematics: π can be found in integrals, in probability theory, in quantum physics, and even in the description of the spirals of mussels.

In the 20th and 21st centuries, computer processing power came into play. Today, π has been calculated to over 62 trillion decimal places (as of 2021). But this dizzying number has little practical use: just a few dozen decimal places are enough to calculate the circumference of the visible galaxy with an accuracy of a fraction of an atom. The rest is—one could say—mathematical luxury.

NASA engineers use just 15 decimal places of π on space missions. Greater precision would be simply unnecessary for navigation calculations.

The fascination of π lies not in its practical necessity, but in its infinity. Many mathematicians compare the number to a treasure chest, which promises ever-new patterns – yet reveals no clear structures. Some hope that certain "messages" or patterns lie hidden in the infinite sequences of digits, such as the entire works of Shakespeare encoded as a sequence of numbers. Indeed, this is not entirely unreasonable: If π truly is a "normal number," then its infinite decimal expansion contains every conceivable sequence of numbers – thus also every text, every image, every melody, if only translated correctly.

But whether π is actually normal remains unproven to this day. The paradox of pi is that we want to know it with infinite precision, even though we know we can never fully understand it. It is the epitome of mathematical beauty: simply defined, infinitely complex.

Every year on March 14, mathematicians around the world celebrate "Pi Day." The date in the American format – 3/14 – corresponds to the first three digits of π. Traditionally, this day features not only mathematical lectures but also cake, or "pie" in English. Thus, advanced mathematics combines with high-calorie bombs.

Pi is no longer just a number, but a cultural symbol. It appears in poems, films, and science fiction novels. Director Darren Aronofsky made the film *p*, a dark psychodrama about a mathematician obsessed with the infinite number. Writers such as Umberto Eco and Jorge Luis Borges have used the infinite nature of π as a metaphor for the human quest for knowledge.

Pi shows us our limitations. We can calculate them with increasing precision, but we can never fully grasp them. We can use it to build bridges and measure the stars, but the infinite depth of its digits remains hidden from us. It mirrors the relationship between humanity and knowledge—we understand enough to live, research, and dream, but never everything.

2.5. The Placebo Effect: How Faith Can Move Mountains

There are moments when medicine seems to border on magic. One of them is the **Placebo Effect**– a phenomenon in which patients experience an improvement in their symptoms despite having received only a "sham treatment": a sugar pill with no active ingredient, a saline infusion, or even an operation that was not performed at all.

What sounds like self-deception has long been an integral part of medical research. Studies repeatedly show that the mere belief that one is being treated can trigger measurable changes in the body – pain relief, lower blood pressure, improved mood, and even improved motor skills in Parkinson's patients.

The history of the placebo effect goes back a long way. As early as the 18th century, doctors noticed that patients sometimes benefited from treatments that were objectively completely useless. However, it wasn't until the 20th century that the effect was systematically researched. Since the 1950s at the latest, it has been considered an indispensable control factor in clinical trials: New drugs are always tested against placebos to determine whether their effects actually go beyond the belief effect.

But how does it work? The placebo effect shows that mind and body are more closely connected than we often believe. Neuroscientists have discovered that when a placebo is taken, the brain actually releases endorphins and other neurotransmitters—the same substances that provide pain relief in real medications. Thus, the body is reacting "real" to a "fake" treatment.

What's particularly astonishing is that placebos work even when patients know they're receiving a placebo. In so-called "open-label" studies, in which doctors disclose that the pill is inactive, patients still report improvements. The ritual, the attention, and the hope alone seem to exert their own healing power.

In the 1990s, US studies showed that patients who underwent sham knee surgery (just a small incision, but no intervention) experienced just as much improvement in osteoarthritis pain as those who had the actual surgery. Believing in the surgery was enough to relieve pain and increase mobility.

The placebo effect has many facets. It depends on expectations, but also on the type of treatment. A large, colored tablet often works better than a small, white one. Two pills are more powerful than one. A shot inspires more trust than a pill—and a surgery more than a shot. The doctor's authority, demeanor, and environment also play a role. One could say: The placebo effect is not just chemistry, but also theater.

Of course, there is also the downside: the **Nocebo Effect** Symptoms worsen because patients have negative expectations. Those who believe a drug has many side effects often experience them even if they have only received a placebo. Thus, the mind can not only heal, but also make people sick.

From a philosophical perspective, the placebo effect raises questions. If belief in a treatment can have healing powers, what does that say about our relationship to illness and health? Are we stronger than we think, or more vulnerable to our own beliefs?

In modern medicine, the placebo effect is viewed not only as a disruptive factor, but also as a resource. Doctors know that even the way they speak to patients can influence their chances of recovery. Positive expectation, empathy, and trust enhance the effectiveness of therapies. One could say: The placebo effect is the invisible medicine that every doctor carries with them—without a prescription pad.

The placebo effect shows that healing is not just a matter of chemistry and technology, but also of rituals, expectations, and trust. It is proof that humans are not just biological, but also deeply psychological beings. And perhaps this also explains the saying that faith can move mountains—sometimes even with a simple sugar pill.

2.6. The mysterious "Wow!" signal

The "Wow!" signal is one of the most exciting and discussed events in the history of the Search for Extraterrestrial Intelligence (SETI). On the evening of August 15, 1977, astronomer Jerry R. Ehman, using Ohio State University's Big Ear radio telescope, received a powerful, 72-second radio signal from deep space that eclipsed all previous signals.

The signal was so extraordinary that when Ehman analyzed the data, he wrote the word "Wow!" in red ink on the margin of the printout. This spontaneous reaction gave the signal its famous name. It came from the direction of the constellation Sagittarius, more specifically, from the vicinity of the star Tau Sagittarii, about 120 light-years from Earth.

The "Wow!" signal had a frequency of 1420 MHz, which corresponds to the hydrogen line. This is the natural emission frequency of hydrogen, the most abundant element in the universe. Many scientists and SETI researchers believe that extraterrestrial civilizations could use this frequency for interstellar communication because it lies in the so-called "watering hole" region of the radio spectrum, which is relatively free of background noise.

Despite intensive searches and repeated attempts to re-obtain the signal, the "Wow!" signal was never observed again. This has led to a variety of speculations and theories about its origin. Some of the most common theories include:

Extraterrestrial Civilization: One of the most exciting theories is that the signal was emitted by an advanced extraterrestrial civilization. The specific frequency and strength of the signal suggest that it may have been sent intentionally to attract attention.

Natural astrophysical phenomena: Some scientists speculate that the signal could have been caused by a previously unknown natural phenomenon. However, there are currently no known astrophysical processes that could explain a signal of this type and intensity.

Earth-like interference: Another possibility is that the signal was caused by human activity or satellite interference. However, this theory is largely ruled out because the 1420 MHz frequency is reserved internationally for astronomical purposes, and terrestrial signals can usually be ruled out.

Movement of objects in space It has also been suggested that the signal originated from a fast-moving object such as a comet or asteroid that randomly reflected or emitted the radio waves. This theory remains controversial, as no corresponding objects have been detected near the signal's origin at the time of the signal.

The "Wow!" signal remains one of astronomy's great unsolved mysteries. It has inspired scientists and enthusiasts alike and remains a symbol of the ongoing search for extraterrestrial life. Although decades have passed, the hope remains that we will one day find a definitive answer.

2.7. The formation of jellyfish inside icebergs

One of many mysterious phenomena is the emergence of jellyfish inside icebergs. These curious discoveries have amazed and challenged scientists and researchers alike, raising questions about the viability and adaptability of marine organisms under extreme conditions.

The phenomenon was first discovered in the early 2000s by polar researchers studying Antarctic waters. While examining ice samples from deep within icebergs, they encountered tiny, frozen jellyfish. This discovery was completely unexpected, as icebergs are considered extremely hostile environments, where temperatures drop well below freezing and light is almost completely absent.

The formation of jellyfish inside icebergs raises several interesting questions:

How do jellyfish get into icebergs? One theory is that the jellyfish larvae are carried near the icebergs by ocean currents. When the seawater around the icebergs freezes, the larvae could become trapped in the growing ice masses. This process could explain how the jellyfish get into the icebergs before they completely freeze.

How do jellyfish survive in the ice? Jellyfish are known for their remarkable adaptability. Some species can significantly slow down their vital functions when temperatures drop, entering a kind of hibernation. It's possible that jellyfish larvae possess similar mechanisms that allow them to survive in a state of dormancy until conditions become more favorable.

What happens when the jellyfish thaw? The biggest surprise came when researchers slowly thawed some of the frozen jellyfish samples. To their surprise, some of the jellyfish showed signs of viability after thawing. These observations raise the possibility that some jellyfish larvae are actually capable of surviving freezing and thawing. The discovery of jellyfish inside icebergs has not only biological and ecological implications, but also scientific and philosophical ones. It challenges our understanding of life and survival under extreme conditions and opens new perspectives for the study of life in extreme environments, both on Earth and possibly on other planets and moons in the solar system. Some researchers also see parallels in these discoveries with the conditions on icy moons like Europa, one of Jupiter's moons, which may conceal an ocean beneath its icy crust. If life can exist in the extreme conditions of an Earthly iceberg, this could support the possibility of life in similar extreme environments in space.

While research into this phenomenon is still in its infancy, the emergence of jellyfish inside icebergs remains an interesting and enigmatic example of the incredible adaptability of life.

2.8 The discovery of water on Mars

The red planet has fascinated humans for centuries. Even early telescopic observations in the 19th century sparked the idea that Mars might harbor traces of life. Astronomers like Giovanni Schiaparelli believed they saw artificial "canals" on its surface—lines supposedly built by a highly advanced civilization. Today we know that these observations were optical illusions. But the question remained: Is there water on Mars—and thus the basis for life?

The answer to this question took on a new dimension in 2015. At that time, NASA announced that there was evidence of liquid salt water on Mars. This statement was based on data from several orbiters, primarily from the Mars Reconnaissance Orbiter, which has been orbiting the planet since 2006. Researchers had discovered dark streaks in the images that appeared on the slopes of craters and canyons. These formations, called "recurring slope lineae," changed seasonally—they grew in the warmer months and disappeared again in the winter.

The obvious explanation: water. More precisely, salty meltwater that remains liquid at low temperatures. Pure water would immediately evaporate or freeze in the extreme conditions on Mars. But salt lowers the freezing point, making the survival of small amounts of liquid possible. This was the first evidence that Mars is not just a dead desert planet, but is still subject to active water cycles.

Why is this so important? Water is the key to life as we know it. Wherever water occurs on Earth—be it in hot springs, crevasses, or the deep sea—microbes are almost always found. So if there is water on Mars, at least microbial life could exist or have existed there.

The discovery also raised hopes for the future colonization of Mars. Water would be the most important resource for astronauts: not only for drinking, but also for producing oxygen and fuel. Instead of bringing everything from Earth, future Mars travelers might be able to harvest water directly on the planet—a crucial step toward making long-term missions possible.

But the euphoria was soon dampened. Further investigations showed that the dark streaks don't necessarily have to be caused by water. They may also be dry debris that shifts seasonally. Other measurements indicated that the amounts of water, if any, are extremely small—more like wet patches than streams. The debate remains ongoing to this day.

One thing is certain, however: Mars is a planet with a turbulent water history. Billions of years ago, it had rivers, lakes, and perhaps even oceans. Satellite images show dried-up riverbeds and coastlines. Mars's current climate is too cold and thin to retain large amounts of water on the surface. But researchers suspect that vast amounts of ice and perhaps even subterranean lakes could still be hidden beneath the surface. Indeed, in 2018, the European Mars Express spacecraft used radar waves to discover a 20-kilometer-wide lake beneath a thick layer of ice at the planet's south pole.

If all of Mars' ice were melted, a global ocean would be created that could cover the entire planet with a layer of water about 30 meters deep. The "red planet" would essentially be a "frozen blue planet."

The discovery of water on Mars has not only scientific but also philosophical significance. It touches on one of humanity's oldest questions: Are we alone in the universe? Even the smallest microbes on Mars would prove that life is not an exclusively terrestrial phenomenon, but a cosmic principle.

Of course, science fiction also plays a role. From H. G. Wells' *War of the Worlds* to modern Hollywood films such as *There Martians* The red planet has repeatedly captured our imagination. The idea that water flows there makes it even more tangible—as a possible second habitat.

After the 2015 NASA press conference, the hashtag #MarsWater trended on Twitter, and some users posted pictures of Mars Bars dissolving in glasses of water. Proof that major scientific breakthroughs are now instantly transformed into memes.

For research, Mars is the most exciting destination in the solar system. Rovers like Curiosity and Perseverance are already drilling for traces of organic molecules. Future missions are expected to bring samples back to Earth. And who knows – perhaps the first Mars colonists will actually drink water that was frozen deep in the planet's depths billions of years ago.

2.9. CRISPR-Cas9 genetic engineering / molecular scissors

Imagine if one could not only read the "Book of Life" but also specifically correct typos. What remains impossible in literature is now reality in biology: Using CRISPR-Cas9 genetic engineering, scientists can precisely cut, modify, and reassemble the DNA of living organisms—almost as easily as using word processing software.

The discovery of this method is one of the most exciting stories in modern science. CRISPR-Cas9 is not based on an ingenious laboratory invention, but on a natural mechanism that bacteria have used for millions of years to defend themselves against viruses.

The name sounds complicated: **CRISPR** stands for **"Clustered Regularly Interspaced Short Palindromic Repeats"**—short, repeating DNA sequences that act like a genetic memory. Bacteria store fragments of viral DNA there that have previously infected them. Should the same virus attack again, the bacterium recognizes it immediately. With the help of the enzyme Cas9—"CRISPR-associated protein 9"—it can cut the foreign DNA at the appropriate point, thus rendering it harmless.

Researchers realized that this principle could be used for other purposes. If bacteria can fight viruses in this way, why not use the same "molecular scissors" to specifically cut DNA in plants, animals, or humans?

The major breakthrough came in 2012. Two scientists, Emmanuelle Charpentier and Jennifer Doudna, first described how CRISPR-Cas9 could be used in the laboratory. Using a type of "guide RNA," Cas9 is guided to the exact location in the DNA. There, the enzyme precisely cuts the double helix. The genome can then be repaired or a new piece of DNA can be inserted. This marked the completion of the revolution: a tool that can modify genes quickly, cheaply, and reliably – something that previously required years of complex experiments.

For this discovery, Charpentier and Doudna received the 2020 Nobel Prize in Chemistry, making them one of the few all-female teams ever to win a Nobel Prize.

The applications are immense. With CRISPR, researchers can switch off genes to understand their function. They can correct mutations that cause diseases. Initial clinical studies show that patients with sickle cell anemia or beta thalassemia could benefit from this technique, as the defective genes in their blood stem cells are repaired. Cancer research is also intensively testing whether CRISPR can be used to "upgrade" immune cells so that they can specifically attack tumors.

But molecular scissors aren't just used in medicine. They're also opening up new possibilities in agriculture. Plants can be made more resistant to pests or droughts without having to insert foreign genes. Instead, existing genes are specifically modified – blurring the line between traditional breeding and modern biotechnology. Tomatoes that stay fresh longer or rice varieties that combat vitamin deficiencies are just the beginning.

Of course, this power also raises questions. If it's so easy to modify genes, what's stopping us from shaping the human genome at will? In 2018, Chinese researcher He Jiankui caused a worldwide stir when he announced that he had genetically modified two babies to make them resistant to HIV. The outcry was enormous—not only because of the ethical issues, but also because no one can predict the long-term consequences of such interventions.

The debate is reminiscent of scenes from science fiction novels: designer babies, tailor-made humans, super soldiers. While reality is still a long way off, science and politics are already struggling to set limits. One thing is clear: CRISPR-Cas9 has opened a door that can no longer be closed.

In an interview, Jennifer Doudna compared the invention to the moment someone first built the atomic bomb. The difference, she said, was that this time, the ethical consequences could be discussed in time—before the tool was misused.

Despite all the risks, CRISPR offers hope. Perhaps in the future, it will be possible to cure diseases like muscular dystrophy, cystic fibrosis, or even Alzheimer's by repairing faulty genes. Perhaps agriculture will become more resilient to climate change. Perhaps we will even learn to save entire species from extinction by genetically adapting them to new living conditions.

Molecular scissors have ushered biology into a new era. They demonstrate that humans can not only observe nature, but also change it at the deepest level—at the very script of life itself. This is both magnificent and frightening.

Thus, CRISPR-Cas9 becomes a symbol of our time: a tool that can bring healing and hope, but also raises the question of whether we are ready to intervene so deeply in the foundations of life.

2.10 The Brain – A Miracle of Nature

There is no organ in our body as mysterious and yet as indispensable as the brain. From the outside, it appears unspectacular: a gray, ridged mass, weighing around one and a half kilograms, soft as gelatin. Yet this inconspicuous lump is the center of our existence. It is here that thoughts and memories are formed, emotions are controlled, and who we are and how we perceive the world are determined. It is no coincidence that some scientists describe the brain as "the most complex object in the known universe."

Its sheer complexity is almost incomprehensible. Approximately 86 billion nerve cells, or neurons, are interconnected within it. Each individual cell can make contact with thousands of others, creating a network of connections whose density exceeds anything humans have ever created artificially. Some researchers compare this interconnectedness to a gigantic cosmos in miniature: While in the universe, galaxies are connected by gravity, in the brain, it is electrical impulses that continuously jump from synapse to synapse. And just as the universe creates stars, the brain creates thoughts, feelings, and memories. What's particularly remarkable is that the brain not only processes information, but also generates consciousness—that elusive phenomenon that allows us to think about ourselves, experience the world, and perceive ourselves as independent beings. Exactly how subjective experience arises from the activity of billions of neurons remains a mystery to this day. Some philosophers call this the "hard problem of consciousness." While we can measure which brain areas are active during certain activities, the bridge from the neural spark to the feeling of pleasure, pain, or self-awareness has not yet been conclusively explained.

The brain is also a master of adaptation. Contrary to what was long assumed, it is not a static organ that remains unchanged after childhood. On the contrary: it is plastic. It changes with every new experience, forming new connections, strengthening used pathways, and weakening unused ones. Anyone who learns a language, practices a musical instrument, or learns to walk again after an accident is literally reshaping their brain. This plasticity makes it possible for stroke patients to often regain abilities because other regions take over the functions of the damaged ones.

The variety of functions that converge in the brain is virtually endless. This is where our emotions arise, which can drive, warn, motivate, or paralyze us. They are not understood as vague "feelings," but rather as concrete biochemical processes that take place in areas like the limbic system. Joy, fear, or anger are not abstract concepts, but the result of finely tuned neurotransmitters. It's no coincidence that we remember happy events more vividly than trivial facts— emotions act as memory amplifiers.

Equally astonishing is the creativity that springs from this organ. Poems and symphonies, technical inventions, and abstract theories are born here. Creativity is the product of a complex interplay of various brain networks – logical-analytical structures meet emotional centers, stored experiences mingle with spontaneous neuronal firings. It's not uncommon for people to experience creative ideas in moments of relaxation, when the brain unconsciously links patterns and finds new paths. The famous "flash of inspiration" is thus less a divine spark than the result of tireless, hidden networking.

A particularly exciting discovery in neuroscience is the so-called mirror neurons. They are activated not only when we perform an action ourselves, but also when we observe others performing the same action. Thanks to these mechanisms, we can learn through imitation and also empathize with the feelings of others. When we see someone cry and feel sadness ourselves, it is the mirror neurons that allow our brain to "empathize." Some researchers see them as the biological basis of empathy—a capacity that made our social communities possible in the first place.

But as far as we know today, the list of unanswered questions is long. How exactly memories are stored in the brain is not fully understood, despite all the progress we have made. We know that certain regions, such as the hippocampus, are important, but how neural activity becomes an experience that can be recalled for life remains a mystery. The same applies to dreams: they are a universal phenomenon that occurs every night, but their exact function is still unclear. Are they a training ground for the brain, a kind of emotional storage device, or merely the byproduct of neural activity during sleep? The only thing that is certain is that sleep itself is vital because it is during this time that the brain sorts through memories and eliminates toxins that accumulate during the day.

Another unresolved issue concerns the role of genes. How much do they determine who we are? Do we inherit not only eye color and height, but also intelligence, character, perhaps even political views? Studies suggest that genes certainly have an influence, but they are never the sole determining factor. Our environment, our experiences, our social circles shape the brain just as strongly—an interplay that scientists call epigenetics.

Despite all the progress, research into the brain is still in its infancy. New technologies such as functional magnetic resonance imaging allow us to observe the brain as it thinks. Optogenetics makes it possible to selectively switch individual nerve cells on or off using light. Artificial intelligence, in turn, helps sift through the unimaginable amounts of data provided by modern brain scans.

These developments are not only exciting but also highly relevant for medicine. Diseases such as Alzheimer's, Parkinson's, depression, and epilepsy could be treated more specifically in the future if we better understand the underlying mechanisms. So-called brain-computer interfaces appear visionary: interfaces that allow prosthetics or computers to be controlled directly with thought. The first patients can already write texts by thinking only of letters. What once sounded like science fiction is now reality in the laboratory.

But with the growing power to research and influence the brain, ethical questions also arise. What does it mean for our privacy if minds become readable? Could we one day not only treat illnesses but also shape personalities? The line between healing and manipulation is thin, and the discussion about it has only just begun.

Some facts about the brain sound almost like anecdotes from a cabinet of curiosities. Although it only accounts for about two percent of body weight, it consumes about 20 percent of the body's total energy. More electrical processes take place in it every second than in all the telephone lines in the world combined. Open brain surgery is possible because the organ itself lacks pain receptors. And despite its incredible performance, it has one distinctly "human" weakness: It is easily fooled, as illusions and optical illusions impressively demonstrate.

Perhaps the greatest miracle of the brain is not even its performance, but its capacity for self-reflection. It is the only organ that examines itself, that asks questions, seeks answers, and at the same time falters due to its own limitations. We can launch rockets into space and perform quantum calculations, but we still don't know exactly how a thought arises.

Thus, the brain remains a mirror of our own existence: incredibly complex, full of possibilities, full of mysteries. It is the source of our identity and our culture, our greatest tool—and our greatest mystery. No other organ in nature combines so many opposites: hardness and fragility, precision and chaos, knowledge and ignorance. We owe the fact that we can reflect on all of this to the brain itself. In this sense, the brain is not just a miracle of nature—it is nature that has become aware of itself.

2.11. The Antikythera Mechanism: A Mystery from Antiquity

The Antikythera Mechanism is arguably one of the most enigmatic artifacts ever recovered from antiquity.

When sponge divers discovered an ancient shipwreck off the small Greek island of Antikythera in 1901, no one suspected they would stumble upon one of the most enigmatic technological artifacts in human history. Found among amphorae, statues, and coins, an inconspicuous, heavily corroded lump of bronze initially received little attention. Only upon closer examination did it become clear: It was the remains of a highly complex mechanism—a device that resembled a modern pocket computer, but originated from a time when such precision was unthinkable.

Today the so-called **Antikythera-Mechanism** Famous as the world's oldest known "analog computer model." It dates back to between the 2nd and 1st centuries BC, likely an era in which Greece was shaped by great scholars such as Hipparchus and Archimedes. The existence of such a sophisticated device during this period has long been a mystery to researchers.

The device was originally housed in a wooden box, of which only remnants remain. Inside were finely crafted bronze gears, the precision of which is still impressive today. A crank powered the mechanism, and the movement set in motion an entire system of interlocking gears. On the front were dials with scales and hands indicating the movements of the sun, moon, and presumably planets as well.

With this design, the mechanism could not only perform simple calendar functions, but also perform astonishingly complex astronomical calculations. It simulated the sun's path through the zodiac, indicated lunar phases, could calculate new and full moons, and even predict solar and lunar eclipses. Evidence also suggests that the Olympic Games cycle was also taken into account—an indication that the device was not only scientifically but also culturally significant.

The big question is: Who could build something like this? A device with over 30 gears, whose ratios precisely replicate astronomical cycles, requires exceptional knowledge of mechanics and astronomy. No comparable device was known until the Middle Ages, and even then, it took centuries before similarly complex clocks were built.

The discovery sparked a debate that continues to this day. Some researchers suspect that the mechanism dates back to the knowledge of scholars such as Hipparchus of Rhodes, one of the most important astronomers of antiquity. Others see influences from Archimedes, who also wrote about gears and mechanical constructions. The only thing that is certain is that the mechanism is unique—nothing comparable from that period has been found to date.

What's particularly spectacular is that modern computer tomography has given researchers completely new insights into the inner workings of the mechanism in recent decades. High-resolution scans made it possible to virtually "x-ray" the gears and thus reconstruct their original function. This revealed that the construction was even more complex than initially thought. Some gears had special notches that made it possible to replicate the irregular motion of the moon—caused by its elliptical orbit. A detail that demonstrates how precisely the ancient builders understood celestial events.

When the mechanism was discovered, researchers initially believed it was a modern hoax. The idea that people in ancient times could have built such a device seemed too fantastic. Only decades later, after thorough analysis, did it become clear: It was real—and added a whole chapter to the history of technology.

The inscriptions on the remaining parts of the mechanism add to the mystery. They are written in ancient Greek and provide clues to its workings. Some describe astronomical cycles, others hint at calendar functions. But they are badly damaged, and so much remains obscure.

The discovery is also fascinating from an archaeological perspective. The ship in which the mechanism was discovered sank around 70 BC and was apparently transporting valuable goods from the eastern Mediterranean to Rome. Was the mechanism a scientific instrument for wealthy Romans? Or did it belong to a Greek scholar on a journey? Such questions remain unanswered to this day.

The fascination of the Antikythera Mechanism lies not only in its technical genius, but also in what it reveals about our perception of antiquity. For a long time, antiquity was considered an era that, while producing philosophy and art, lagged behind modern times in terms of technology. The construction of the mechanism requires a profound understanding of astronomy, mathematics, and mechanics.

This device proves that even then, engineering skills of the highest level existed – knowledge that was later lost.

Some researchers therefore refer to it as the "first computer in human history." While it couldn't perform complex calculations like modern machines, it was an analog model of celestial mechanics, a device that translated the cosmos into gears.

Today, replicas of the mechanism are on display in museums—and many visitors immediately consider them modern steampunk works of art. Only upon reading the explanation does it become clear: This is 2,000 years old.

One mystery of the mechanism is not only how it worked, but also why only this one exists. Was it a one-off, a kind of prestige project by a brilliant inventor? Or were there several such devices that were lost? To this day, the mystery remains unsolved.

To this day, no comparable device from ancient times is known.

2.12. The Pavlov Experiment: The Discovery of Conditioning by a Drooling Dog

When people talk about "Pavlov's dog" today, it sounds like a common saying that has long since found its way into everyday language and pop culture. But behind this familiar phrase lies one of the most famous experiments in the history of science – and a researcher who actually had entirely different goals when observing the behavior of his test animals. Ivan Petrovich Pavlov himself probably couldn't have imagined that a drooling dog would one day revolutionize psychology when he began his research in the late 19th century. Pavlov was a physiologist, a man who studied the internal workings of the body. He was particularly interested in the digestive system. His goal was to discover how saliva, gastric juice, and other digestive juices are produced and how these processes can be measured. To this end, he set up a large laboratory in St. Petersburg in which dogs played the main role. With surgical precision, he had small tubes inserted into their salivary glands so that he could precisely observe and collect the flow of saliva. What initially seemed like a sober, medical examination would soon take on a completely different dimension.

Pavlov noticed that his dogs didn't only produce saliva when they actually had food in their mouths. Even before the meal was served, it would drip from their mouths, for example, when the assistant who usually brought the food entered the room. The mere sight of the bowl or the sound of footsteps was enough to trigger salivation. For Pavlov, this was both a mystery and an opportunity. He wondered: Can this effect be produced systematically? Can an animal be taught to respond to a specific signal in the same way as it responds to food itself? This began what later became world-famous as classical conditioning. Pavlov paired neutral stimuli, meaning things that actually had no meaning for the dog, with food. Sometimes it was the click of a metronome, sometimes the hum of an electrical device. At first, the animals ignored these signals. But as soon as the food followed the tone each time, something changed: The dog began to drool at the sound of the signal, even if no food appeared. The neutral stimulus had become a signal that triggered salivation, as if it were the food itself. Pavlov had thus discovered a mechanism that went far beyond digestion. For the first time, it was shown that behavior can be learned through the repeated pairing of two stimuli. The animal associated a previously meaningless event with a biologically important trigger and subsequently showed the same response. Pavlov called this process the "conditioned reflex." This was a small revolution: Until then, reflexes had been understood primarily as rigid, innate reactions—a blow to the knee produces the typical flinch reflex, a bright light causes the pupils to constrict. But here it was shown that reflexes could be learned and modified through experience.

Interestingly, the myth of the bell triggering salivation only came about later. Many textbooks and popular depictions still mention a ringing bell, even though Pavlov himself never used it systematically. The story is probably so persistent because the idea of a ringing bell is simpler and more catchy than a metronome. The fact that this detail has stuck so strongly is almost itself an example of conditioning: We have learned to inextricably link the dog and the bell, even though this isn't historically true.

The significance of the discovery quickly became clear. Pavlov himself initially remained firmly rooted in his physiological perspective, but other researchers took up the idea and applied it to human behavior. If dogs could learn to salivate in response to a sound, couldn't humans also develop feelings, actions, or fears through similar couplings? This very idea became the basis of behaviorism, the school of psychology that studied human behavior from a strictly scientific perspective.

Pavlov was by no means a dry theorist who viewed his dogs merely as measuring instruments. Many of his laboratory animals had names, and he described them in his notes almost as if they had idiosyncratic personalities. He called some dogs "courageous" or "fearful," others "obstinate" or "nervous." The fact that the great scientist attributed character traits to them shows how close his laboratory animals were to him. And here's a little fun fact: The very dogs that became known only for the dripping tube in their mouths actually had a special significance for Pavlov.

A particularly exciting aspect of his experiments was the so-called "extinction." When the tone was presented repeatedly without subsequent food, the dog eventually stopped drooling. However, this extinction was not permanent. After a certain pause, "spontaneous recovery" often occurred: The dog began producing saliva again as soon as it heard the signal. This shows that once learned associations remain deeply anchored in the memory, even if they are temporarily suppressed. An echo of this finding can still be found today in psychotherapy when it comes to treating anxiety or understanding relapses in addictive behavior.

One could say that Pavlov's dogs inadvertently laid the foundation for a new understanding of human experience. Suddenly, it became understandable why someone develops a fear of dentist drills after previously experiencing painful treatments. Or why advertising works so successfully with music, scents, or certain images: We associate positive feelings with products that actually have nothing to do with these emotions. The model's smile or the soothing melody in the background become the signal that whets our appetite for a chocolate bar or a new car.

Even in everyday life, we constantly stumble upon such mechanisms. The smell of freshly baked bread makes us hungry, even if we've just eaten. The ringing of a cell phone message immediately triggers the urge to look at the screen, even if the message may be completely irrelevant. And anyone who has ever witnessed how pets react to the mere rustling of a bag of food knows that Pavlov's discovery didn't stay in the laboratory, but has long since migrated into our kitchens and living rooms.

Yet, despite all the fascination, a critical undertone remains. Pavlov's experiments impressively demonstrated how easily behavior can be controlled. This later led to questions about how far conditioning can go and whether people become susceptible to manipulation as a result. Indeed, psychologists and educators in the 20th century resorted to these methods to specifically influence learning processes. The military and intelligence agencies also experimented with them to control behavior. What began in the laboratory with dogs quickly became a tool that promised power over humans. For supporters of conspiracy theories, this is precisely what they see as a godsend: They see Pavlov's findings as the key to mass manipulation, be it through advertising, the media, or political propaganda.

Pavlov himself would likely have rejected this interpretation. He saw himself as a scientist who explored sober mechanisms and remained lifelong inspired by the functioning of the brain. In 1904, he received the Nobel Prize for his work on digestive physiology—not for conditioning, which later established his fame. But it is this story of the drooling dog that immortalized his name.
Today, classical conditioning is part of the basics of psychology. Students learn it right from the start because it so vividly illustrates how learning works. At the same time, the image of "Pavlov's dog" has long since had its own career. It appears in cartoons, films, and political commentaries, often as a metaphor for reflexive behavior. The fact that behind this metaphor lies a real experiment that reveals more about our behavior than we sometimes realize makes the story all the more impressive.

2.13 The iron lung – a breathing device between fear and hope

Anyone who sees photos from the 1940s or 1950s depicting entire wards of children lying in long metal cylinders is quickly reminded of a scene from a dark movie. Only the heads stick out, the rest of the bodies are stuck in the giant tubes. For many people, the iron lung therefore seems like a symbol of hopelessness. But in reality, it was the exact opposite: a device that saved countless lives – and for most patients, it provided only temporary relief until they could breathe independently again.
The iron lung was developed in the late 1920s in response to the dreaded polio epidemics. Polio could attack the nervous system, particularly paralyzing the muscles necessary for breathing. Those who could no longer breathe independently were at risk of suffocation within hours. There were no medications, and no vaccinations either. The iron lung was the only way to save lives at the time—and it worked in a surprisingly simple way.

While today's ventilators actively pump air into the lungs, the iron lung relied on the principle of negative pressure. The patient was placed in an airtight cylinder, and the neck was closed with a cuff, leaving only the head exposed. An electric pump then changed the air pressure inside the tube. When air was sucked out, negative pressure was created, which expanded the chest. The lungs filled with oxygen. As soon as the pressure rose again, the chest contracted, and the air escaped. In this way, the natural breathing process was mimicked—not from within, but from without.
For the patients, this meant they could continue living even though their respiratory muscles were completely paralyzed. At first, the sensation of lying in the device was unusual; some spoke of a frightening pressure, while others described the steady movements as almost soothing, like a gentle rocking. It soon became clear that those who survived a polio attack and continued breathing in the iron lung had a good chance of survival.
Crucially, however, most patients did not have to remain in this device for their entire lives. For many, the paralysis of their respiratory muscles subsided after days or weeks. While the virus had caused damage, the nervous system was able to partially recover. As soon as their muscles were strong enough again, the children and adults were able to leave the iron lung. Some continued to use it at night or for short intervals to relieve pressure on their lungs, but otherwise led a largely normal life.

Of course, there were also more serious cases. Some patients remained in the machine for months while doctors and therapists attempted to train their breathing skills through targeted exercises. They used methods such as "frog breathing": a technique in which patients gulped air into their lungs to be able to function without the machine, at least for a short time. For many, this was a small step toward freedom.

Only a very small minority actually remained permanently dependent on the iron lung. These people suffered such severe nerve damage that their respiratory muscles never functioned again. For them, the iron lung became a lifelong companion. Today, there are only a handful of such patients left worldwide—the last witnesses to an era when polio was ubiquitous. One of the most famous is the American Paul Alexander, who has lived in an iron lung since the 1950s and even used it to complete his studies and practice as a lawyer. He shows that a fulfilling life is possible even under such circumstances.

So why are there still people in iron lungs today, even though polio has long been almost eradicated? The reason is that some patients became ill in the 1950s and have been dependent on the device ever since. While modern ventilation technologies could offer an alternative, many of these people have learned to live in the rhythm of the iron lung and feel safer with it. For them, the device is more familiar than any modern high-tech device. That's why they cling to it to this day.

Images of entire rooms filled with iron lungs may seem threatening, but they are also a symbol of how medicine made the impossible possible. As recently as the 1920s, most polio patients with respiratory paralysis would have inevitably died. With the invention of the iron lung, doctors were able to gain time. Time during which most patients' bodies recovered. The hum of the pumps, the unison rising and falling of chests, was not just a mechanical rhythm, but a reassuring signal: Here, life fought, and often won.

Today, no one needs to fear ever ending up in an iron lung. Thanks to vaccination programs, polio has been eradicated in almost every part of the world, and ventilation technologies are so advanced that even the most severe respiratory problems can be treated with mobile devices. The iron lung is therefore a relic: both eerie and impressive. It recalls a time when a disease paralyzed entire societies and the courage of doctors and patients who used simple technology to ensure survival.

Chapter 3: Mystical Events

This chapter will transport you to a world of mystical events and unexplained phenomena. Whether it's the mysterious Bermuda Triangle, spooky ghost ships, or the famous Loch Ness Monster, these stories capture our imaginations and remind us that there are still many mysteries in this world. Stay curious and open to the unknown, for the wonders and mysteries of our world are numerous and often surprising.

3.1. The Bermuda Triangle: Myths and Facts

The Bermuda Triangle, an area in the western Atlantic Ocean between Bermuda, Miami, and Puerto Rico, is known for the mysterious disappearance of ships and aircraft. Since the 1950s, numerous stories of eerie incidents and unexplained phenomena have emerged.

There are places on Earth whose very name evokes a mixture of awe and fascination. One of these places is the Bermuda Triangle, an area in the western Atlantic marked by Miami, Puerto Rico, and the Bermuda archipelago. If you connect these three points on a map, you get the famous triangle, which for decades has been the setting for stories of mysterious incidents, vanished airplanes, and lost ships. Since the mid-20th century, it has been synonymous with enigmas and the unexplained, with alleged gateways to other worlds or secret powers that are said to operate beyond scientific explanation.

The legend of the Bermuda Triangle did not arise out of nowhere, but has its roots in several real-life incidents whose circumstances were unusual enough to fuel people's imaginations. The fate of Flight 19 became particularly famous. On December 5, 1945, five Avenger bombers took off from Fort Lauderdale, Florida, on a routine training flight. The route was simple enough, but during the flight, squadron leader Charles Taylor reported that his instruments were no longer accurate, that his compasses were acting up, and that he was lost. His radio messages to headquarters became increasingly confused; he spoke of a sea that looked different than expected and of the feeling that he was no longer in the right area. Eventually, contact was lost altogether. The five aircraft disappeared without a trace, and the rescue plane that took off shortly afterwards never returned. 27 men disappeared in one night, and the fact that, despite extensive searches, no wreckage, no fuel film, and no bodies were found made the case one of the greatest mysteries in aviation history.

But decades before Flight 19, the Bermuda Triangle was already a place where mysterious things were said to have happened. The legend dates back to the 19th century. In 1881, the British "Ellen Austin" reported that she had encountered an abandoned ship in the region. The crew sent men on board to bring the ghost ship to safety, but shortly thereafter the ship disappeared along with the men who had crewed it. When it resurfaced, it was once again completely empty. Whether this story actually happened or was later embellished is still debated today, but it contains all the elements that later made the Bermuda Triangle so famous: sudden disappearance, the lack of logical explanations, and a hint of the supernatural.

Another famous example is the USS Cyclops, a U.S. Navy coal freighter that disappeared without a trace between Barbados and Baltimore in 1918 with a crew of over 300. Here, too, neither wreckage nor survivors were found. The accident is still considered the largest non-combat-related maritime disaster in the history of the U.S. Navy. The fact that a ship of this size disappeared without a distress call, without a radio message, and without any trace provided ample fuel for the Bermuda Triangle myth.

Over the course of the 20th century, reports of missing aircraft and ships increased. In the 1940s and 1950s, several cargo ships in the region either ran into trouble or disappeared completely. In 1941, the USS Proteus disappeared along with its 58-man crew, followed by the USS Nereus, both sister ships of the Cyclops. In the 1960s, several small passenger aircraft en route from Florida to the Bahamas were lost. In most cases, neither debris nor survivors were found, creating a picture of a region where the laws of physics seem to defy them.

However, the popularity of the Bermuda Triangle only became so great through media coverage. Journalist Edward Van Winkle Jones published an article in 1950 in which he described the region as a place of "unexplained disappearances." But it was Charles Berlitz who, with his 1974 book *The Bermuda Triangle* made the myth known worldwide. Berlitz combined facts, eyewitness accounts, and much speculation, suggesting that supernatural forces were at work in this part of the world. His book became an international bestseller, selling millions and making the triangle a staple of pop culture. From that moment on, the Bermuda Triangle was no longer just a geographical area, but a synonym for the unexplainable.

The explanations offered since then have been as varied as they are fantastic. Some authors spoke of aliens abducting ships and aircraft for research purposes. Others suggested that the triangle was the entrance to another dimension, a wormhole in the ocean that swallowed objects. Still others invoked the legendary sunken city of Atlantis and claimed that remnants of highly advanced technology were still active in the seabed. In the 1970s and 80s, numerous TV documentaries took up these ideas, and the Bermuda Triangle became a staple in any collection of unexplained mysteries.

But beyond these speculative explanations, there are numerous theories attempting to explain the incidents with natural causes. One of the most well-known concerns weather conditions. The western Atlantic is notorious for its sudden and violent storms. Tropical cyclones, hurricanes, and tornadoes regularly form in this region. A small aircraft or a medium-sized ship caught in such a storm can be destroyed or sunk within minutes. Sudden downdrafts and dense fog have also been discussed several times as causes of accidents.

Another factor is ocean currents. The Gulf Stream runs directly through the Bermuda Triangle and is one of the strongest currents in the world. A wreck caught in its current can be carried far out to sea or sunk completely in a very short time. This also explains why, in many cases, no debris was found: it simply disappeared too quickly.

The topography of the seabed also plays a significant role. In this region, the Atlantic drops abruptly into deep-sea trenches several kilometers deep. A ship sinking there may disappear so deep that it is difficult to locate even with modern technology. Just a few decades ago, it was completely impossible to penetrate such depths, and so many fates remained unknown.

The theory of **magnetic anomalies** Pilots and sailors repeatedly report that their compasses are unreliable in the Bermuda Triangle. Some explain this to variations in the Earth's magnetic field. In rare regions, magnetic north and geographic north coincide, which can cause compasses to show seemingly incorrect directions. An inexperienced navigator could easily be thrown off course in such situations, and in the past, an error on the open sea was often fatal.

Another theory involves methane hydrate, frozen methane stored in large quantities on the seafloor. If this methane is suddenly released in large bubbles, it can reduce the density of the water. A ship caught in such a bubble loses its buoyancy and can sink within seconds. Laboratory experiments have shown that such effects are possible, although no direct evidence has yet been found in the Bermuda Triangle.

Last but not least, there's the explanation of giant waves, so-called rogue waves. These unpredictable monster waves can reach heights of 20 to 30 meters and are powerful enough to break even large ships. Their occurrence is likely in a region where the weather and currents are particularly turbulent. Satellite images have shown that they occur worldwide, but in combination with the myth of the Triangle, they seem particularly threatening.

Despite all these explanations, the Bermuda Triangle remains a place of eerie mystery for many people. It's remarkable, however, that scientific studies repeatedly show that the accident rate in this region is no higher than in other heavily trafficked maritime areas. Many accidents simply occur there because of the extremely high volume of shipping and air traffic. The legend arises from a mixture of statistical coincidence, selective perception, and the human desire for mystery.

The Bermuda Triangle is therefore less a real geographical phenomenon than a cultural one. It has its place in books, films, and documentaries; it appears in novels and science fiction stories; it serves as a projection screen for fears and fantasies. Cruise ships and airlines cross the region daily without incident, but that doesn't diminish its fascination.

3.2. The eerie ghost ships of the seas

Ghost ships are ships that drift on the seas without a crew and are often associated with mysterious stories.

The idea of a ship drifting without a crew on the high seas leaves room for countless speculations. Here are some real, documented cases of ghost ships:
The "Mary Celeste"
Hardly any other ship has become such a symbol of a maritime mystery as the "Mary Celeste." Her name still stands today for the mysterious disappearance of an entire crew, for the inexplicable encounter with a ghost ship drifting abandoned across the Atlantic. The discovery in December 1872 is one of the great unsolved stories of seafaring and has become deeply etched in culture—a mixture of real incident, legal investigation, and countless speculations that have not abated to this day.

The "Mary Celeste" wasn't a particularly striking ship. Launched in 1861 in Nova Scotia, Canada, as a schooner under the name "Amazon," she initially had a rather unspectacular career. After minor incidents, she changed owners, was rebuilt in 1868, and registered under the new name "Mary Celeste." She was a typical merchant ship of the time, just under 30 meters long, with two masts, and stable enough for Atlantic voyages. No one would have expected that this ship would one day achieve world fame—not through its voyages, but through a mystery.

In November 1872, the "Mary Celeste" left New York with a cargo of 1,701 barrels of industrial alcohol, bound for Genoa. On board were Captain Benjamin Briggs, an experienced and respected man, his wife Sarah and their two-year-old daughter Sophia, along with seven crew members. Briggs was known to be devoutly religious and responsible. His decision to take his wife and child with him suggests that he did not consider the voyage particularly dangerous. It was a normal commercial voyage, one of countless others undertaken.

But on December 4, 1872, the "Dei Gratia," a Canadian freighter under Captain David Morehouse, made an unusual discovery. About 600 miles west of Portugal, the sailors spotted a ship drifting without a clear direction. They sent a boat across to investigate—and found the "Mary Celeste." What awaited the men there was far beyond routine.

The ship was abandoned. The sails were damaged but mostly set, the rigging sound. There were no signs of a struggle, no indications of looting or violence. Below deck, there was plenty of food and drinking water, enough to last for months. The crew's personal belongings were untouched, and tobacco tins and pipes were within easy reach. The hold was largely intact, with the valuable cargo still on board. The only noticeable thing was that one of the lifeboats was missing. Furthermore, the ship's log was incomplete: the last entry dated November 25, when the ship was near the Azores. After that, the trail goes cold.

This is where the great mystery began. Why would an experienced crew abandon a seaworthy ship with supplies, functioning equipment, and valuable cargo? What were they fleeing from? Why didn't they return? And how could it happen that an entire lifeboat, complete with crew, disappeared without a trace, never to be seen again?

Theories abounded. Possible explanations were discussed shortly after the discovery. One of the most obvious was a problem with the cargo. Some barrels of industrial alcohol were leaking during salvage, and the escaping fumes may have worried the crew. In a confined, poorly ventilated space, an alcohol gas explosion can be devastating, even without an open flame. Perhaps Briggs feared an explosion and ordered the ship to be temporarily abandoned until the fumes dissipated. Perhaps he had the lifeboat secured with a rope so they could return at a moment's notice. But if the boat had accidentally become detached from the ship—perhaps due to wind or waves—the crew would have been lost while their ship drifted on. This theory is still considered plausible today, even though there is no conclusive evidence.

Other explanations are more dramatic. Pirate attacks were suspected early on, but the cargo was complete, and there were no signs of violence or plunder. A mutiny would have the same problem: why leave the ship intact? The assumption that Briggs himself was driven to suicide, perhaps by religious fanaticism, also doesn't fit the picture, given his impeccable reputation.

Natural phenomena were also discussed. Some historians consider a seaquake, an underwater earthquake, a possibility that could have violently shaken the ship. Combined with rising gas bubbles, the crew mistakenly believed the ship was sinking. In a panic, they climbed into the boat – and never returned. A sudden, massive wave was also suggested. It could have flooded the deck and forced the crew into the boat. But here, too, there is no concrete evidence.

Over time, more imaginative ideas emerged. Attacks by sea monsters, the sudden pull of an underwater whirlpool, or even alien abductions found their way into literature. In the 20th century, the "Mary Celeste" was even occasionally associated with the Bermuda Triangle, despite its discovery being far outside it. But for mystery writers, this was irrelevant—the story fit the "devouring ocean" image too well.

A particularly fascinating chapter in the story is the prize trial that followed the salvage. The crew of the "Dei Gratia" took the "Mary Celeste" to Gibraltar to claim the finder's fee. There, a judicial investigation was launched, forcing the British authorities to determine whether a crime had been committed. Had the men of the "Dei Gratia" possibly murdered the crew of the "Mary Celeste" in order to take possession of the ship? This suspicion was investigated intensively, as such a safe and sound ship full of cargo seemed suspicious. However, the investigation yielded no conclusive evidence. While doubts remained, in the end the crew of the "Dei Gratia" received part of the finder's fee, albeit less than hoped. The rest remained an unsolved mystery.

The story didn't end there. The "Mary Celeste" sailed for another thirteen years after her return, but she remained a "ship of misfortune." Time and again, she suffered breakdowns, accidents, and unfortunate business dealings. In 1885, her last captain finally ran her aground on a reef off Haiti, apparently to commit insurance fraud. Thus ended her real existence, but her posthumous fame was just beginning.

Arthur Conan Doyle, in particular, contributed to the ship's immortality. In his 1884 short story, "J. Habakuk Jephson's Statement," he described a "Marie Celeste" that had been abandoned by a crew. Although the story was fictional and Conan Doyle altered many details, it made a huge impact. It was picked up by newspapers, misinterpreted as a factual account, and left a lasting impression on the public imagination. From then on, the "Mary Celeste" became the ultimate ghost ship, a symbol of the unfathomable on the high seas.

Since then, the mystery has been revisited in countless books, articles, films, and TV documentaries. Some authors sought serious explanations, others enjoyed the allure of the supernatural. For the general public, the "Mary Celeste" remained the perfect enigma: mysterious but not threatening, a piece of seafaring romance in a world that seemed increasingly explainable.

Even today, historians debate the most likely explanation. The most popular theory is the alcohol gas and panic reaction. This best fits the findings, even if it cannot explain the complete absence of the lifeboat. Others see human error, perhaps a fatal error by the captain. Still others cling to natural phenomena. But until conclusive evidence emerges, the "Mary Celeste" will likely remain a mystery.

The reasons for the crew's disappearance remain unclear to this day.

Die „Carroll A. Deering"

When the "Carroll A. Deering" was discovered abandoned and stranded on the coast of North Carolina in January 1921, it had everything it took to go down in history: a modern, imposing ship, a crew that had vanished without a trace, and a scene that seemed like something out of a horror story. Within a very short time, the event became the stuff of rumors, legends, and conspiracy theories—and the ship itself joined the long line of famous ghost ships that continue to capture the imagination to this day.

The "Carroll A. Deering" was a true giant of her time. The proud five-masted schooner was launched in 1919 in Bath, Maine, a town already world-renowned for shipbuilding. At almost 80 meters long and capable of carrying 3,300 tons of coal, she was a symbol of post-World War I American shipbuilding. She was named after the son of shipowner Benjamin Deering, who commissioned the ship. As a merchant and cargo ship, she was designed for use on international routes, a floating workhorse that made an impression in every port.

In the summer of 1920, she set out on what would be her last voyage. Under Captain William H. Merritt, an experienced seaman, and with a crew of eleven, she was loaded in Norfolk, Virginia. Her destination was Rio de Janeiro, where she was to transport 3,300 tons of coal. However, complications arose shortly after the voyage began: Captain Merritt fell seriously ill and was forced to resign his command. He was replaced by Captain Willis B. Wormell, a man over 60 years old who was considered an experienced but also headstrong seaman. The crew was a diverse group and apparently not free from tensions, as later reports suggested.

The voyage to Rio initially passed without major incidents. In Brazil, the "Carroll A. Deering" unloaded its cargo of coal, and Captain Wormell spent a few days in port, talking with other captains and acquaintances. He hinted that he was dissatisfied with his crew and sensed tensions on board. His remarks were later interpreted by some as a harbinger that something ominous might be about to happen.

The decisive events occurred on the return voyage. On January 28, 1921, the "Carroll A. Deering" was sighted by a lighthouse keeper at the Cape Hatteras Lighthouse. It was noted that she was sailing unusually close to the coast, but no one suspected that this would be the last confirmed sighting of the crew. Two days later, on January 31, the crew of another lighthouse discovered the "Carroll A. Deering" stranded on a sand reef in what is known as Diamond Shoals—a notorious region off North Carolina nicknamed the "Graveyard of the Atlantic" because of its dangerous shoals.

Upon boarding the ship, a ghostly scene presented itself. Although the proud schooner had been stranded and partially damaged, it was overall in relatively good condition. The officers' cabins were untouched, the crew's personal belongings were still in place, and the storerooms were full. There were no signs of violence, no fire, and no looting. What was striking, however, was that the navigation instruments and the steering wheel were missing – as were the lifeboats. There was no trace of the crew.

News of this discovery spread quickly. Speculation soon began. Was it a mutiny? Some suspected that the disgruntled crew had overpowered the aging Captain Wormell and taken control of the ship. But why, then, would they have run the ship aground and disappeared without a trace? An attack by pirates or smugglers was also discussed. In the years following the First World War, the North American coast was not free of crime at sea, but even here, there were no signs of an attack – the cargo had long since been unloaded, and valuables remained on board.

Another theory involved German submarines. Although the war ended in 1921, fears of secret operations by the former enemy were still present in people's minds. The idea that a German submarine had abducted or killed the crew didn't seem far-fetched at the time, but it could never be substantiated with evidence.

Other attempts at explanation have pointed to natural forces. The Diamond Shoals are notorious for their dangerous currents and sandbanks, which have been the downfall of countless ships. It's possible that the Carroll A. Deering encountered a storm, the crew abandoned ship in panic, and perished in the lifeboat. However, this theory is also not entirely convincing, as the schooner was found in a condition that hardly indicated acute distress.

As is often the case in such cases, fantastic speculation soon mingled with the sober hypotheses. Some saw the "Carroll A. Deering" as another victim of the Bermuda Triangle, even though its discovery site was strictly outside of it. Others suggested supernatural phenomena, from ghost sightings to alien abductions.

The US government intervened, which only made the mystery more intriguing. Several agencies investigated the case, including the FBI, which was still in its infancy at the time. Ultimately, investigators were unable to determine a definitive cause. The official file simply noted that the reasons for the crew's disappearance were unknown.

The legend was born. The "Carroll A. Deering" was soon dubbed the "Mary Celeste of the 20th Century" because it was found abandoned in much the same way as its famous predecessor. Both ships shared the eerie fact of being discovered drifting or stranded in relatively good condition—with all supplies and equipment on board, but without their crew.

The cultural impact was not long in coming. Newspapers reported extensively on the ghost ship, authors picked up on the subject, and to this day the "Carroll A. Deering" is mentioned in mystery collections and documentaries. Some researchers see it primarily as an example of the dangers of shipping at that time, before modern communications and satellite navigation existed. A ship could disappear without a trace within days, and often only speculation remained. Others consider the "Deering" one of the great unsolved mysteries of maritime history, comparable to the "Mary Celeste."

To this day, there's no definitive answer. Was it an unfortunate chain of misunderstandings, natural forces, and human error? Or is there more to it, a mutiny, a secret attack, perhaps a crime that was never solved? The files provide no certainty, and therein lies the mystery.

The "Carroll A. Deering" thus stands in a series of fates that make the ocean a place of the uncanny. A ship, large and modern, suddenly found stranded without a crew. And so the legend lives on, even more than a hundred years after that winter day in 1921, when the men of Cape Hatteras boarded the abandoned ship and wondered where the sailors had disappeared to, their traces forever erased by the ocean.

The "Tai Ching 2"

In November 2008, the Tai Ching 21, a Taiwanese trawler, was found drifting in the Pacific Ocean off the Phoenix Islands. The ship was partially burned, and its entire 29-person crew was missing. No evidence of a struggle or assault was found on board.

The story of the "Tai Ching 21" serves as proof that the sea still holds secrets in the 21st century. It reminds us that, despite GPS, satellite monitoring, and international communications, the ocean remains a place where people and entire crews can disappear as if they had never existed. When the Taiwanese trawler was discovered abandoned in the Pacific in November 2008, it was as if a modern chapter in the ancient legend of ghost ships had been opened—and this time, the drama unfolded not in the 19th century, but in our own time.

The "Tai Ching 21" was a modern deep-sea trawler, equipped for long, dangerous voyages deep into the Pacific Ocean. With a crew of 29 men, presumably mostly from Taiwan, China, and Southeast Asia, it was part of the vast fleet of vessels that roam the world's oceans day after day, catching fish, squid, or crustaceans. Deep-sea fishing means weeks, sometimes months, away from land, living in close quarters, shift work, constant contact with machinery and the sea, and often dangerous working conditions. Anyone who goes to sea knows that the ship itself is both a home and a prison—and that every mistake can have fatal consequences.

In 2008, the "Tai Ching 21" operated in the waters around the Phoenix Islands, a remote archipelago in the central Pacific, now part of Kiribati. This region is so isolated that even experienced sailors describe it as a kind of "forgotten corner" of the ocean. Between Hawaii, Fiji, and Samoa lies a vast area that, while not completely untouched, is one of the most remote regions on Earth. If something happens here, it takes days, sometimes weeks, for help to arrive.

On November 9, 2008, a US search aircraft became aware of the vessel. The "Tai Ching 21" was drifting through the sea, unable to maneuver. From the air, it was immediately apparent that something was wrong: The trawler's superstructure showed clear signs of burning, the deck was partially charred, and yet the hull appeared intact overall. There were no more plumes of smoke, no active fire, only the silent traces of a previous fire. And what was even more eerie: There was no one on board.

When the ship was finally boarded, the scene resembled the great ghost ship stories of centuries past. There were no signs of a struggle, no traces of blood, no broken cabins. Supplies were still there, as were the men's personal belongings. But the entire crew—29 men—had disappeared. The lifeboats were also missing, suggesting that the crew had deliberately abandoned the ship. But why?

The most obvious explanation was fire. Fire on board is one of the worst nightmares for sailors. Wooden ships of past centuries often went up in flames, but even on modern steel ships, fires are a constant danger: in the engine rooms, in the galley, from cable fires. Smoke spreads rapidly, toxic gases fill the cramped cabins, and even a small fire can trigger panic. Presumably, the men noticed the fire and decided to abandon ship. But why hadn't any of them called for help?

This is where the mystery begins. Modern trawlers are equipped with radios, satellite communications, and emergency buoys. In the event of a fire, at least a short Mayday signal could have been sent. But not a single distress call came from the "Tai Ching 21." Some experts suspect that the communications system had already been destroyed by the fire before anyone could respond. Others consider it possible that in a chaotic moment—perhaps at night, perhaps in thick smoke—the crew climbed into the lifeboats so quickly that no one thought about the radio.

But even if the men hastily abandoned the ship, the question remains: Where did they disappear to? The Phoenix Islands may be located in a remote region, but searches covering several thousand square kilometers were conducted. Neither lifeboats nor remains were found. No drifting wreckage, no bodies, no clues. It was as if the entire crew had vanished into thin air.

Some observers drew parallels to other famous ghost ships, such as the "Mary Celeste" or the "Carroll A. Deering." In those cases, too, the ship was found abandoned but intact, with supplies and equipment, but without its crew. The difference: These cases occurred more than a hundred years ago, in times without modern technology, without radio, without satellites. That such a case could occur in 2008, in the midst of the age of global surveillance, made the story of the "Tai Ching 21" all the more disturbing.

Naturally, speculation soon arose. Some suspected that pirates might have played a role. While the Western Pacific is not as notorious as the Somali coast, attacks occasionally occur there as well. Pirates were said to have kidnapped or killed the crew and set fire to the ship to cover their tracks. But there were no clear signs of this. No valuable equipment was missing, nor were there any signs of violence. Furthermore, a kidnapping would likely have resulted in demands – but no such report ever came to light.

Other theories point toward internal conflicts. Deep-sea fishing is known for extreme working conditions. Long shifts, cramped cabins, monotonous work, and isolation often lead to tensions and violence. There are documented cases of mutinies or murders on fishing vessels. Could there have been a conflict that ended in arson and escape? Here, too, concrete evidence is lacking, but some historians don't rule it out.

Still others consider a chain of unfortunate circumstances the most likely solution. Perhaps a fire had spread, the crew abandoned ship in the lifeboat, but lost contact with the mother ship. Without an emergency radio or satellite buoy, the men drifted in the Pacific, helplessly at the mercy of the currents. The Pacific is so vast that even a major search effort can easily come to nothing. Just a few days in the wrong direction are enough for survivors to disappear forever. The lack of any evidence makes the "Tai Ching 21" a modern myth. It is an example of how, even today, with all our technology, the sea can swallow people without leaving a trace.

The "Tai Ching 21" was later salvaged and examined by authorities, but the results provided little insight. The fire was real, but its cause remained unclear. No evidence of explosions, sabotage, or attacks was found. There was also no trace of the crew. Thus, the ship remains a modern-day ghost ship to this day, comparable to the legends of past centuries.

Die „Baychimo"

When one imagines a ghost ship, one often thinks of tropical waters, foggy coasts, or the stormy seas off Bermuda. But even in the icy waters of the Arctic, there is a legendary ship that has captured people's imaginations for decades: the "Baychimo." She was neither a pirate ship nor a proud ocean liner, but a cargo ship built for the rigors of everyday merchant shipping. Yet her fate made her a legend—a ship that repeatedly appeared like a ghost among icebergs and drifted through the Arctic waters for decades, as if she simply refused to sink into the depths.

The story begins in Sweden. Launched in 1914 under the name "Ångermanelfven," the ship was a typical cargo ship of the era. After the First World War, it was sold to Great Britain as part of the war reparations and acquired in 1921 by the Hudson's Bay Company, which renamed it "Baychimo." From then on, it served the trade between Canada, Alaska, and Europe, transporting furs, goods, and equipment—a maritime workhorse, designed primarily for the harsh Arctic. The Baychimo was not an elegant steamer, but it was robust and reliable.

In the fall of 1931, the events that would make the ship immortal occurred. While voyaging along the Alaskan coast, the "Baychimo" encountered a severe storm. Soon after, it became trapped in drifting ice. For ships operating in Arctic waters, this was always a nightmare: When the ice gripped the ship, it threatened to crush the hull like a nutshell. After days of hardship, the crew managed to cross the ice to safety, but the ship had to be abandoned. When the ice broke up and they later returned to the scene, the "Baychimo" was gone. It was presumed to have sunk.

But that was a mistake. Just a few weeks later, the Hudson's Bay Company received news that the ship had been sighted again—unharmed, but abandoned, drifting in the ice. This began a series of sightings that would span decades. Inuit hunters reported encounters with the ship, sailors unexpectedly stumbled upon the "Baychimo," and time and again, it was briefly located before disappearing again.

Sometimes she resurfaced hundreds of kilometers from her last known location. Sometimes she drifted peacefully among ice floes, at other times she was carried far out to sea by storms and currents. Several attempts were made to salvage the ship. Expedition groups and sailors tried to board, but Arctic conditions made it almost impossible. Once, a few men spent several days on the "Baychimo" but were forced to abandon it when the ice became too dangerous. Another time, the Hudson's Bay Company planned to destroy it to put an end to the ghost story. But this attempt also failed—nature thwarted every intervention.

Thus, the "Baychimo" became a phantom that could never be fully grasped. It wasn't a wreck in the true sense of the word, but an abandoned freighter that survived for decades despite storms, ice, and cold. For the Inuit, it was a familiar sight: a steely stranger that repeatedly resurfaced, as if it had become part of the landscape. For sailors, however, it was a mystery that defied all logical explanation.

Even more remarkable is the lengthy period over which the sightings occurred. Time and again, just when the ship was thought to have vanished for good, it reappeared. The last confirmed sightings date back to the 1960s, more than 30 years after it was abandoned. This means that the "Baychimo" drifted for decades as an abandoned freighter through some of the world's most inhospitable oceans. No storm, no pack ice, no collision could completely destroy it.

To this day, it remains unclear where the "Baychimo" ultimately met its end. Some believe it sank unnoticed in the Arctic Ocean at some point, swallowed by the icy depths. Others consider it possible that it still lies somewhere encased in the ice, preserved like a relic from a bygone era, and perhaps one day released by meltwater. The idea that a rusting 1920s cargo ship lies hidden in the ice somewhere north of Alaska has its own appeal.

The legend of the "Baychimo" is not only a maritime curiosity, but also a symbol of the harshness and unpredictability of the Arctic. It demonstrates how inaccessible and mysterious this region still was in the 20th century. In a world where the oceans had long been mapped and shipping routes seemed standardized, there were still places where ships could disappear without a trace and reappear decades later.

The last confirmed sightings of the Baychimo date back to the 1960s. Since then, it has been considered lost. Where exactly the ship ultimately sank, or whether it is still trapped somewhere in the ice, remains unknown.

3.3. The Mystery of Loch Ness: Does the Monster Really Exist?

Hardly anyone is unfamiliar with the name "Nessie," even if they've never set foot in Scotland. It's a myth that has persisted for centuries, reshaping itself with each new generation, and symbolizes humanity's longing for the mysterious, for the last blank spot on the map. While almost every continent has been surveyed, every mountain range climbed, and every corner of the Earth mapped, Loch Ness remains a place where the unexplainable is supposedly still possible.

The first stories of a creature in the waters of the River Ness date back to the 6th century. The Irish monk Columba, later venerated as Saint Columba, is said to have encountered a giant beast on the river's banks that threatened humans. By making the sign of the cross, he sent the creature back into the depths. Such stories are typical of Christian missionary work at that time – they demonstrate the triumph of faith over the unknown. But for some, this is the oldest written reference to a creature that would later become world-famous as "Nessie." For centuries, anecdotes continued to surface: fishermen reported seeing large shadows beneath the water, farmers who supposedly saw a massive figure emerge from the lake. But these remained isolated stories that never spread beyond the Highlands.

Everything changed in the 20th century. In 1933, a new road was built along Loch Ness, opening up views of the lake to motorists. Suddenly, many more people than ever before had the opportunity to observe the body of water up close. That same year, a couple reported seeing a large, slithering creature in the water. The local newspaper picked up the story, and soon other eyewitness accounts appeared. Within weeks, a local story had become a national story. The real breakthrough came in 1934, when a photograph was published that supposedly showed the head and long neck of an animal protruding from the water. This image, later known as the "Surgeon's Photo," became iconic. Newspapers around the world reprinted it, and suddenly Loch Ness was a household name from New York to Tokyo. People traveled there to catch a glimpse of the monster for themselves. For decades, the photo was considered the most important proof of Nessie's existence. It wasn't until the 1990s that it was revealed to be a fake—a model mounted on a toy submarine. But the truth didn't diminish its impact. The myth had long since grown too big to be shattered by a revelation.

In the decades that followed, sightings became more frequent. Fishermen reported long shadows beneath the water, tourists of unexplained movements on the surface. Some saw multiple humps reminiscent of the back of a giant animal, others described a swan's neck protruding from the waves. The number of eyewitness accounts grew so rapidly that, in the 1960s, research groups began conducting systematic investigations. Using sonar equipment, they combed the lake, which is over 230 meters deep, making it one of the deepest bodies of inland water in Europe. In fact, they repeatedly recorded large, moving objects in the depths that could not be easily explained. Were they schools of fish, large catfish, or something else unknown? The results remained vague and raised more questions than answers.

The lake itself contributes significantly to the myth. Loch Ness is not an idyllic bathing lake, but a long, murky body of water, eerie in its depth and dark color. The water is interspersed with peat particles, making it almost opaque. Darkness reigns just a few meters below the surface, and what happens down there remains hidden from the human eye. This natural feature reinforces the feeling that something might be lurking down there.

With technological advances, the search changed. In the 1970s, underwater cameras were used, but they produced rather blurry images that raised more questions than answers. Some of these shots showed indistinct shapes reminiscent of fins or large bodies. But no image was clear enough to convince the scientific world. Forgeries arose time and again – from manipulated photos to staged videos. Any "proof" was immediately questioned with skepticism, and yet often even a blurry image was enough to rekindle the imagination around the world.

Scientists remained reluctant. Biologists pointed out that Loch Ness doesn't provide enough food to sustain a population of large animals for centuries. Even if a single animal had existed, it would have died long ago—and bones or remains would have been found somewhere. Moreover, while the loch is deep, it isn't infinite. It's connected to rivers at both ends, but these are too narrow to offer a giant animal a means of escape to the sea. All these arguments clearly speak against the existence of a prehistoric creature like a plesiosaur, as some Nessie enthusiasts like to claim.

But there are always new theories, less spectacular but more plausible. Some researchers suspect that these could be large fish like sturgeons, which actually reach lengths of several meters. Others see the sightings primarily as optical illusions. The light over the lake, the unusual wave patterns, drifting tree trunks – all of these can give excited observers the impression of a monster. Even reflections in the unusually still water surface can simulate movement.

In recent years, state-of-the-art methods have been used, including DNA analysis. In 2018, researchers took water samples from various depths in Loch Ness to examine the DNA traces left behind by every living creature in the water. The results were intriguing: They found numerous references to familiar fish species such as eels, but no DNA traces pointing to an unknown large animal. Some scientists concluded that the most frequent Nessie sightings might be due to giant eels.

But while science tends to spread disillusionment, the myth remains unbroken. Nessie not only lives in the loch, but has long since become a fixture in pop culture. She appears in films, cartoons, and novels, is a popular motif for souvenirs and advertising campaigns, and attracts hundreds of thousands of tourists to the shores of Loch Ness every year. In Inverness and the small villages along the loch, you'll find museums, exhibitions, and boat tours all featuring Nessie. The monster has become an important economic factor for the region, almost as real as a living animal.

The psychological side of this phenomenon is just as interesting as the biological one. People often see what they want to see. Anyone standing at Loch Ness, gazing into the dark waters, almost expects to discover a secret. Every rippling ripple, every drifting branch can become a sensation if the desire is strong enough. It is this interplay of expectation, fascination, and cultural influence that keeps the myth so alive. Nessie is thus also a mirror of human longing: the longing for the inexplicable, for a remnant of magic in a world that seems ever more explainable.

Even if the probability of a prehistoric monster is vanishingly small, there remains that one tiny crack of possibility that is enough to capture the imagination of millions of people.

As long as there is no definitive answer, the Loch Ness Monster, whether real or not, remains one of the great mysteries.

3.4. The Prophecies of Nostradamus

Michel de Nostredame, who would later become world-famous under the Latinized name Nostradamus, was born in 1503 in the southern French town of Saint-Rémy-de-Provence. He grew up in a time marked by upheaval, fear, and hope. Europe suffered from recurring waves of plague that depopulated entire cities; at the same time, the Renaissance flourished in Italy, challenging old worldviews. Christianity experienced the Reformation with Martin Luther, and new worlds were opened up through the voyages of discovery across the Atlantic. In this mixture of fear and progress, Nostradamus developed his reputation as a healer, astrologer, and ultimately, as a prophet.

Initially, his path led him into medicine and pharmacy. As a pharmacist, he manufactured medicines that he used to treat the plague. He became famous for rose pastilles, which were said to clear breath and ward off disease. Thus, Nostradamus was by no means a mysterious fortune-teller from the outset, but rather a man who sought to help the people of his time in a very practical way. Nevertheless, he lived in an era in which stargazing and interpreting signs were an integral part of everyday life. Astrology was a recognized practice, often practiced in the courts of the powerful. Nostradamus began to draw horoscopes and engage in celestial observations. He soon combined his medical knowledge with astrological forecasts – a combination that made him both popular and dangerous. Anyone who looked too clearly into the future quickly risked coming into conflict with the Church.

His main work, the "Propheties," first appeared in 1555. It consisted of several "centuries," collections of one hundred four-line verses each, called quatrains. In total, he wrote almost a thousand of these verses, in which he supposedly foresaw the future of humanity. The language was deliberately cryptic: Nostradamus mixed French with Latin, ancient Greek, and even a few Italian terms. He played with anagrams, distorted place names, and employed metaphors and allegories. This made the texts difficult to understand, sometimes almost cryptic. His defenders say he did this to protect himself from the Inquisition; his critics suspect that the ambiguity was a method—the more obscure the verses, the easier it was to find a suitable interpretation later.

Even in his own time, the prophecies attracted attention. The French Queen Catherine de' Medici was particularly impressed by his predictions and even invited him to court. Thus, Nostradamus was transformed from a provincial pharmacist into a man with direct access to the powerful. Many saw this as a sign that he knew more than others.

One of his most famous alleged predictions concerns the death of King Henry II of France. One verse speaks of a "young lion" defeating the "old lion" in a duel, with the spear piercing his eye through the "golden grille." In 1559, Henry II actually died in a tournament fight when his opponent's lance pierced the visor of his helmet, mortally wounding him. For Nostradamus' followers, this was the definitive proof of his gift for prophecy. Skeptics, however, point out that tournament accidents were not uncommon at that time and that the metaphors could have applied to many other scenarios. Yet therein lies the power of his verses: they are formulated so generally that, in retrospect, they can apply to numerous events.

Over the centuries, Nostradamus's texts have been repeatedly cited to explain major historical events. Some saw his verses as heralding the French Revolution, others interpreted them as references to Napoleon Bonaparte. Later, many believed that Nostradamus also predicted the First and Second World Wars. A verse in particular is cited in which a "great leader from Western Europe" appears and "Hister" is mentioned. Many saw this as an allusion to Adolf Hitler. Historians point out, however, that "Hister" was an old name for the Danube River – and the connection to Hitler only emerged through subsequent interpretation. Nevertheless, this supposed prophecy made Nostradamus world famous again in the 20th century.

Even the catastrophes of the recent past have been linked to Nostradamus. After the terrorist attacks of September 11, 2001, alleged Nostradamus quotes circulated in the media, speaking of "fires in the sky" and "twin brothers torn apart." Many of these verses, however, did not come from his writings at all, but were completely fabricated. Nevertheless, the aura of his name alone was enough to make people feel that a man from the 16th century had foreseen the fate of the modern era.

Another reason for Nostradamus's enduring popularity lies in the psychological workings of his texts. People tend to recognize patterns even where none exist. This phenomenon is called pareidolia. In Nostradamus's nebulous verses, believers see exactly what they want to see. In times of uncertainty—wars, epidemics, economic crises—people were particularly drawn to his writings. His prophecies gave them the feeling that there was meaning in the chaos, that someone had recognized the order behind it.

It's also remarkable how flexibly his verses have been used throughout history. During World War II, they were used for propaganda purposes by both sides. The Nazis interpreted Nostradamus's words in such a way that they made Hitler's victory seem preordained. At the same time, the Allies published their own interpretations, which recognized the Nazis' downfall in his verses. The fact that the same texts could be interpreted so contradictorily demonstrates how open they were to projections.

Today, Nostradamus has long been part of pop culture. His prophecies regularly appear in books, television documentaries, and even computer games. Whenever a new millennium or a significant date approaches, his name is invoked. The year 1999 played a particularly significant role, as a verse spoke of a "great king of terror" who would descend from heaven in the "seventh month of 1999." Many people saw this as a herald of an apocalypse. When the year passed without catastrophe, the interpretation was simply shifted to other years. Thus, the prophecies remain ever relevant, because they are never definitive.

A little fun fact shows how down-to-earth Nostradamus was, despite everything: In addition to his prophecies and astrological writings, he also wrote recipes for jams and guides for dealing with bad smells. The fact that this man, of all people, was stylized as the greatest prophet in world history illustrates how strong the human desire for predictability and secret knowledge is.

From a scientific perspective, Nostradamus's writings are hardly reliable. Historians view them more as a mixture of poetic talent, astrological vocabulary, and vague metaphors. Nevertheless, they remain impressive to this day precisely because they defy any definitive interpretation. Perhaps the real mystery lies not in his prophecies themselves, but in people's unwavering willingness to see in them the key to the future. Nostradamus knew how to tap into this longing by not offering clear answers, but just enough ambiguity to allow each generation to reinterpret his verses.

3.5. The mysterious crop circles: Messages from space?

Crop circles are large-scale patterns that appear in crop fields, often overnight. Some believe them to be the work of extraterrestrial intelligence, while others consider them human hoaxes or works of art.

The first complex patterns: The crop circles that appeared in England in the 1980s, which went beyond simple circles and featured complex geometric patterns, caused a great stir.
There are numerous examples of crop circles whose origins remain unconclusively unclear. Although many crop circles were clearly man-made, often using simple techniques such as boards and ropes, there are some where the circumstances are so complex and the patterns so distinctive that they cast doubt on human origin. They have therefore given rise to many theories and speculations.
What makes some of these crop circles so mysterious?
Complexity of patterns: Some crop circles exhibit extremely complex geometric shapes and mathematical precision that seem difficult to create with simple human tools.
*Sudden onset:*Crop circles often appear overnight without any witnesses noticing.
*Lack of traces:*In some places, no footprints or other evidence of human intervention were found.
*Scientific puzzles:*In some cases, physical changes in the plants or soil were observed that cannot be simply explained by mechanical action.
Examples of mysterious crop circles:
*Crop circles with unusual properties:*There are reports of crop circles in which the plants were bent at the kinks without being broken, or in which the nodes of the plants were twisted in unusual ways.
*Crop circles in remote areas:*The appearance of crop circles in remote and inaccessible areas raises questions about how the creators got there and how they could have created the complex patterns without modern tools.
There are theories about the origin of crop circles. Most experts assume that most crop circles are created by humans to attract attention or to convey a certain message.
Some theories suggest that crop circles could be caused by natural phenomena such as hurricanes or electromagnetic fields.
A popular, albeit scientifically unproven, theory is that crop circles are created by aliens as messages or as landing sites for UFOs.

Whoever or whatever creates the crop circles remains unclear as to what such complex and artistic patterns are meant to express.

Crop circles are certainly interesting, and probably not only for lovers of geometric images.

3.6 The Dyatlov Pass Incident

The Dyatlov Pass Incident is one of the most mysterious and disturbing events in recent history. In 1959, nine experienced hikers, eight men and one woman, led by Igor Dyatlov, set out on an expedition into the remote mountains of the Northern Ural Mountains in what was then the Soviet Union. They would never return home.

In early 1959, in the midst of the freezing Soviet winter, a group of ten young hikers set out to cross the snowy wilderness of the Northern Urals. It was an expedition prized in universities of the era as a testament to physical toughness and sporting spirit. Led by 23-year-old Igor Dyatlov, the group consisted primarily of students and graduates of the Sverdlovsk Polytechnic Institute. They were experienced, disciplined, and familiar with the rigors of nature. Eight men and two women shouldered their skis, backpacks, and tents to tackle a demanding tour that would ultimately earn them a "Difficulty Level III" rating, the highest classification for such an undertaking. But the journey that was supposed to bring them recognition and sporting glory became the stage for a tragedy that remains incomprehensible to this day.
The participants were young and full of joie de vivre. Photos taken along the way show smiling faces, improvised evenings of music with guitars, and cooking together in the snow. Among them was a woman, Lyudmila Dubinina, only 20 years old but already an experienced mountaineer. The group gelled; they were not daredevil adventurers, but carefully planned hikers. When one of the participants had to abandon the trek early due to illness and return home, a group of nine remained behind to set out on the final stages toward Kholat Syakhl, a remote mountain. The name of the mountain in the Mansi language, "Mountain of the Dead," seemed like an ill omen to many – but for experienced hikers, it was little more than cultural background, nothing more than a legend. On February 1, 1959, the nine camped on the slopes of Kholat Syakhl. The decision to camp on the slope rather than in a nearby forest was unusual. Some researchers speculate that they wanted to practice the technique of pitching tents in difficult locations or to avoid wasting any more time. It was bitterly cold, with temperatures between minus 20 and minus 30 degrees Celsius. The wind whipped, the snow drifted. But for the group, this was nothing out of the ordinary. They found shelter in their tent, prepared their dinner, laughed, and wrote in their diaries. Everything seemed normal.
Then, during the night, something must have happened that sent the entire group into a panic. When search parties found the camp weeks later, the tent was still standing on the hillside, half-covered in snow, but ripped open from the inside. Personal belongings, shoes, warm clothing—everything had been left behind. The nine had left the tent as if every second were precious to them. Barefoot, lightly dressed, with no chance of survival in this cold.

The tracks in the snow suggested that they had initially descended the slope together, not running, but hurrying, as if trying to gain distance. The first two bodies were discovered a few hundred meters away, near a fallen tree. They were wearing barely any clothing, their hands torn open, as if they had been desperately trying to tear firewood from branches. Later, three more bodies were found between the tree and the tent, as if they had been trying to return. The last four victims were discovered months later, buried under several meters of snow in a ravine. This was where the most severe injuries were found: broken ribs, skull injuries, injuries that experts compared more to car accidents or explosions. The condition of Lyudmila Dubinina, whose tongue and eyes were missing, was particularly eerie.

The autopsies provided no clear answers. Some had died of hypothermia, others from severe injuries. But what caused these injuries remained unclear. There were no external wounds, no cuts, no blows. The bodies were severely damaged internally, but almost intact externally – as if an enormous, yet diffuse force had acted upon them. Things became even stranger when traces of elevated radioactivity were discovered on some items of clothing.

The official investigation took a strange course. The cause of death was soon summarized with the vague phrase "an overwhelming force of nature." The files were closed, the area was closed to hikers, and many relatives never received satisfactory answers. For the Soviet authorities, the case seemed closed, but for the public, this was just the beginning of the mystery.

A variety of theories quickly emerged. The obvious explanation was an avalanche. Perhaps an avalanche had broken loose, or perhaps the hikers feared that their tent would be buried under an approaching avalanche. However, no signs of a classic avalanche were found. The tent was not destroyed, and the slope was not marked by large masses of snow. Many experts still consider this incompatible with the avalanche theory.

Others speculated that the group had witnessed secret Soviet military tests. In the 1950s, the Red Army did indeed experiment with rockets and parachute mines, even in remote regions. Some injuries resembled pressure waves that might be caused by explosions. The radioactive traces on some items of clothing also fit the picture for some. However, a direct connection could never be proven.

More exotic explanations also circulated. The local Mansi people were suspected but quickly ruled out – they were considered peaceful, and no traces of foreign attackers were found at the camp. Animals were equally out of the question. Some even spoke of an attack by yetis or UFOs, as eyewitnesses from surrounding villages claimed to have seen strange lights in the sky that night. To many, such hypotheses sounded absurd, but they persisted because the more realistic explanations left too many questions unanswered.

Another theory that has gained popularity in recent years is that of infrasound. Certain wind conditions could generate low-frequency vibrations that trigger panic attacks in humans. Perhaps this caused the hikers to become irrationally afraid and flee their tents. This hypothesis could explain why they left without clothing, but not the serious injuries suffered by the four victims in the ravine. In 2019, sixty years after the incident, Russian authorities reopened the case. They examined modern simulations and concluded that a rare form of slab avalanche, triggered by the weight of the tent and the specific slope conditions, could have been the cause. The injuries, the researchers argued, could have been caused by the pressure of snow and ice. But this official explanation did not convince many. Too many details remain unexplained—for example, why the tent was ripped open from the inside, why some victims continued to light fires for days while others lay far away in a ravine.

To this day, the Dyatlov Pass Incident remains a magnet for speculation. Books, films, and countless documentaries have reopened the case, and internet forums and conspiracy theorists fiercely debate every detail of the investigation files. The appeal lies less in the possibility that we may ever find a definitive answer, but rather in the fact that the mystery has become a kind of modern legend. It is the interplay of eerie scenery, unexplained injuries, official silence, and human imagination that makes the Dyatlov Pass Incident one of the greatest unsolved mysteries of the 20th century.

Perhaps it was indeed a force of nature that struck that night—a combination of snow, wind, and darkness that sent the hikers into a panic. Perhaps it was a military secret that was never meant to be revealed. Or perhaps it was something that defies rational explanation. All that is certain is that the "Mountain of the Dead" lived up to its name when nine young people lost their lives there—and that, decades later, their story reminds us that even in a scientifically enlightened world, the wilderness holds secrets we don't understand.

3.7 The Tunguska Event

On the morning of June 30, 1908, a mysterious and powerful event occurred in the remote region of Siberia, which became known as the Tunguska Event. A massive explosion shook the taiga and devastated an area of approximately 2,150 square kilometers. This explosion was so powerful that it uprooted and burned trees and generated shock waves that triggered seismic and atmospheric effects worldwide.
The Tunguska event began around 7:17 a.m. local time, when a bright flash of light appeared in the sky, followed by an intense explosion. Eyewitnesses near the explosion reported a massive fireball illuminating the sky and a pressure wave that threw people to the ground and shattered windows in villages hundreds of kilometers away.
One survivor, the shepherd Semyon Semyonov, described the scene this way: "The sky split in two, and high above the forest the entire northern part of the sky appeared as if it were covered in fire."

Although the event caused immense destruction, due to its remote location, the area wasn't thoroughly investigated until 1927 by a scientific expedition led by Russian geologist Leonid Kulik. Kulik and his team found unimaginable devastation: millions of trees lay flat on the ground, all in a radial arrangement that indicated the point of explosion. Curiously, however, they found no impact crater or obvious meteorite fragments.

The exact cause of the Tunguska Event remains unclear, but the most likely explanation is that a large meteor or comet entered the Earth's atmosphere and exploded at an altitude of approximately 5 to 10 kilometers. The explosion released an energy estimated at about 10 to 15 megatons of TNT—about 1,000 times more powerful than the atomic bomb dropped on Hiroshima.

Several theories have been proposed to explain the Tunguska event:
Meteorite or comet impact: The most widely accepted theory is that a cosmic object, probably a meteor or comet, exploded in the atmosphere. The enormous heat and pressure wave destroyed most of the object before it reached the ground, which explains the lack of a crater.
Geological or volcanic activity: Some early theories speculated about geological or volcanic causes, but the evidence did not support these theories.
Antimatter or exotic particles: A less common theory proposes that the event was caused by the collision of antimatter or exotic particles with Earth. However, this hypothesis remains speculative and is not widely accepted.
Experimental or extraterrestrial technology: Conspiracy theories and science fiction stories have linked the Tunguska Event to secret experiments or alien spacecraft, but there is no credible evidence to support these claims.

The Tunguska event remains a disturbing example of the potentially catastrophic effects of cosmic events on Earth. It spurred the scientific community to take the risk of asteroid impacts seriously and to develop monitoring and mitigation systems to detect and prevent future threats.

While the exact nature of the object that caused the explosion may never be fully understood, the Tunguska event reminds us that the universe is full of unpredictable and powerful forces.

3.8. The mystery of the ship "SS Ourang Medan"

In 1947, a distress call was reportedly intercepted from the ship "SS Ourang Medan," a Dutch cargo ship traveling in the Strait of Malacca.

The message was disturbing: All crew members had been found dead, their faces contorted in horror. The cause of death remained unclear, but the message spoke of a "deadly force" on board.
Several ships rushed to the scene to provide assistance. Upon reaching the ship, they found the crew dead, just as described in the radio message. But as the rescuers boarded, something inexplicable happened: Some of them also mysteriously died.
The cause of the crew's death was never conclusively determined. Speculation ranged from poisonous gases to an attack by a sea monster to paranormal phenomena.
The descriptions of the dead crew members with their distorted faces create an eerie atmosphere and leave room for numerous interpretations.
There is little concrete evidence of what happened aboard the SS Ourang Medan. Most of the information comes from unconfirmed radio messages and sailors' reports. It's conceivable that the story was embellished over time to make it more exciting.

The story of the ship "SS Ourang Medan" is an example of how quickly rumors spread and how difficult it can be to distinguish between fact and fiction.

3.9 The Philadelphia Experiment

The Philadelphia Experiment is arguably one of the most well-known and frequently discussed conspiracy theories of modern times. The story surrounding this alleged experiment is both exciting and enigmatic. It promises to transcend the boundaries of human imagination and raises questions about the nature of space and time.

Legend has it that during World War II, the US Navy conducted a secret experiment to make a warship, the USS Eldridge, invisible using electromagnetic fields.

However, the experiment is said to have gone wrong, and the ship is said to have disappeared for a short time and then reappeared in another location, with some crew members merging with the ship or being transported to other dimensions.

The USS Eldridge was a real warship of the U.S. Navy. It was a destroyer escort that was commissioned in 1943 and served until 1955.

The story of the Philadelphia Experiment first appeared in the 1950s in letters from science fiction author Morris K. Jessup. Jessup had received several letters claiming that the experiment had actually taken place.

These letters were later disseminated by UFO researcher Carl Allen and published in a book that popularized the legend of the Philadelphia Experiment.

People's enthusiasm for this story can be attributed to several factors:

The idea of making a ship invisible or teleporting through space and time has a strong appeal to science fiction fans.

The idea that the government is conducting secret experiments that the public wants to keep secret appeals to many people.

However, the story raises more questions than it answers, which stimulates the imagination and leads to numerous speculations.

From a scientific perspective, the Philadelphia Experiment is highly improbable, if not impossible. There is no evidence that such an experiment ever took place. The story is based more on rumors, anecdotes, and speculation.

The laws of physics as we understand them today do not allow such manipulation of space and time.

The Philadelphia Experiment is nevertheless an example of how quickly a story can become a legend, even though there is no evidence for it.

3.10. El Dorado: The Lost City of Gold

The legend of El Dorado, the Gilded City, has captured the human imagination for centuries. It originates from the stories of Spanish conquistadors who came to South America in the 16th century to search for gold and other treasures. The indigenous people told of a powerful king who lived in a city of gold. During religious ceremonies, he is said to have covered himself with gold dust and then jumped into a lake to offer the gold to the gods. These tales were taken up by the Spanish and expanded into a mythical story of infinite wealth. The image of a king covering himself in gold and jumping into a golden lake was so impressive that it sparked a veritable gold-rush-like search. Numerous expeditions set out into the unexplored jungles of South America to find the legendary city. But despite centuries of searching and countless explorers, El Dorado remained hidden.

The enthusiasm for El Dorado can be attributed to several factors:
The dream of wealth: The idea of infinite gold treasures has always fueled human greed.
The unknown: For Europeans at that time, South America was a largely unexplored continent full of secrets and dangers.
The missing evidence: Since no concrete evidence of the existence of El Dorado was found, the legend was able to live on and become anchored in people's minds. Historians today agree that El Dorado was not a real city, but rather a mythological figure created from the stories of indigenous peoples and the imagination of Europeans. The idea of a king covering himself in gold may have been based on religious rituals of some indigenous peoples in which they covered themselves with dyes or minerals. The Spanish exaggerated these rituals and created the legend of El Dorado.
Although El Dorado was never found, the legend has left a lasting impression on culture. It symbolizes the human longing for wealth, adventure, and the unknown. El Dorado has been featured in numerous books, films, and games and continues to inspire the imagination of people around the world.
An artifact often mentioned in connection with El Dorado is the so-called *"Goldfloß von Pasca"*. It was discovered in 1969 in a cave near the ancient Muisca settlement of Pasca, southwest of Bogotá.

The raft depicts a ceremony in which a leader is rubbed with gold dust and floats out onto a lake on a raft. It is cited as evidence of the authenticity of the El Dorado legend, as it confirms the Muisca rituals described. However, the raft represents only a small part of the story and does not prove the existence of a golden city.
The legend of El Dorado is more than just a story about lost treasure; it is a reflection of human nature, dealing with desires, hopes, greed, and fears.

El Dorado has been featured in numerous books, films and games and continues to inspire the imagination of people around the world.
Even though El Dorado will probably never be found, it is an interesting subject for speculation.

3.11. Encounters with unknown underwater objects

Reports from Russian submarines about encounters with unidentified underwater objects (**USE**s) are a mysterious chapter in the history of maritime research and the military. These incidents, which occurred particularly during the Cold War, raise questions about the nature and origin of these enigmatic phenomena.

During the Cold War, Soviet submarines patrolled the world's oceans, conducting secret missions. Crew members of these submarines occasionally reported encounters with unusual objects moving underwater at tremendous speeds and maneuverability. These objects, known as USOs, could not be explained by known technologies or natural phenomena.

Known incidents:

The K-222 Encounter

In 1970, the world was still in the midst of the Cold War, and few places were the rivalries between the superpowers more tangible than beneath the ocean waves. Where radar was of limited use and secrecy reigned supreme, the submarines of the Soviet Union and the United States patrolled in constant vigilance. It was a world where every unexplained signal, every unusual shadow, immediately fired the imagination. It was in precisely this climate that the mysterious encounter of the Soviet submarine K-222 with an object that transcended all known physical boundaries occurred.

The K-222 was a technical sensation at the time. It belonged to the Project 661 class, aptly codenamed "Papa class" by NATO. This submarine was the fastest nuclear-powered submarine ever built, officially capable of speeds exceeding 40 knots – a speed that even then broke records and put Western militaries on high alert. With its titanium-reinforced hull and considerable propulsion power, the K-222 was considered a prime example of Soviet engineering. But even this masterpiece was unprepared for what its crew encountered one day in the Atlantic.

During a routine operation, the sonar operators reported a strong signal. It was an object moving at a speed that exceeded all previous experience. The sonar registered over 300 knots – approximately 555 kilometers per hour. By comparison, the fastest torpedoes of the time reached perhaps 50 to 60 knots. Even today, decades later, the fastest underwater weapons are far below the speed recorded by the Soviet crew at that time. It was immediately clear to the officers on board: This could not be allowed to happen.

Even more bizarre was the description of the object. The sonar reflection suggested a metallic structure, and its shape seemed unusual—unlike any submarine or torpedo the men were familiar with. Not only was it moving at breathtaking speed, but it was also changing direction abruptly, as if the physical laws of water had been suspended for this thing. Normally, high speed underwater creates enormous pressure and drag. An object traveling at 300 knots should leave a massive pressure wave behind it, creating sounds that would be heard far and wide. But according to the crew's records, it was almost as if this thing was gliding through the water, oblivious to the laws of fluid mechanics.

The officers aboard the K-222 took the signal very seriously. It wasn't a one-time measurement or a sonar flare, but a stable track observed over several minutes. The men were adept at distinguishing between errors and real objects—after all, their survival often depended on detecting enemy ships and torpedoes in time. They were convinced they had detected something real.

But what could it have been? Shortly after the incident, rumors circulated in Soviet naval circles. Some suspected a top-secret American project, perhaps a new type of underwater drone or an experimental torpedo far superior to the Soviet Union's. But no one could explain how even the technologically advanced United States could have developed such a device without it ever coming to light through espionage or intelligence reports.

Others resorted to an explanation that would be heard more frequently in the decades to come:**USE**s, „**unidentified submerged objects**Underwater UFOs, so to speak. Since the 1960s, both Soviet and American sailors have repeatedly reported unidentified objects beneath the water's surface, moving at unimaginable speeds and abruptly submerging or surfacing. Some described glowing spheres gliding through the depths, others describing disc-shaped structures that disappeared without a trace. Unofficially, many of these reports were dismissed, but officially, both the US and the Soviet Union meticulously collected data on such encounters. Because, whether extraterrestrial or not, every unknown object in the ocean posed a potential risk.

In the case of the K-222, the incident remained unexplained. Neither the Soviets nor Western intelligence services were ever able to identify a technical device that even came close to the recorded speeds. Some later analyses attempted to attribute the event to sonar errors, such as overlapping signals or reflections from particular stratification in the water. But to the men on board, this sounded like an unsatisfactory excuse. They were certain: they had been tracking a real object.

The idea that alien technologies might not originate from space, but from the depths of the oceans, fascinated many. After all, the oceans are still less explored than the moon. Over 70 percent of the Earth's surface is covered by water, and large parts of the deep sea remain largely unexplored. Who could say with certainty that things beyond our imagination don't exist there?

Perhaps it was a measurement error, perhaps a top-secret military experiment we'll never know about. Perhaps it was something else entirely—a technological phenomenon from another world. The only thing that is certain is that for a few minutes, those men sitting in the stuffy corridors of the world's fastest submarine believed they had encountered an enemy superior to them in every way.

Despite intensive surveillance, the origin of the object could never be determined.

The Lake Baikal Encounters

Lake Baikal in Siberia is a place of superlatives. It is not only the deepest lake in the world, at over 1,600 meters deep, but also the oldest, formed around 25 million years ago. Approximately one-fifth of the world's freshwater is stored in its basin, and its isolation in the heart of Siberia gives it an almost mythical aura. Legends have long surrounded this lake, which the locals reverently call "the sea." In the folklore of the Buryats, who have lived on its shores for centuries, Lake Baikal has always been a sacred place, populated by spirits, gods, and mysterious beings. But in the second half of the 20th century, the lake took on a new place in stories—as the setting for inexplicable encounters with objects and creatures that seem to come from another world.

Since the 1970s and 1980s, reports from Soviet fishermen, divers, and even military personnel have been accumulating, speaking of unusual phenomena in and above the lake. Repeatedly, lights were observed flashing beneath the surface, then moving at tremendous speed and disappearing without a trace. Some witnesses reported seeing giant shadows gliding beneath boats, larger than any known watercraft. Machine-like sounds echoed from the depths, their source never being pinpointed.

The statements of Russian military divers from the 1980s attracted particular attention. During secret training missions in Lake Baikal, they allegedly encountered humanoid figures at depths of 50 meters, gliding through the water in shimmering silver suits. These beings were unusually large, almost three meters tall, and moved with an ease impossible for humans without heavy diving equipment. The encounters became so threatening that the divers attempted to throw nets over the figures – whereupon they were thrown back by an invisible force. Three of the divers involved are said to have died in this incident. Officially, no declassified files exist regarding this incident, but the stories circulated in military circles for decades and leaked out to the public after the collapse of the Soviet Union.

There were also numerous civilian reports. Fishermen described seeing cones of light shooting up from the lake at night, as if an invisible machine were piercing the water's surface. Others saw enormous objects hovering just below the surface before disappearing at a speed that exceeded any known submarine. Even pilots flying over Lake Baikal reported anomalies, unexplained radar contacts, or lights that seemed to rise directly from the water.

The Soviet authorities reacted ambivalently. On the one hand, the reports were collected and kept secret; on the other, they attempted to dismiss them with rational explanations. Lake Baikal is a geologically active area: earthquakes and volcanic processes are not uncommon, and luminous phenomena could be due to geophysical causes. Methane gas bubbles rising from the sediment can, in the right light, appear like mysterious flares. Acoustic illusions are also conceivable in the vast depths, where water currents and geological movements produce sounds reminiscent of machines.

But many of the military reports cannot be dismissed so easily. In particular, the combination of speed, size, and maneuverability of the described objects defies all that is technically possible. Submarines, even the most modern of the Soviet Navy at the time, could barely exceed 40 knots—and only for short periods of time. However, the described objects moved at hundreds of knots, changed direction abruptly, and surfaced and submerged as if the water presented no resistance.

With the end of the Soviet Union, some archives opened, and former officers reported more freely about the unusual phenomena in Lake Baikal. Some spoke of a "hot zone," a region of the lake that had repeatedly been the source of sightings. In this region, it is said, boats also disappeared without a trace on several occasions, while the crews reported nothing unusual.

The stories of underwater humanoid beings remain a mystery to this day. Were they merely legends, exaggerated memories of diving accidents at great depths? Or did the divers actually encounter something beyond human comprehension? Proponents of the extraterrestrial hypothesis see Lake Baikal as an ideal hiding place for a hidden civilization. The lake is deep enough, remote enough, and its gigantic masses of water provide perfect camouflage.

Even though skeptics point out that many phenomena can be explained geologically or meteorologically, Lake Baikal remains an intriguing place for UFO and USO researchers. Even the Russian Navy is said to regularly collect data on unusual occurrences there. For the locals, there's no question: Lake Baikal is a lake full of mysteries, and not all of them are of terrestrial origin.

The Shag Harbour Sightings

Although Shag Harbour is located in Canada, there are reports of Soviet submarines operating near this region and observing USOs.
On the evening of October 4, 1967, several eyewitnesses, including military personnel, observed and reported strange orange lights in the sky over Shag Harbour. These lights appeared to be moving toward the sea and eventually crashing near the coast.
Although it was officially investigated as a plane crash, divers found no wreckage, leading to further speculation about USOs.
The eyewitness accounts are remarkably detailed and consistent. Many described the object as luminous and oval. It reportedly continued to glow underwater for some time after the crash.
The Royal Canadian Mounted Police (RCMP) was alerted and launched a search. Despite intensive efforts, no wreckage or other physical evidence was found.
Soviet military and scientists took these reports seriously and conducted investigations.

There is evidence that the Soviet Navy established special units to investigate USOs and that these phenomena were documented in secret archives. Some of these reports were published after the end of the Cold War and the collapse of the Soviet Union, but many details remain secret.

The nature of the USOs remains a mystery. Various theories and speculations exist, ranging from advanced human technology to extraterrestrial origins:

Some researchers believe the USOs may represent secret military projects using highly advanced technologies. These may have been developed by the Soviet Union, the United States, or other nations and were kept secret.

Other scientists suspect that some USO sightings could be natural phenomena such as unusual ocean currents, gas emissions, or optical illusions.

Another theory is that USOs are of extraterrestrial origin. Proponents of this theory argue that the maneuverability and speed of these objects indicate technologies far beyond what human science and engineering could achieve at the time of the sighting.

Chapter 4: Incredible Coincidences

This chapter explores some of the most astonishing coincidences and unbelievable events in history. Whether they're literary prophecies, recurring natural phenomena, or remarkable life stories, these tales demonstrate that the unexpected often plays a larger role in our lives than we might think. Stay tuned, because the world is full of surprising twists and inexplicable coincidences.

4.1. The Titanic and the fictional ship Titan: An eerie prediction

Few shipping disasters have shocked the world as much as the sinking of the Titanic in April 1912. The passenger ship, hailed as "unsinkable," collided with an iceberg on its maiden voyage, killing over 1,500 people. This tragedy remains a symbol of human hubris and a reminder of the limits of technological progress. Less well known, however, is that just 14 years earlier, a novel was published that foreshadowed this catastrophe with uncanny accuracy.
In 1898, the American author Morgan Robertson published the book*Futility, or the Wreck of the Titan*In it, he describes the sinking of a gigantic, luxurious steamer, which its builders described as virtually unsinkable. The ship's name was Titan, and like the later Titanic, it struck an iceberg in the North Atlantic in April and sank because it didn't have enough lifeboats for all the passengers on board.
The parallels between Robertson's Titan and the later Titanic are so numerous and precise that many readers got goosebumps upon first comparing them. The names of the two ships differed by only two letters. In Robertson's story, the Titan measured 244 meters, while in reality the Titanic measured 269 meters. Both were therefore among the largest ships of their era. Both the Titan and the Titanic were capable of speeds of over 20 knots, both were considered luxurious passenger ships with the latest

technology, and were touted by their builders as virtually unsinkable. In both cases, there were far too few lifeboats for the number of passengers, a decisive factor in the high number of casualties. And finally, in April, both ships collided with an iceberg in the North Atlantic, killing more than half of the people on board in each case.

Morgan Robertson himself was by no means an unworldly writer who had conceived the story at his desk. He was the son of a ship's captain and had himself spent several years at sea in his younger years. He knew the risks of the North Atlantic, the power of storms, the danger of icebergs, and the thin safety margins of shipping at that time. His depictions were therefore not mere literary fantasy, but based on the experiences of a man who had witnessed the maritime world with his own eyes. The fact that he predicted the sinking of a luxury liner so precisely therefore seems less like a supernatural prediction than the result of keen observation and sober analysis.

A curious detail that further reinforces the myth surrounding the Titanic concerns its fourth funnel. Of the four massive chimneys that made the ship appear so imposing, only three were actually in use. The fourth served no technical function whatsoever, serving solely as a symbol of symmetry and prestige. It was intended to make the ship appear more powerful and impressive than it actually was. At a time when the outward appearance of strength and technical superiority was almost as important as its practical function, this nonfunctional funnel became a symbol of the Titanic's self-image: more show than substance, a prestige object that placed safety behind the demands of grandeur and elegance.

After the sinking of the Titanic, Robertson's novel was reissued and enjoyed unexpected success, as readers were now amazed to discover how many details of the fictional story paralleled the gruesome reality. Robertson himself, however, rejected any mystical interpretation. He explained that he had simply observed the developments of his time and drawn logical conclusions. Nevertheless, the story of Titan and Titanic remains one of the most striking examples of how fiction and reality sometimes merge in uncanny ways.

4.2. The story of the two Kennedys: coincidence or fate?

Sometimes history seems to contain so many strange reflections that one wonders whether coincidence alone is truly a sufficient explanation. This phenomenon is particularly striking when comparing two American presidents who both became icons – Abraham Lincoln and John F. Kennedy. Both were assassinated, both are considered symbolic figures of an era, and both are inextricably linked to a whole series of astonishing parallels that have occupied historians, journalists, and even conspiracy theorists for decades.

Abraham Lincoln was elected the 16th President of the United States in 1860, in the midst of a period of political tension that would soon explode into the Civil War. John F. Kennedy, in turn, became the country's 35th president exactly a century later, in 1960, also during a period of great uncertainty, marked by the Cold War, the Cuban Missile Crisis, and the Civil Rights Movement. These election years, exactly 100 years apart, are considered the first striking coincidence.

Both men were assassinated on a Friday, and both died of gunshot wounds to the head. Lincoln was shot on April 14, 1865, at Ford's Theater in Washington, D.C., and Kennedy was shot on November 22, 1963, in Dallas—in a Lincoln car manufactured by the Ford Motor Company. The fact that the names "Ford" and "Lincoln" are so eerily intertwined in both stories is one of those details that appears countless times in riddle lists and history books.

The murderers also share striking similarities. Lincoln's assassin was named John Wilkes Booth, Kennedy's assassin officially Lee Harvey Oswald. Both are known by their three names, and both consist of fifteen letters. Booth was born in 1839, Oswald exactly 100 years later, in 1939. Both were killed after their crimes, before they could be brought to justice: Booth by soldiers who arrested him on a farm in Virginia, Oswald by nightclub owner Jack Ruby, who shot him in front of live cameras.

Even more curious is the look at the two presidents' successors. After Lincoln's assassination, Andrew Johnson took office, and after Kennedy's death, Lyndon B. Johnson. Both not only had the name Johnson, but were also born in the South and had previously served as senators. Andrew Johnson was born in 1808, Lyndon B. Johnson in 1908—again, a coincidence, exactly 100 years apart.

Even their personal circumstances sometimes seem like mirror images. Both presidents were known for their charisma, but also for the divisiveness their policies provoked in the country. Lincoln led the United States through the Civil War and ushered in the end of slavery; Kennedy represented the hope of a young, modern politics, one that, however, was also accompanied by enemies and critics. Both died in the presence of their wives, both in moments when they were in the public spotlight, and both assassinations shocked not only the USA but the entire world.

Since these parallels were first systematically collected and published—particularly in popular magazines of the 1960s and '70s—they have captured people's imaginations. For many, they exemplify the enigmatic patterns that fate sometimes seems to weave. Others see them as nothing more than a series of coincidences that, in retrospect, appear particularly striking due to selective perception. Finally, there are also many differences between the two men and their times that are often overlooked in such lists.

The man who was struck by lightning seven times

When talking about unlucky people, one might think of a forgotten umbrella in a sudden shower or an unfortunate trip over a curb. But compared to Roy Sullivan, all of this seems almost ridiculous. The American park ranger from Virginia went down in history as the "human lightning rod" because he was struck by lightning seven times between 1942 and 1977 – and survived each time. Not a fabricated anecdote, not a modern myth, but a documented life whose absurdity is almost unsurpassed.

Roy Sullivan was born in 1912 and later worked as a ranger in Shenandoah National Park. This park, full of mountains, forests, and canyons, was his workplace, his second home, and apparently also the preferred playground for the forces of nature when it came to targeting him. While millions of people never even come close to a lightning strike in their lifetime, Sullivan managed to find himself in the center of it time and time again.
His first documented incident occurred in 1942 while he was serving on an observation tower. The tower itself was new, but the lightning arrestor system hadn't yet been installed. As a thunderstorm approached, lightning struck the tower and jumped onto Sullivan. He survived but suffered severe burns to his legs and feet. This single incident alone would have been enough to make him cautiously watch for the weather for a lifetime. But it was only the beginning.
Further lightning strikes struck him in a variety of situations. Once he was driving, another time he was walking. In 1969, lightning struck a tree next to him, and the force knocked him to the ground. In 1970, he was struck again, this time burning his shoulder. In 1972, while on duty in the park, another strike knocked him to the ground. Each time, he survived, but his body bore the effects. His hair burned, his nails splintered, and his skin was scalded. Sometimes his clothes even caught fire, and he had to extinguish the flames himself.
People soon began calling him "the Lightning Man" or "the human lightning rod." He later spoke of feeling persecuted, as if a higher being had specifically targeted him. Indeed, after the repeated strikes, he avoided large crowds during thunderstorms, fearing that lightning might find him again and strike innocent people. In his hometown, it was no joke, but a serious reflex, for people to keep their distance whenever dark clouds appeared in the sky and Sullivan was nearby.

Statistically speaking, Sullivan's story is almost impossible to grasp. The probability of being struck by lightning even once in a lifetime is approximately 1 in 500,000. Being struck multiple times is a probability so small it would be practically impossible. Yet Sullivan repeatedly refuted these statistics until he finally survived the seventh strike in 1977.

The press regularly reported on his incredible streak, and he soon even made it into the Guinness Book of Records. To this day, he remains listed as the person who has survived the most lightning strikes. A bizarre mixture of misfortune, perseverance, and a tenacious will to live made him a legendary figure.

But the story also has a tragic side. Despite his spectacular ability to survive in the face of the forces of nature, Sullivan remained a man of worries and injuries. The constant fear of being hit again accompanied him until the end of his life. Friends reported that he often checked the sky with a stick when dark clouds appeared, and that he became so nervous during thunderstorms that he could hardly sit still.

While scientists explain that lightning tends to strike the highest or most conductive point, and Sullivan's workplace in the mountainous Shenandoah National Park was located in a lightning hotspot, his string of tragedies remains extraordinary. Millions of people have lived, worked, and hiked there without ever experiencing a strike. That a single man was struck seven times seems like a twist of fate that defies all logic.

Today, Sullivan is often mentioned in collections of curious stories, in television documentaries, articles, or record lists. His nickname as the "human lightning rod" sounds almost like a comic book character, yet he was a real, flesh-and-blood human being who felt the power of nature on his own body, time and time again.

His story also raises a peculiar question: Was he truly just the victim of a series of unfortunate coincidences, or did he actually attract lightning through his work, his surroundings, and perhaps even a certain susceptibility? Science has no definitive answer. Perhaps it was simply a chain of circumstances that repeatedly brought him to the wrong place at the wrong time.

4.4. The Incredible Coincidence by Edgar Allan Poe

Edgar Allan Poe, the master of gothic fiction, wrote the novel "The Narrative of Arthur Gordon Pym of Nantucket" in 1838. In it, he tells the story of four shipwrecked sailors who kill and eat a cabin boy named Richard Parker in order to survive. Approximately 46 years later, in 1884, the British ship Mignonette ran aground, and the surviving crew also chose to kill and eat a cabin boy named Richard Parker. This uncanny coincidence has led many people to reflect on Poe's prophetic abilities and speculate about the role of chance in literature and life.

4.5 The two hurricanes that hit the same village – exactly 100 years apart

In 1920, a hurricane struck the small village of Yallahs, Jamaica, causing devastating damage. Exactly 100 years later, in 2020, the same village was hit again by a hurricane. This incredible recurrence has baffled many people and reminds us how nature can inexplicably exhibit recurring patterns. Although such events are rare, they demonstrate the enchanting nature of our planet.

4.6. The twin brothers and their parallel lives

Sometimes life delivers stories that sound so improbable that you almost think they're made up—and yet they're well-documented. One such story is that of identical twin brothers Jim Lewis and Jim Springer, who were separated shortly after birth and grew up in completely different families. For decades, they knew nothing of each other, lived in different cities, and led their own separate lives—and yet their lives unfolded in a way that later astonished psychologists, geneticists, and laypeople alike.

The brothers were born in 1940 in the US state of Ohio. Shortly after their birth, they were adopted – by two different families who had no contact with each other. One detail, which in retrospect seems like the beginning of a curious anecdote, shaped their lives from the very beginning: Both adoptive families gave their child the same name. They simply christened their boys "James." Thus, Jim Lewis and Jim Springer grew up, unaware of each other, yet with an identical first name that, in a sense, subconsciously connected them.

When they finally met again at the age of 39, a chain of discoveries ensued that could hardly have been more astonishing. Both had a dog they named "Toy." Both married for the first time at a young age—and both married a woman named Linda. When their marriages fell apart, they both remarried—and again, their wives shared the same first name: Betty. Even their children mirrored each other. Jim Lewis had a son named James Alan, while Jim Springer named his boy James Allan. A difference in the letter, but essentially the same choice.

The parallels didn't end there. Both worked in the security sector for a while, both had a passion for woodworking, both smoked the same brand of cigarettes, both drank the same beer, and both independently made similar vacation plans. Even their headaches, sleeping habits, and minor quirks seemed similar. When researchers at the University of Minnesota studied the two, they discovered that the "Jim Twins," as they soon became known in the press, became a prime example of the importance of genetic factors in personality development.

The story interested not only scientists but also the general public. Newspapers enthusiastically picked it up, television shows invited the brothers, and they became symbolic figures for the age-old question: What determines humanity—genetics or nurture? At first glance, the case seemed clear: So many identical decisions and preferences could hardly be coincidence, so genetics must play a huge role in shaping life.

But it wasn't that simple. Critics pointed out that people generally tend to look for patterns. In a world full of millions of name combinations, "Linda" and "Betty" for wives suddenly seem less unusual when you consider the frequency of these names in the USA in the 1960s and 1970s. "James" was also among the most popular boys' names of the time. The fact that both brothers also named their sons James seemed spectacular, but statistically speaking, it wasn't quite as unlikely as it seemed at first glance.

Nevertheless, the multitude of similarities remains remarkable, and for psychologists, the "Jim Twins" are a prime example. The famous twin study at the University of Minnesota, which examined twins who had grown up apart for decades, used the brothers as a memorable example to demonstrate the powerful influence of genetic factors on personality, intelligence, and behavior. The fact that the brothers not only made similar decisions but also showed strong similarities in cognitive tests, reaction patterns, and preferences actually suggests that genes have more influence on our lives than we often assume. For the public, however, it was the small, almost comical details that stuck with them. Two brothers who separately named their wives Linda and Betty, who had the same dog, "Toy," who both raised James Alan as their son—it sounds like a story you'd tell at the pub to leave the audience wide-eyed.

4.7 The Incredible Survival of Violet Jessop

Some people seem to be dogged by fate, others by luck—and in rare cases, both are true at the same time. Violet Constance Jessop, an Irish stewardess and nurse, undoubtedly falls into this category. Her life is a unique testament to the early era of the great passenger ships, a time when ocean liners were considered not only technological marvels, but also symbols of progress, luxury, and human pride. Violet Jessop's survival of three serious disasters at sea made her a legend—and earned her the nickname "Miss Unsinkable."

Violet Jessop was born in Argentina in 1887 to Irish immigrants. She experienced a hard life early on: Her childhood was marked by illness and deprivation, and as a young girl, she herself survived a severe bout of tuberculosis that doctors deemed fatal. However, she recovered and eventually followed in her mother's footsteps, working as a stewardess on passenger ships. For many young women, this profession offered a way to earn a steady income and see the world—even if the work on board was anything but glamorous.

In 1911, Violet Jessop began her service on the RMS Olympic, one of the White Star Line's most modern ships at the time. The ocean liner was considered the pride of British shipping, a technical masterpiece that combined luxury and safety in an unprecedented way. But that same year, an incident occurred: The Olympic collided with the British warship HMS Hawke near Southampton. Although the ship was able to tow itself back to the shipyard despite massive damage, it was a shock for the passengers and crew – and for Violet Jessop, her first encounter with the uncanny vulnerability of these supposedly unsinkable giants.

Just a few months later, she transferred to the RMS Titanic, arguably the most famous ocean liner of all time. When the ship set sail on its maiden voyage from Southampton to New York on April 10, 1912, Violet Jessop was on board as a stewardess. She looked after the first-class passengers, served tea and food, assisted with changing, and was part of the invisible but indispensable staff who made the on-board luxury possible. Four days later, on April 14, the Titanic famously collided with an iceberg in the North Atlantic. As chaos and panic spread on deck, Violet Jessop was ordered to help the passengers board the lifeboats. She later wrote in her memoirs that she was told to set a good example for the passengers and get into a boat. This is how she ended up in one of the last lifeboats, clutching a strange baby that a panicked woman had pressed into her hands at the last moment. She survived the disaster, in which over 1,500 people died, and was brought ashore in New York along with the other rescued people.

But the story didn't end there. Three years later, in the midst of the First World War, Violet Jessop was once again serving at sea – this time on HMHS Britannic, a sister ship to the Titanic, which was used as a hospital ship. On November 21, 1916, the Britannic struck a mine or was possibly hit by a torpedo in the Aegean Sea; the exact causes are still unclear. Within a very short time, the enormous ship began to sink. Violet Jessop later recalled that she climbed into a lifeboat, but it was sucked into the massive propellers of the Britannic, which was still running. At the last second, she jumped into the water, survived – albeit with a head injury – and was picked up by another boat. She survived this disaster too, although 30 people lost their lives in the accident. Violet Jessop had thus experienced three serious shipping disasters – and survived each one. Her colleagues nicknamed her "Miss Unsinkable," half mockingly, half admiringly. Nevertheless, she remained a loyal employee of the White Star Line. After the war, she continued to work as a stewardess on various ships and remained active in the maritime profession until the 1950s. Her extraordinary fate made her a legend among sailors, and her memoirs, which she wrote down in later years, gave the world a unique insight into the life of a woman who seemingly overcame everything.

Fun fact: Decades after the Titanic disaster, Violet Jessop recounted receiving an anonymous call one night. A woman's voice said, "Thank you for saving my baby." The person then hung up. Whether this was actually the child placed in her arms on that fateful night on the Titanic remains uncertain—but the story further contributed to the legend surrounding Violet.

4.8. The incredible survival story of Juliane Koepcke

On Christmas Eve 1971, the then 17-year-old student boarded a plane in Lima operated by the Peruvian airline LANSA. It was Flight 508, a scheduled flight from the capital to the city of Pucallpa in the Peruvian Amazon. More than 90 people were on board, including Juliane's mother. For most, it was a routine flight – but within a few hours, it would become a catastrophe, from which Juliane was the only survivor.

During the flight, the plane encountered a severe thunderstorm. Powerful lightning flashed through the clouds, turbulence jolted the passengers, and the crew desperately tried to maintain control. Then, suddenly, lightning struck the aircraft. Within seconds, the plane began to break apart. Juliane later recalled seeing her mother sitting next to her, and then being swept into the depths—strapped in her seat, surrounded by nothing but the clouds and the vast emptiness of the sky.

Miraculously, she survived the fall from a height of approximately 3,000 meters. The seat she was still strapped to apparently cushioned the impact, and the dense canopy of the rainforest did its part to slow her speed. Nevertheless, Juliane suffered severe injuries: a broken collarbone, deep lacerations, and a concussion. When she came to, she was lying alone in the Peruvian jungle—injured, disoriented, yet alive.

Her survival wasn't just luck. Juliane was the daughter of two German zoologists who conducted research in the Peruvian rainforest and had raised her there. Even as a child, she had learned which plants were edible, how to navigate in the dense vegetation, and what dangers lurked. This knowledge now became her lifeline. She knew that water means life in the rainforest, and so she set out to find a stream, because small streams lead to larger rivers, and rivers are home to people.

For eleven days, she fought her way through the wilderness. She lived on sweets she found in the wreck and drank water from rivers. She was repeatedly plagued by infections—a deep wound on her arm was infested with maggots—but Juliane knew she couldn't blindly face the maggots, as they ate the flesh off dead tissue and could thus prevent dangerous blood poisoning. Knowledge she gained from her parents' research helped her not to panic.

The jungle was merciless: tropical heat, poisonous snakes, swarms of insects, and the feeling of being completely alone in an endless green hell. Juliane fought with dizziness, hunger, and fever, but she didn't give up. She followed the watercourse as she had been trained to do, and after days, she finally found a larger river. On its banks, she discovered traces of people, the first sign of civilization.

On the eleventh day, she came across a small hut used by lumberjacks. Weakened and semi-conscious, she waited there until the men returned. They immediately recognized the half-starved girl as a survivor of the plane crash that was now the talk of the whole country. They provided her with emergency care and eventually brought her to safety.

Of the more than 90 people on board Flight 508, Juliane Koepcke was the only one to survive. Her mother had not survived the crash. For the girl, it was not only a physical struggle for survival, but also a psychological ordeal that would shape her for the rest of her life. Later, she studied biology and, like her parents, became a zoologist. She worked for many years in Peru, where she campaigned for rainforest conservation.

Her story made her famous worldwide. She was called "the girl who fell from the sky," and her survival fascinated people all over the world. Documentary filmmakers, journalists, and writers repeatedly sought contact with her. Juliane herself dealt with this interest very thoughtfully. She later wrote about her experiences in a book, emphasizing that it was less a miracle than a combination of luck, experience, and the iron will not to give up.

Fun fact: German director Werner Herzog had already planned a project with the same airline before the crash. He actually wanted to be on board LANSA 508, but rebooked – a coincidence that deeply moved him, too. Decades later, he made the documentary "Juliane's Fall into the Jungle," in which she herself told her story.

4.9. The lottery winner: Bill Morgan

In 1999, Australian truck driver Bill Morgan experienced a series of incredible coincidences that changed his life in remarkable ways. Morgan, who lived in Melbourne, had been going through a difficult time. After a serious truck accident, he was in a coma for 12 days.

Doctors gave him little chance of survival and even advised his family to turn off life support. But contrary to expectations, Bill made a full recovery and returned to life.

To celebrate his newfound joy in life, Bill decided to buy a Scratchies lottery ticket. To his amazement, he won a new car worth approximately $17,000. This win was a sign of happiness and hope for him after his dramatic recovery.

A few weeks after his first win, a local television station wanted to document his amazing story. During filming, Bill bought another scratch card to demonstrate on camera how he had won the first time. Incredibly, he won again, this time the top prize of 250,000 Australian dollars.

The moment Bill won the second jackpot on camera caused great excitement and joy for both him and the film crew. The coincidence of winning the same lottery twice in such a short period of time made Bill Morgan a local hero, and his story spread worldwide.

After his second win, Bill Morgan continued his modest life.
He used part of his winnings to buy a house, significantly improving his quality of life. Despite his sudden wealth, he remained down-to-earth and grateful for the unexpected turns in his life.

Bill Morgan's story shows that life can sometimes take incredibly surprising turns. His two-time lottery win, especially on camera, is a rare and remarkable coincidence that garnered worldwide attention and earned him local hero status.

4.10 The Savior in Need

In 1965, a five-year-old boy named Kevin Stephan from Cheektowaga, a small town in New York, was saved from certain death by a stranger.

Kevin was playing Little League Baseball when he was hit in the chest and collapsed.

By chance, a man named John McCarthy, a trained paramedic, was on the scene. Without hesitation, he performed cardiopulmonary resuscitation on the unconscious boy, saving his life.

Kevin recovered fully.

Years passed, and life went on. Kevin grew up and decided to follow in his savior's footsteps by becoming a paramedic himself. He eventually became part of an emergency medical team in the same city.

In 2006, more than 40 years after the incident on the baseball field, the incredible coincidence occurred.

John McCarthy, who had grown older by then, had a severe heart attack in a restaurant in Cheektowaga.

The guests and staff present panicked when they saw him collapse and stop breathing.

At that time, Kevin Stephan also happened to be in the restaurant and immediately recognized the urgency of the situation. Without knowing who he was dealing with, he began CPR and used a defibrillator to restart John's heart.

Only after John was stabilized and taken to the hospital did Kevin realize he had saved the man who had once saved his life. The realization that he had saved the life of his own savior was overwhelming for both Kevin and John and their families.

Kevin Stephan and John McCarthy were interviewed on the popular television show "Good Morning America" on January 31, 2007. During the program, they shared their story and offered insights and thoughts on the extraordinary event.

Chapter 5: Curiosities from Nature

This chapter explores some of the most fascinating and curious aspects of the natural world. From unusual animals to astonishing natural phenomena, nature displays incredible diversity and complexity that never ceases to amaze us. The stories in this chapter remind us how much there is still to discover and how the wonders of nature can enrich our understanding of life and existence.

5.1. The strangest animals in the world: From the axolotl to the naked mole rat

Nature is not only creative, it is also sometimes astonishingly eccentric. Alongside the majestic lions, the swift cheetahs, and the intelligent dolphins, there are creatures that, at first glance, seem more like freaks of evolution. Some of them look so bizarre that they are reminiscent of fantasy figures; others possess abilities that seem almost supernatural. Among the most famous examples of these "wonderful creatures" are the axolotl and the naked mole rat—two animals that could hardly be more different, yet both demonstrate the astonishing nature's adaptive strategies.

The axolotl, also called the "Mexican salamander," seems like a cross between a salamander, a mythical creature, and eternal youth. Its most striking feature is the fact that it never grows up—or rather, that it remains in a permanent juvenile stage. While other amphibians lose their gills and move to land, the axolotl retains its larval stage and lives its entire life in the water. With its fringed gill branches, which protrude from the sides of its head like small, red feathers, it appears almost fairytale-like. But its true miracle is its ability to regenerate. The axolotl can regrow not only lost limbs, but also heart tissue and even parts of its brain. This makes it an invaluable research object for modern medicine, as it may hold the key to healing serious injuries that are currently irreversible in humans.

Completely different, but no less impressive, is the naked mole rat. This almost hairless rodent lives in the underground tunnels of East Africa and, at first glance, looks more like a shriveled caricature of a mole. But its appearance is deceptive. Naked mole rats are masters of adaptation and possess characteristics that make them one of the most extraordinary animals of all. They live in tightly organized colonies, similar to insect colonies of ants or bees. A single queen breeds offspring, while the remaining animals, with clearly assigned roles—from workers to guards—ensure the survival of the colony. Even more remarkable is their physiology: Naked mole rats can survive extremely low oxygen levels, are almost completely insensitive to pain, and numerous studies have shown that they develop an unusual resistance to cancer. They also reach an almost biblical age for rodents: up to 30 years, while normal mice barely live longer than two years.

The fascination with such animals lies not only in their bizarre appearance, but also in the scientific questions they raise. Why does an animal like the axolotl develop the ability to regenerate organs, while we humans have almost completely lost this gift? How does the naked mole rat manage to stay healthy for decades without suffering from age-related diseases? Such questions drive researchers worldwide and transform these unassuming creatures into true "superstars" of biology.

But axolotls and naked mole rats aren't the only curiosities nature has to offer. Just consider the platypus, an animal that looks as if it were assembled by an eccentric creator from the remains of other living creatures: a body like a beaver, a duck's beak, webbed feet, and the ability to deploy poisonous spines on its hind legs. For a long time, European naturalists considered the platypus a hoax, a stuffed "mythical creature" from Asia. Only after thorough investigation did they realize it was, in fact, a real animal.

Or the axis deer of the deep sea: the anglerfish, whose females have a luminous lure protruding from their heads, attracting prey in the pitch-black waters of the deep sea. Even more bizarre is the love life of these animals: tiny males permanently bite the bodies of the females and fuse with them, so that from then on they exist as a kind of living appendage.

The diversity of these animals demonstrates how incredibly inventive evolution can be. Some adaptations seem bizarre to us, yet they serve a purpose: survival under extreme conditions. Whether it's the axolotl that never leaves its youth, the naked mole rat that defies age and disease, or the platypus that seems to stand between the worlds of mammals, birds, and reptiles – each of these creatures proves that nature has far more to offer than we might think at first glance.

Fun fact: The axolotl has inspired not only scientists but also pop culture. In Mexico, it's a national symbol and has long since become a favorite of gamers in computer games like "Minecraft." The naked mole rat, on the other hand, has even made it into animated series as a quirky supporting character—a silent testament to how much these strange creatures also capture our imaginations. Ultimately, these strange animals show us that we still don't fully understand the world. Behind every trait, no matter how strange, lies an ingenious adaptation to the environment, a secret of evolution that may also provide us humans with new insights.

5.2. The tree that bears 40 fruits

It sounds like a fairy tale from One Thousand and One Nights or a fantasy from an old gardening book: a single tree growing not just one, but forty different types of fruit. Yet this marvel actually exists—and it is neither a product of nature alone nor the result of genetic engineering, but the work of an artist who has combined science and art in an extraordinary way.

The "Tree of 40 Fruits" is the work of American artist and professor Sam Van Aken. Van Aken, who teaches at Syracuse University in New York, had an early interest in the connection between nature and art. When he was given the opportunity to take over an old orchard that was on the verge of being abandoned, he used it not only to preserve heritage fruit varieties but also as a starting point for a unique project. His goal was to create a tree that embodies diversity, beauty, and wonder—while also serving as a symbol of biodiversity.

The basis for this botanical work of art is an ancient technique: grafting. This involves inserting branches or buds from one plant into the trunk or branches of another, allowing them to grow and survive. This method has been used in agriculture for centuries to propagate fruit varieties or to breed more resilient plants. However, Van Aken used this technique not for mass production, but as a means of artistic expression. With patience, precision, and an eye for aesthetics, he joined dozens of different fruit varieties into a single tree.

Over the years, trees have grown that offer an unparalleled spectacle in spring: While most trees bloom in a uniform color, the tree of 40 fruits explodes into a mosaic of white, pink, violet, and deep red. Each fruit variety has its own blossom color, making the tree appear as if it had sprung from a dream in spring. But the real surprise comes in summer, when the fruit ripens: On a single trunk, peaches hang next to apricots, cherries next to plums, nectarines next to almonds. This diversity is not only an aesthetic pleasure, but also a small homage to the significance of plant diversity in times of increasing monocultures.

Van Aken himself describes his work not only as an art object, but also as a living archive. Many of the varieties he preserves in his trees come from old, almost forgotten stands. By grafting them and allowing them to continue to live, he preserves a piece of agricultural cultural history. The tree thus becomes simultaneously a work of art, a statement for biodiversity, and a practical contribution to the preservation of old fruit varieties.

The project attracted worldwide attention. Van Aken planted the first trees on university campuses, in parks, and in museums. They became symbols of the connection between nature and culture.

For children, they seem like magic trees from a fairytale book; for botanists, they are a masterful example of applied grafting; and for artists, they are a living work of art that is constantly growing, changing, and never completely finished.

It's also curious that Van Aken didn't originally intend to create the tree for the mass market. Each tree is unique, requiring years of care, planning, and attention. The "Tree of 40 Fruits" is therefore not a product you can simply buy and place in your garden, but a unique project that requires patience, knowledge, and dedication. And therein lies part of its magic: It cannot be reproduced at will, but remains a work of art that can be admired without being able to own it in large numbers.

5.3. The mysterious singing sand dunes

Singing sand dunes are an interesting natural phenomenon in which, under certain conditions, sand dunes produce sounds that sound like singing or humming. This phenomenon occurs when dry sand grains of a certain size and shape slide over each other, creating vibrations. These vibrations produce harmonious tones that can last for several minutes. Singing dunes can be found in various places around the world, including the Gobi Desert, Namibia, and Death Valley in California.

5.4. The Wandering Rocks in Death Valley

Death Valley in California, one of the hottest and most inhospitable places on earth, is known for its extremes. But alongside scorching heat and endless salt flats, it also harbors one of the strangest natural phenomena that has amazed scientists, adventurers, and tourists alike for decades: the shifting rocks of Racetrack Playa.

Imagine a vast, barren plain, flat as a mirror, framed by mountains, with a ground of hard, dried mud. Scattered across this plain are boulders of various sizes, some barely larger than a soccer ball, others as heavy as a refrigerator. And these boulders are doing something that actually seems impossible: They are moving. Slowly, almost imperceptibly, but steadily. Across the dried clay soil, they leave long, straight or curved tracks behind them – as if they had been moved by invisible hands.

This phenomenon was first documented in the 1910s, but the tracks themselves were likely known to the people living there for much longer. For decades, it remained unclear how the stones could move. Some theories were as bizarre as the tracks themselves. They said magnetic forces were at play, perhaps earthquakes, or even supernatural forces. In the 1940s and 1950s, some visitors believed the rocks might be evidence of extraterrestrials—after all, the image of mysterious movements in the middle of a hostile desert fit perfectly with the UFO fantasies of the time.

But it wasn't just speculation: The stones were actually moving, and their tracks could be traced over months and years. Some stones traveled distances of hundreds of meters. Their paths weren't always smooth: some snaked in curves, others ran parallel to each other, as if the rocks were marching in lockstep. Scientists took the mystery seriously, but the solution was slow to arrive. Several research teams examined the beach, made measurements, and put forward hypotheses. Wind alone seemed insufficient to move the heavy rocks across the ground. Some weighed several hundred kilograms—how could even the strongest storm push them across the plain?

The crucial discovery only came in the 2010s, when modern camera technology and GPS measurements were used. In 2014, scientists were able to observe the process directly for the first time. After a rare rainfall, a thin layer of water formed over the plain, which froze at night and left a wafer-thin layer of ice in the morning. When the sun came out again, the ice broke into large, flat sheets. These ice floes, driven by light winds, pressed against the rocks, sliding them across the soft, slippery ground with surprising ease. The speed was extremely slow, often only a few centimeters per second, and barely perceptible to the human eye. But over time, the stones left deep marks in the ground – the mysterious pattern that has puzzled visitors for so long.

This solved the mystery: the wandering stones were not the work of ghosts or aliens, but an interplay of rain, frost, sun and wind – an interplay that only occurs under the extremely special conditions of Death Valley.

However, the explanation doesn't diminish the phenomenon's fascination. On the contrary: it demonstrates how subtle yet powerful the forces of nature can be. The idea that rocks weighing tons can be moved by wafer-thin ice sounds almost poetic and is a striking example of how, through rare combinations of circumstances, nature creates images that seem like a mystery to us.

Today, Racetrack Playa is a popular destination for curious travelers. But the phenomenon is fragile. The beach's soil is so fragile that even a single footprint or tire mark can remain visible for years. Therefore, visitors must exercise extreme caution: the rocks are not allowed to be moved, and entry into certain areas is prohibited to preserve this natural wonder.

One of the most famous "wandering stones" was stolen by visitors in the 1990s and anonymously returned years later—with a handwritten note in which the thieves apologized and promised never to enter Death Valley again. Apparently, even the "guilt" of a stolen stone had given rise to a guilty conscience—or the fear that the mystical phenomenon would somehow haunt them.

5.5. The immortal jellyfish organism

Nature has many tricks to cheat death. But an animal that not only survives but defies old age itself sounds almost too unbelievable to be true. This is precisely what makes the jellyfish *Turritopsis dohrnii* so interesting, an inconspicuous sea creature only a few millimeters in size, which researchers reverently call the "immortal jellyfish."

Jellyfish have been part of the Earth for hundreds of millions of years, predating the dinosaurs and remaining virtually unchanged in form. They are often considered primitive creatures—translucent, without a brain, without a heart, without bones. Yet they hold a secret that perhaps reveals more about life itself than we have previously understood. *Turritopsis dohrnii*, originally discovered in the Mediterranean, has an amazing ability: it can reverse its life cycle.

A jellyfish's life normally progresses through several stages. A fertilized egg first develops into a tiny larva, which attaches itself to the seafloor and grows into a polyp. This polyp then develops into tiny medusae—the actual jellyfish—which detach themselves from the seafloor, grow, age, and eventually die. *Turritopsis dohrnii* However, this cycle can be interrupted. When the jellyfish is threatened by injury, starvation, or other stress factors, it transforms its cells back into their original polyp state. It begins its life cycle all over again, young, fresh, and full of energy. From a purely biological perspective, this means it is potentially immortal—because it can always reset the aging process.

This process, called transdifferentiation, is unique in the animal kingdom. Mature cells, which already have a fixed function, are returned to a kind of "stem cell state." This is of great interest to medicine: If a similar mechanism could be applied to humans, aging processes could perhaps be stopped or even reversed. Cancer research, regenerative medicine, and aging research are therefore intensively studying the "immortal jellyfish."

Of course, immortality in nature does not mean that jellyfish live forever. They can be eaten by predators, weakened by disease, or destroyed by environmental changes. But theoretically, there is no natural death from aging for them. This makes *Turritopsis dohrnii* a small but powerful symbol of humanity's dream of defeating aging.

The discovery of this ability was a coincidence. In the 1980s, researchers noticed that some of these jellyfish didn't die as usual, but instead transformed back into life. Initially, this was thought to be a freak of nature or a misunderstanding, but repeated observations confirmed the phenomenon. The immortal jellyfish has now been detected in many of the world's oceans, having spread as stowaways in ships' ballast water.

To the general public, the story of this jellyfish sounds like a fairy tale. No wonder it quickly appeared in newspaper articles and television documentaries and made headlines. While we humans invest billions in trying to understand aging, somewhere in the ocean swims an inconspicuous creature that has long since solved this very mystery for itself.

Fun fact: Despite her unique ability, *Turritopsis dohrnii* not on the endangered species list. On the contrary – it is now found almost worldwide, but due to its small size and inconspicuous appearance, it often remains hidden even from researchers. While other animals impress with their size, strength, or intelligence, this small jellyfish fascinates with its mysterious biology alone. The image of the immortal jellyfish also raises philosophical questions. What would it mean for us humans if we could simply reverse the aging process, as they did? Would that be a liberation or a burden? *Turritopsis dohrnii* gives no answers – it simply swims on, eternally young, eternally new.

5.6. The case of the "pig cloud" in Australia

In 1997, an extraordinary and unexplained natural phenomenon occurred in the remote Kimberley region of Western Australia, becoming known as the "pig cloud." This unusual event was so named by locals because the affected animals—primarily pigs—appeared strangely dazed and ill, as if afflicted by an invisible cloud.

The first reports came from the small town of Wyndham, where ranchers observed that their pigs suddenly suffered extreme behavioral changes. The animals showed signs of disorientation, loss of appetite, and lethargy. Some pigs began behaving unusually, running in circles or seemingly wandering aimlessly. These symptoms worsened over the following days, and some animals died for no apparent reason.
Concerned livestock farmers alerted local authorities and veterinarians, who quickly rushed to investigate the phenomenon. Despite intensive efforts and numerous tests, experts were unable to find a clear cause for the pigs' strange symptoms.

Neither known diseases nor poisonous plants could be used as an explanation. Water and soil samples also revealed no evidence of contamination.
One theory put forward by locals is that the phenomenon was caused by an unusual weather phenomenon.

Some believed that some kind of toxic cloud—possibly a buildup of gases from the Earth's interior or a chemical cloud from industrial activities—had hit the region. This cloud may have contained hydrogen sulfide or other toxic gases that affected the animals.

Another theory suggested that the "pig cloud" could be the result of a natural phenomenon such as a gas burst from underground volcanoes or hot springs. Such gas emissions occur in some parts of the world and can be released suddenly and in high concentrations, leading to poisoning and other health problems in animals and humans.

Although none of these theories has been conclusively proven, reports of the "pig cloud" led to increased awareness of the potential dangers of invisible environmental phenomena. Authorities took measures to better monitor the region and prevent further occurrences. This included installing air quality sensors and establishing emergency plans for similar events.
The case of the "pig cloud" in Australia is an example of the unpredictable and often inexplicable forces of nature.

5.7. The "Zone of Silence" in Mexico

In northern Mexico, near the Bolsón de Mapimí, lies a mysterious place known as the "Zone of Silence" (Zona del Silencio). This remote desert area has earned a reputation as a place of unusual and unexplained phenomena, attracting scientists, researchers, and adventurers alike.

The "Zone of Silence" extends across parts of the states of Chihuahua, Coahuila, and Durango. It became known in the 1960s when reports of strange disturbances and unusual occurrences emerged in the region.

The name "Zone of Silence" comes from the alleged fact that radio waves are blocked or severely disrupted in this area, rendering communication devices such as radios and mobile phones unusable.

One of the first documented incidents that drew attention to the zone was the crash of an American test rocket in 1970. The rocket, launched from the White Sands Missile Range in New Mexico, went out of control and crashed in the "Zone of Silence."

The recovery team reported unusual magnetic anomalies and problems with their communications equipment, cementing the zone's reputation as a mysterious place.
In addition to the communication disruptions, there have been numerous reports of strange lights and unidentified flying objects sighted in the skies of the zone. Locals and visitors frequently report bright, glowing spheres that silently move across the sky or suddenly appear and disappear. These lights have led to speculation about extraterrestrial activity in the region.

Another phenomenon attributed to the Zone of Silence is the report of unusual plants and animals. Some researchers have claimed that certain plant species in the zone appear mutated or grow unusually large. Animals in the region are also said to exhibit strange behavior. However, these reports are controversial and viewed critically by the scientific community.
One possible explanation for some of the phenomena in the Zone of Silence is the high concentrations of magnetite and other mineral deposits in the soil. These could be the cause of the magnetic anomalies and radio wave interference.

In addition, the zone is located at the same latitude as the Bermuda Triangle and the Pyramids of Giza, which has led to further speculation about geomagnetic lines and energy fields.

Despite numerous theories and attempts at explanation, the "Zone of Silence" remains a mystery. Scientific expeditions and investigations have so far failed to provide definitive answers, and many of the reported phenomena remain unexplained. The mixture of scientific curiosity and mystical flair makes the zone a mysterious place for researchers and adventurers.

5.8. The Taos Hum

The Taos Hum is one of the most mysterious and discussed acoustic phenomena of modern times. This strange, low-frequency humming sound is heard by some residents and visitors of the small town of Taos, New Mexico. The phenomenon first came to public attention in the early 1990s and has since attracted scientists, engineers, and curious onlookers from all over the world trying to find the source of this enigmatic sound.

People who hear the Taos hum describe it as a deep, persistent hum, similar to the sound of a distant diesel engine. The noise is often most noticeable indoors and is generally more intense at night and in the early morning hours. Reports suggest that the Taos hum can be unbearable for some people, leading to sleep disturbances, headaches, and other health problems.

Interestingly, only a small percentage of the population hears the Taos hum. Estimates suggest that approximately 2% of Taos residents perceive the sound. This phenomenon is not limited to Taos; similar humming sounds have been reported in other parts of the world, including the United Kingdom, Australia, and Canada.

Since the Taos hum was first publicly reported, various scientific teams have attempted to investigate and explain the phenomenon. In 1993, U.S. Congressman Bill Richardson conducted an official investigation, inviting physicists, geologists, and acoustic experts to Taos to identify the source of the hum.
The investigation yielded inconclusive results. Despite using sensitive equipment, scientists were unable to detect any measurable sound waves or vibrations that matched the victims' reports. This lack of physical evidence has made explaining the Taos Hum even more difficult and has led to various hypotheses and speculations.

Several theories have been proposed to explain the Taos Hum, but none have been conclusively proven:
*Industrial noises*One of the most plausible theories is that the Taos hum is caused by industrial activities such as nearby gas lines, compressors, or other machinery. However, no specific industrial sources have been identified to explain the phenomenon.
*Geological activity*Another theory suggests that geological processes such as tectonic plate movements or subterranean lava flows could be responsible for the sound. However, there is no concrete evidence to support this hypothesis.

*Electromagnetic radiation*Some researchers believe that the hum could be caused by electromagnetic radiation from high-voltage power lines or other electrical devices. This theory remains controversial and unproven.

*Otoacoustic emissions:*One medical explanation suggests that the hum is due to otoacoustic emissions, in which the inner ear itself produces sounds that are then perceived by the affected individual.

*Psychological factors:*Some experts suspect that the Taos hum may be partly psychological in nature, with stress, anticipation, or other mental factors playing a role. This would explain why only a small percentage of people perceive the hum.

The Taos Hum remains an unsolved mystery, challenging the limits of our understanding of acoustic phenomena and human perception. Despite numerous investigations and theories, there is no definitive explanation for this strange sound.

5.9. frozen birds

Nature holds many mysteries, but few are as bizarre and surprising as the case of the "Frozen Bird." This strange phenomenon, reported in various parts of the world, continues to amaze and astonish. In this event, a bird seemingly suspended in mid-air is found in a completely frozen state—a sight that raises many questions and is difficult to explain.

One of the most famous reports comes from Alaska, where fishermen discovered a frozen bird suspended in mid-air. It appeared as if the bird had suddenly stopped mid-flight and frozen completely. The bird was in a flight position with its wings spread, as if it were about to soar again at any moment. Similar reports have also been reported from other cold regions, such as Canada and Russia.

The "Frozen Bird" phenomenon has given rise to several theories attempting to explain the strange event:
Black ice and extreme cold: One of the most commonly proposed explanations is that the bird was hit by black ice during a particularly cold and stormy spell. Black ice occurs when super-cool raindrops freeze instantly upon contact with a surface. A bird flying through such super-cool droplets could theoretically be encased in a thick layer of ice and freeze in a fraction of a second.
Catastrophic weather events: Some scientists suspect that extreme and sudden weather events, such as cold air bursts or blizzards, could catch birds by surprise and cause a rapid drop in temperature. This could cause birds flying in these conditions to freeze in mid-air before falling to the ground.
Liquid nitrogen or cryogenic technology: An unusual and less accepted theory is that the bird was frozen by human intervention, possibly through the use of liquid nitrogen or other cryogenic technology. This theory is often considered unlikely, as there is no evidence of such intervention.

To date, there has been little scientific research into this phenomenon because reports of frozen birds are rare and difficult to trace.

Most cases are reported by eyewitnesses, and there is little documented evidence or physical specimens available for examination. However, scientists who study extreme weather conditions and their effects on wildlife believe a natural explanation is possible.

5.10 The phenomenon of "green flashes"

The phenomenon of "green flashes" is one of the most impressive and rare optical phenomena observed in nature. These fleeting green flashes of light appear shortly after sunset or just before sunrise and have captured people's imaginations for centuries. They are not only a striking natural spectacle, but also an example of the complex and often surprising interactions between light and atmosphere.

A green flash typically occurs for only a few seconds, immediately before the sun completely disappears below the horizon or just appears. Observers see an intense, green flash of light at the top edge of the solar disk. This phenomenon is so short-lived that it can easily be overlooked, but those who witness it often describe it as an awe-inspiring and unforgettable experience.

The phenomenon of green flash can be explained by the refraction and dispersion of sunlight in the Earth's atmosphere.

While the classic green flash is the most commonly observed, there are also other variations of the phenomenon:
Blue Flash: In rare cases, the phenomenon can also appear as a blue flash when conditions are particularly favorable and the refraction of light is more intense.
Green beam: Sometimes the green flash can appear as a kind of green beam or as a green cap on the solar disk.

The best chance of seeing a green flash is in a location with a clear, unobstructed view of the horizon, such as by the ocean or on a mountaintop. This time is either shortly before sunrise or immediately after sunset.

Clear atmospheric conditions without clouds, fog, or haze are crucial to maximize the dispersion of light and make the phenomenon visible.

Since the phenomenon occurs right at the edge of the sun, don't forget your sunglasses!

5.11 The Legend of the Kraken

One of the most mythical creatures is the Kraken, a giant, ink-spewing sea monster. It has captured the imaginations of sailors, writers, and adventurers for centuries. This mysterious creature, said to lurk in the deep, cold waters of the North Atlantic, is one of the most recognizable and terrifying sea monsters in the world. Stories about the Kraken tell of its gigantic size and its ability to drag entire ships into the depths.

The legend of the Kraken originated in the Scandinavian countries, particularly Norway and Iceland. The first accounts of the Kraken appeared in medieval Norwegian sagas and legends. These early stories describe the Kraken as a monstrous creature with countless tentacles that rises from the depths of the sea to attack ships.

The Kraken is often described as incredibly large, with a wingspan exceeding several ship decks. Some reports claim it could be as large as a small island. The kraken is said to possess numerous, powerful tentacles with which it can wrap itself around ships and pull them into the depths. These tentacles are covered with suction cups that have a deadly grip.

One of the most famous early accounts of the kraken comes from the 18th-century Norwegian bishop Erik Pontoppidan. In his work "The Natural History of Norway," Pontoppidan describes the kraken as a massive monster capable of destroying entire ships and making the sea appear like a seething cauldron.

In 1861, the crew of the French warship "Alecton" claimed to have seen and attacked an octopus off the coast of Tenerife in the Atlantic Ocean. The crew's account told of a giant, ink-spewing creature that escaped back into the depths after a fierce battle. These and similar stories contributed to the spread and confirmation of the legend.

Modern scientists believe that the legend of the Kraken originates from sightings of giant squid (Architeuthis), which actually exist in the deep oceans. Giant squid can reach lengths of over 13 meters and possess large, strong tentacles. Their rare sightings and the ignorance of early sailors about these creatures may have contributed to the creation of the legend.

The most popular theory is that reports of the kraken originated from sightings of giant squid. These deep-sea creatures are rare and difficult to study, leading to mysterious and exaggerated reports.

Some theories suggest that the legend of the Kraken was also influenced by sightings of sea serpents or other large sea creatures that fueled the imagination of sailors.

The legend of the Kraken has found its place in numerous books, films, and works of art. The Kraken is a symbol of the untamed power and mystery of the seas. Well-known works such as Jules Verne's "20,000 Leagues Under the Sea" and films like "Pirates of the Caribbean" have further popularized the legend.

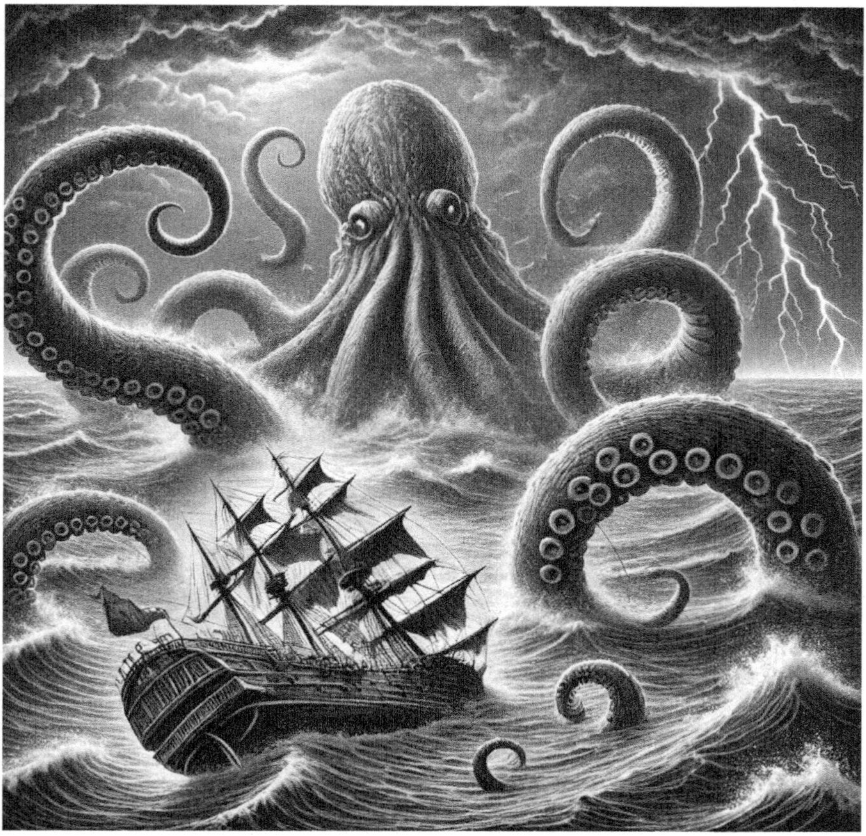

5.12 The Bombardier Beetle: A Walking Flamethrower

The bombardier beetle is a truly remarkable insect known for its unique defense strategy. When threatened, it triggers a chemical reaction that results in the explosive release of a hot, toxic spray. This ability has earned it the apt name "bombardier beetle."
The bombardier beetle has two special chambers in its abdomen. One chamber stores hydroquinone and hydrogen peroxide. The other chamber contains a catalyst enzyme.

When the beetle senses danger, it contracts its muscles and forces the two chemicals into the catalyst chamber. There, they trigger an exothermic reaction, generating a large amount of heat and releasing oxygen. The mixture is heated to nearly 100 degrees Celsius and expelled with great force as a fine mist from an opening in its abdomen.
What's special about this defensive reaction is its precision. The bombardier beetle can precisely control the direction of the spray, thus directly targeting its attackers. The spray's range is up to several centimeters, an impressive distance for such a small insect.
The hot, toxic spray serves the bombardier beetle both as a defense and for hunting. It repels predators such as spiders, ants, and birds. It also kills small prey such as other insects, which the beetle then uses as food.
The development of these complex defense mechanisms was a major evolutionary advantage for the bombardier beetle. The ability to fend off its enemies and kill its prey enabled it to assert itself in its environment and increase its chances of survival.

5.13. The Secret of Carmine – Red from a Louse

Beauty has its price, sometimes even that of a tiny insect. Anyone who touched rouge or lipstick in the 18th or 19th century unknowingly carried a piece of natural history on their face: the cochineal bug. For centuries, a particularly intense shade of red, carmine, was a symbol of wealth and beauty.

But hardly anyone thinks that this color does not come from a flower or a mineral, but from a tiny insect: the cochineal louse (*Dactylopius coccus*This inconspicuous little creature lives on prickly pear cacti in Central and South America and produces carminic acid, which is supposed to protect it from predators. However, for humans, it has become one of the world's most valuable pigments.

The Aztecs and Mayans already used cochineal to dye textiles. Their garments glowed in a rich red, a color almost unattainable with plant pigments. When the Spanish conquered America in the 16th century, they discovered the dye's exceptional quality and quickly turned it into an export of global importance. For three centuries, cochineal was one of New Spain's most important trading products, at times even more valuable than silver. It is said that smugglers in Spain caught illicitly trading cochineal risked draconian punishments—so great was the economic and strategic value of this tiny louse.

In Europe, the vibrant carmine red soon became a fashion phenomenon. Courtly robes shone in a red that symbolized power and influence. Painters like Velázquez and Rembrandt used it for particularly expressive accents, and in cosmetics, the pigment found its way into the makeup kits of the upper classes as rouge and lip color. Over time, carmine also found its way into everyday life: Even in the 20th century, it colored candy, yogurt, and red drinks – an idea that initially spoils the appetite of many when they hear that the color is derived from a louse that sucks on cacti.

Yet as inconspicuous as the insect was, the properties of its pigment were astonishing. Carmine was not only brilliant in color, but also almost unbeatable in its durability. Lipsticks tinted with real carmine often lasted longer than modern products. The reason lies in its chemistry: carminic acid binds extremely well to proteins and fats, including lipids and the uppermost horny layer of the skin. On the lips, carmine acts like a natural mordant – once applied, it adheres strongly, is smudge-proof, and light-stable. For many women, that was exactly what made a good lipstick: a radiant red that didn't fade even after a long evening.

With the development of synthetic dyes, the situation changed. Many modern red shades are water-soluble and less absorbent. They tend to fade more quickly when exposed to UV light or oxygen. Almost every lipstick wearer is familiar with the result: The color loses its intensity more quickly and needs to be reapplied more frequently. The cosmetics industry has responded by combining synthetic pigments with special binding agents such as waxes, silicones, or oils. This makes it possible to achieve a durability comparable to that of carmine—but only through complex formulations that must be chemically precisely matched.

Carmine hasn't completely disappeared, however. Even today, the colorant with the E number E120 can still be found in cosmetics, artistic applications, and occasionally even in food. However, it's not as widely used as before. Some people are allergic to the animal-derived colorant, and the idea of "lice in yogurt" doesn't exactly sound appealing. Therefore, many manufacturers are now turning to plant-based alternatives such as beetroot or paprika extract.

Chapter 6: Myths, Monsters, Cryptozoology

In this chapter, you'll learn about the terrifying tales of the Dogman in Michigan, the ominous sightings of the Mothman in West Virginia, and the fascinating sightings of the Yeti. Explore the boundaries between myth and reality. From the snow-capped peaks of the Himalayas to the dense forests of North America, this chapter compiles accounts of mysterious creatures from many parts of the world into an interesting and entertaining blend.

6.1. The Yeti – The Snowman of the Himalayas

The Yeti, also known as the Snowman, is a creature that has captured people's imaginations for centuries. A cryptic being said to live in the remote regions of the Himalayas, the Yeti is the subject of numerous legends, myths, and expeditions. Whether it is a real animal, a misinterpretation, or a pure invention remains unclear to this day.

The roots of the Yeti legend reach deep into the mythology of the Himalayan peoples. The Sherpa, the indigenous people of Nepal, have numerous stories about the Yeti, whom they call "Met Bar Sengwa" (the man of the wild snowfields). In their tales, he is described as a large, hairy creature that lives in the highest regions of the mountains and poses a threat to travelers.

Descriptions of the Yeti vary widely, but some commonalities can be identified. It is often depicted as a large, humanoid creature with thick, brown or gray fur. Its height is said to be between two and three meters, and its footprints are said to be unusually large and round.

Numerous sightings of the Yeti have been reported over the years. Many of these reports come from mountaineers and expeditions to the Himalayas. For example, in 1951, the famous mountaineer Eric Shipton reported large footprints he had found during an expedition on Everest. These prints sparked worldwide interest and fueled speculation about the Yeti's existence.

In the decades that followed, there were repeated reports of sightings and the discovery of traces. Hair, bone fragments, and even film footage were presented as supposed evidence of the Yeti's existence. However, in most cases, these finds could not be scientifically identified as the Yeti and often turned out to be the remains of other animals or even fakes.
Scientists have proposed various explanations for the Yeti sightings and discoveries.
Some suspect that the large footprints are bear tracks distorted by the snow. Others consider it possible that the reports are the result of hallucinations or misinterpretations.

Another theory states that the Yeti legend is based on the existence of an unknown primate species. This theory was supported by the discovery of the gibbon, an ape-like primate, in the forests of Southeast Asia.

It is questionable, however, how such a large and striking animal as the Yeti could remain undiscovered and unexplored for so long in the remote regions of the Himalayas.

Whether the Yeti truly exists remains an open question. To date, there is no scientifically undisputed evidence for its existence. However, the numerous reports and legends surrounding the snowman testify to the mystical attraction this creature exerts on humans. The Yeti is more than just a creature; it is a symbol of the unknown, the mysterious, and the adventurous.

It's possible that the legend of the Yeti is based on a true observation that has been exaggerated and embellished over time. Or perhaps the Yeti is simply a projection of our longing for the inexplicable and the miraculous.

6.2. The Best of Gévaudan

France in the mid-18th century was a land of contrasts. While the splendor of the court shone in Versailles and the ideas of the Enlightenment matured in Paris, people in remote regions like Gévaudan lived in another world. This isolated area in what is now the Lozère department was characterized by mountains, forests, and fields; it was barren and poor, full of myths and superstitions. Here, far from the courtly splendor, a terror so intense that it still haunts people today struck in 1764: the story of the Beast of Gévaudan.
In the summer of that year, the first victim was found. Jeanne Boulet, a 14-year-old girl, was out with her cattle when she was attacked. When she was found, her throat had been torn to pieces and her body mutilated. The death of a child at the hands of an animal was tragic, but nothing that would send the entire region into a panic. But just a few days later, there was the next attack. In Chanaleilles, a woman was attacked and seriously injured. She reported seeing a huge animal, larger than any wolf, with bristling fur and a long, whip-like tail. The next attack soon followed in Le Malzieu. It seemed as if a sinister creature was roaming the woods, hunting not cattle like other animals, but specifically humans.
The series continued. In the following months, dozens died, many of them women and children, who were surprised while working in the fields or on lonely paths. The wounds were almost always the same: deep bites on the neck and head, as if the beast were deliberately trying to kill. Some bodies were so disfigured that the families barely recognized them.
Panic spread. Farmers only ventured out into the fields in groups, and children were no longer sent to school alone. Villages locked their doors in the evenings, as if fearing the monster might emerge from the shadows at any moment. Tradition tells of entire regions being paralyzed.
Descriptions of the beast were disturbing. Some said the beast was wolf-like, but twice as large. Others swore it had reddish fur with black stripes. Some claimed it had a horse's chest, while others claimed its head was flat and broad, like that of a calf. There were rumors that the beast could stand upright, that it was bulletproof, or even a demon in animal form. The superstition of the time did the rest, and quickly, a predator became a supernatural threat.
The first organized hunts soon began. Jean-Baptiste Duhamel, captain of the local infantry, and his men attempted to capture the beast. Hundreds of farmers and hunters joined in. But the beast repeatedly escaped. On several occasions, hunters swore they had shot at the animal and hit it, but it had continued running unharmed. Rumors of supernatural invulnerability circulated, and preachers interpreted the beast as God's punishment for human sins.

The number of victims grew. Some chronicles speak of over a hundred deaths in the years up to 1767. The fear was so great that the case attracted the attention of the capital. Newspapers reported in detail on the attacks, and drawings of the terrifying figure spread throughout the country. Soon, the "Bête du Gévaudan" was being talked about throughout France.

Finally, King Louis XV himself intervened. He didn't want France to be exposed by a monster while his power seemed unchallenged throughout the country. So, in 1765, he dispatched the famous wolf hunters Jean-Charles Marc Antoine Vaumesle d'Enneval and his son Jean-François. They combed the forests for weeks, but the beast remained untraceable. The press began to mock him: Even the king's men couldn't catch it.

In September 1765, another specialist arrived: François Antoine, the lieutenant of the royal huntsmen. And indeed, he seemed to be successful. On September 21, he killed a massive wolf, almost the size of a calf. The animal was stuffed, brought to Versailles, and presented to the king. Antoine received a reward, and, as far as the public was concerned, the matter was settled: the beast had been vanquished.

But the reality was different. Just a few months later, there were new attacks, each with the same ferocity. For the people of Gévaudan, this was proof: the slain wolf was not the beast—or at least there were several of them. Panic returned, worse than before. Now people believed the beast was immortal. The church preached of divine punishment. Chroniclers recorded that expiatory processions were held in the churches, in which entire villages begged for forgiveness. At the same time, new hunts were constantly being organized. Entire armies marched through the forests, but the beast escaped.

The story didn't end until June 1767. A simple farmer named Jean Chastel, known as an experienced hunter, confronted the beast. According to legend, he had previously had a silver bullet blessed at mass, which he then loaded into his musket. When the beast appeared, he fired and hit. The beast collapsed. It was a gigantic wolf, even larger and more powerful than the one killed by François Antoine. After that day, the attacks abruptly stopped.

The danger was averted, but the mystery remained. What was the beast really? Theories are varied. Some researchers simply consider it an exceptionally large wolf or a line of wolves that had learned to hunt humans. Others believe it was a cross between a dog and a wolf that became unusually aggressive. Zoologists have suggested exotic animals, such as a hyena that might have escaped from a menagerie or traveling circus. Hyenas do fit many descriptions: their broad head, their mottled fur, their massive jaws.

There are also speculative approaches. Some historians suspect that a human perpetrator was behind the attacks, perhaps a serial killer exploiting the fear of wolves. Since many of the victims were mutilated, this could also be plausible. However, there is no evidence for this.

One thing is certain: The Beast of Gévaudan was more than just an animal. It was a social phenomenon that paralyzed an entire region, challenged the power of the crown, and fueled the superstitions of the time.

The legend lives on to this day. In Gévaudan, museums, monuments, and even festivals commemorate the Beast. Tourists visit the sites of the attacks, and historians still debate the creature's true nature. In pop culture, the Beast has already become immortal—most notably through the film.*The Pact of the Wolves*from 2001, which artfully interweaves reality and myth.

Whether it was a wolf, a hyena, a serial killer, or even a product of collective fear remains unclear.

6.3. The Legend of the Living Dinosaur in the Congo: Mokele-Mbembe

Mokele-Mbembe, meaning "he who stops the river" in the native Bantu languages, is a mythical creature said to live in the remote rivers and lakes of the Congo Basin in Central Africa.

This legend has captured the imagination of adventurers, researchers, and cryptozoologists. The Mokele-Mbembe is described as a large, dinosaur-like sauropod.
Some therefore believe that prehistoric animals may still exist in unexplored regions of the Earth.

The Congo Basin, one of the largest and most densely forested regions in the world, stretches across several countries in Central Africa, including the Republic of Congo, the Democratic Republic of Congo, Gabon and Cameroon. However, the legend of Mokele-Mbembe focuses primarily on the Likouala Swamp in the Republic of Congo. This swamp is a remote, little-explored region because it is difficult to access.

It is approximately 55,000 square kilometers in size.
The dense forests, winding rivers, and murky swamps provide an ideal backdrop for a creature that could hide from the eyes of the modern world.

The earliest written accounts of Mokele-Mbembe come from the records of Western missionaries and colonial officials in the early 20th century. In 1913, the German captain Freiherr von Stein zu Lausnitz reported stories from the local population about a large, herbivorous animal resembling a dinosaur that lived in the rivers and lakes of the Likouala Swamp.

These reports described the animal as about 10 to 15 meters long with a long neck, a small head and a powerful tail.

Throughout the 20th century, numerous expeditions attempted to uncover the mystery of Mokele-Mbembe.

One of the most famous expeditions was that of Ivan T. Sanderson, a British biologist and explorer who crossed the Likouala Swamp in the 1930s. Although Sanderson found no direct evidence of the creature's existence, he reported numerous sightings and stories from local people describing the creature.

Perhaps the most famous expedition was organized in 1980 by Dr. Roy P. Mackal, a biologist at the University of Chicago. This expedition aimed to find scientific evidence for the existence of Mokele-Mbembe. The researchers interviewed numerous locals who claimed to have seen the animal and collected stories of encounters in which the animal overturned boats and blocked rivers. Despite their efforts, the scientists were unable to provide any physical evidence such as bones or photographs.

In the following decades, further expeditions were organized by enthusiasts and cryptozoologists, including those accompanied by television stations and documentary film crews.
A notable expedition took place in 2006, when Japanese explorer Yoshiaki Matsumoto crossed the Likouala Swamp. He, too, was unable to provide definitive evidence, but his reports of local stories contributed to the perpetuation of the legend.

The scientific community remains skeptical about the existence of Mokele-Mbembe. There is no physical evidence to support the existence of such a large animal in the dense forests of the Congo Basin. Zoologists and paleontologists point out that a large, herbivorous animal like Mokele-Mbembe would leave significant traces of feeding and life that have not yet been found.

Some scientists suggest that the reports of Mokele-Mbembe may have been based on sightings of familiar animals such as crocodiles, hippos, or large snakes living in the murky waters of the Likouala Swamp. The overlay of local legends and oral tradition may have contributed to these reports being embellished over time into stories of a living dinosaur.

The legend of Mokele-Mbembe remains a mystery that blurs the boundaries between myth and science.

6.4 The Legend of the Dogman in Michigan

The legend of the Dogman in Michigan is a mysterious tale that has spawned numerous sightings and reports for over a century. Often described as a hybrid of man and dog, the Dogman has captured people's imaginations and remains a mystery to this day. This creature has reportedly been sighted primarily in the Wexford County area, but reports extend throughout the state of Michigan.

The first documented sighting of the Dogman dates back to 1887. In Wexford County, two lumberjacks reported seeing a strange creature standing on two legs, with a human body and a dog-like head. The creature reportedly frightened them with an eerie howl before disappearing into the forest. This encounter marked the beginning of a series of sightings that extended into the 20th and 21st centuries.

In the 1930s, several sightings of the Dogman were reported in northwest Michigan, particularly in the Manistee National Forest. A particularly notable sighting occurred in 1938, when a man named Robert Fortney, near Paris, Michigan, reported being attacked by a large, wolf-like creature that walked on two legs. Fortney shot the creature, and it fled into the woods. He described the creature as about two meters tall, with a muscular body and glowing eyes.

The 1960s saw another wave of Dogman sightings in the Big Rapids area. One notable incident occurred in 1961, when a night watchman at North Central Michigan College reported seeing a large, dog-like creature roaming the campus on two legs. This encounter led to several more reports from students and residents claiming to have seen similar creatures in the surrounding woods.

Sightings continued to be reported throughout the 2000s, particularly in the Reed City and Luther areas. In 2001, a woman named Lori Andrade reported that she and her son had seen a large, hairy creature walking through the woods on two legs. Her description matched previous reports of the Dogman.

Despite numerous reports, there are no confirmed cases of death or injury caused by the Dogman. Most encounters describe the creature as fearsome but not aggressive toward humans. However, some witnesses have reported the Dogman chasing or attacking them, though without causing serious injury.

The existence of the Dogman remains controversial, and there are various theories about the nature of these sightings. Some believe the Dogman is a real, unknown species living in the forests of Michigan.

Others suspect that these are misinterpretations of familiar animals such as bears, or that the reports are based on a combination of hoaxes, hallucinations and collective imagination.

Another element that contributes to the mystique of Dogman is the supernatural explanations that some suggest.
There are theories that consider the Dogman a type of cryptid, a werewolf, or even a supernatural apparition. These theories are often supported by unusual aspects of the reports, such as glowing eyes or the ability to walk on two legs.

The Michigan Dogman remains a legend of modern cryptozoology. Despite the many reports and eyewitnesses, there is no hard evidence of his existence. However, the stories and sightings of the Dogman continue to be told and studied, and the creature remains an integral part of Michigan folklore. The eerie tales, often passed down from generation to generation, contribute to the mystical aura.

6.5 Discovery of Denisovans

The discovery of Denisovan Man in Denisova Cave, also known as Star Cave, marks one of the most poignant advances in paleoanthropology in recent decades. This discovery has significantly expanded our understanding of human evolution and contributed to our understanding of the various human species in the past.

Denisova Cave is located in the Altai Mountains in southern Siberia, Russia, about 150 kilometers south of the city of Barnaul. This cave has proven to be a significant archaeological site, providing evidence of various prehistoric cultures and human activities spanning tens of thousands of years.

In 2008, Russian archaeologists excavating Denisova Cave discovered a tiny finger bone fragment dated to about 40,000 years ago.
This fragment belonged to a young girl, whom scientists dubbed "X-Woman." Initially, it was assumed that the bone belonged to a Neanderthal or modern human. But genetic analysis, conducted by an international team of researchers led by Svante Pääbo at the Max Planck Institute for Evolutionary Anthropology in Leipzig, revealed something completely new.

DNA analysis revealed that the finger bone belonged to a previously unknown human species, genetically distinct not only from modern humans but also from Neanderthals and other known hominin groups. This new human species was named Denisovan Man (Homo denisova) after the cave.

In addition to the finger bone, other fossils were also found in Denisova Cave, including a molar and a toe bone, which could also be attributed to Denisovans. The genetic data from these fossils showed that Denisovans interacted and interbred with Neanderthals and modern humans in a complex manner.

In particular, Denisovan DNA has been found to be detectable in the genomes of modern human populations in Asia, particularly among indigenous peoples in Melanesia and Australia.

The discovery of Denisovans raises many questions and offers exciting insights into human evolution. It shows that the prehistoric world was a complex mosaic of different human species that interacted, interbred, and learned from each other. Denisovans lived contemporaneously with Neanderthals and early modern humans, and there is evidence that they may have exchanged technologies and cultural practices.

Denisova Cave itself is a rich archaeological site containing tools and artifacts from various prehistoric periods. These artifacts provide clues to the lifestyles and skills of the Denisovans. The finds include finely crafted stone tools, bone tools, and even jewelry, suggesting that the Denisovans possessed advanced technological skills and possibly a symbolic culture.

The exact number of individuals who lived in Denisova Cave is difficult to determine due to the limited archaeological evidence. Nevertheless, genetic analyses have shown that the Denisovans exhibited significant genetic diversity, indicating that they were a widespread and successful human species.

From the small bone fragments found, such as a finger bone, a molar, and a toe bone, it is difficult to make precise estimates of the height and weight of this human species. However, based on the available materials and comparisons with Neanderthals and modern humans, some assumptions can be made:
It is believed that Denisovans were of similar height to Neanderthals, who averaged between 1.55 and 1.65 meters. However, this is only an estimate, as no complete skeletal remains are available.
Here, too, the weight is assumed to have been similar to that of Neanderthals, who averaged about 70–80 kilograms. Again, this is an estimate based on the limited fossil data available.
Denisovans lived between 50,000 and 300,000 years ago. The exact time period is difficult to determine, but the remains suggest that they existed during the late Pleistocene. This was a period in which several human species coexisted and interacted with each other.
The oldest fossil finds attributed to Denisovans come from Denisova Cave and are about 200,000 to 300,000 years old.
The youngest known remains that can be attributed to Denisovans are about 50,000 years old.
The study of Denisovans is far from complete. The cave continues to be intensively studied, and new discoveries could further deepen our understanding of this human species.

6.6. Bigfoot

Bigfoot, also known as Sasquatch, is one of the most famous and discussed creatures in modern cryptozoology. Accounts of this mysterious creature have appeared in the legends of North America's indigenous peoples for centuries. Bigfoot stories are diverse and include numerous sightings and encounters reported from various regions of North America, particularly the Pacific Northwest of the United States and Canada.

Indigenous peoples' stories tell of large, hairy creatures that lived in the forests and were known as "Sasquatch."
However, the name "Bigfoot" only emerged in the 1950s, when reports of large footprints in remote areas began to appear.
One of the first modern sightings to attract widespread attention occurred in 1958 when a construction worker named Jerry Crew discovered giant footprints in Bluff Creek, California.

This discovery was widely reported in the media and led to the popularization of the term "Bigfoot."

One of the most famous Bigfoot sightings was filmed by Roger Patterson and Bob Gimlin near Bluff Creek, California, in 1967. The Patterson-Gimlin film depicts a large, upright, hairy creature walking through the forest.

Although this film continues to be intensely analyzed and discussed, its authenticity remains controversial. Many cryptozoologists consider it one of the best pieces of evidence for the existence of Bigfoot, while skeptics believe it to be a fake.

Most reports describe Bigfoot as a large, bipedal, ape-like creature with thick, dark fur. The creature is said to be between 2 and 3 meters tall and walks upright. The eyes are often described as deep-set and luminous, and many witnesses report a strong, unpleasant odor accompanying the creature.

Bigfoot is said to live in remote, forested areas and has been reported particularly frequently in the Pacific Northwest of the United States and the western provinces of Canada. However, reports also come from other parts of North America, including the Appalachian Mountains, the Rocky Mountains, and even the Southern United States.

The exact number of Bigfoot sighting reports varies widely. There is no official count. However, thousands of people claim to have seen the creature. The reports include not only sightings, but also stories of loud, unexplained screams, strange smells, and large footprints found in remote areas.

Some stories tell of aggressive encounters in which people were persecuted or threatened.
The scientific community remains skeptical about Bigfoot's existence. There is no physical evidence such as bones, hair, or feces that can be conclusively attributed to the creature.

Many scientists argue that Bigfoot reports are the result of a combination of misidentifications of known animals or mass hysteria. Some also believe that the legends and reports are cultural artifacts deeply rooted in the folklore and myths of indigenous peoples and modern society.

Bigfoot enthusiasts who continue to search for evidence of the creature's existence are undertaking expeditions into remote forests, using camera traps, and continuing to search for footprints.

Bigfoot has a firm place in pop culture. Films, television series, books, and documentaries have explored the subject and helped keep the legend alive. Events such as Bigfoot conferences and festivals attract enthusiasts and researchers who share their experiences and theories.

Whether Bigfoot is a real creature or merely a product of mythology and misidentification, or perhaps just an unshaven, unkempt hillbilly, remains an unsolved mystery. However, the numerous reports and sightings help keep the legend alive.

The search for Bigfoot continues.

6.7. The legends of the Mongolian death worm

The legends of the Mongolian death worm, also known as the "Olgoi-Khorkhoi," are impressive and frightening stories that have been part of Mongolian folklore for many decades. These tales tell of a terrifying creature that lives in the Gobi Desert and is supposedly capable of killing humans and animals through electric shocks or poisonous secretions.

The Gobi Desert, which stretches across Mongolia and parts of northern China, is one of the largest and harshest deserts in the world. The region is characterized by extreme temperatures and barren landscapes, yet boasts a rich history and diverse flora and fauna. Legends of the Mongolian death worm originate primarily from the indigenous nomads who live in this inhospitable region.

The first documented mention of the death worm dates back to the early 1920s. Mongolian Prime Minister Damdinbazar told paleontological researcher Roy Chapman Andrews about a creature capable of killing humans in horrific ways. Andrews, who was traversing the Gobi Desert in search of dinosaur fossils, initially considered the story a legend, but it piqued the interest of many cryptozoologists and adventurers.

The Mongolian death worm is described as being approximately 60 to 150 centimeters long, with a thick, worm-like body that is said to be red or yellow in color. Some reports describe it as a "bloodworm" because of its bright red color. The creature is said to have no visible eyes or mouth and to slither through the desert. It is claimed that the death worm lives beneath the surface of the sand, only occasionally rising to the surface.

The Death Worm's frightening abilities are what make it particularly fearsome. According to legend, the worm can kill its victims in two ways: by delivering an electric shock or by injecting a deadly poison. These abilities make it a particularly dangerous creature, threatening both humans and animals in its environment.

There are numerous reports of encounters with the Death Worm, but exact casualty figures are difficult to determine. Most reports come from nomads who claim to have seen the creature or heard of its deadly abilities. Scientific evidence for the Death Worm's existence, however, is lacking, which has led to much skepticism and debate.

Despite the lack of physical evidence, the Mongolian death worm has piqued the interest of many researchers. Several expeditions have been undertaken to find and document the creature. One of the most famous expeditions was led by Czech cryptozoologist Ivan Mackerle in 1990. Mackerle traveled to the Gobi Desert, interviewing locals and searching for evidence of the death worm's existence. Although he found no physical evidence, his reports and documentation helped spread the legend further.

Even in the 21st century, researchers and adventurers continue their search for the death worm. Expeditions like that of Richard Freeman, a cryptozoologist at the Centre for Fortean Zoology, have scoured the region but found no definitive evidence. Modern technologies such as drones and satellite surveillance have also been used to track down the creature, but so far without success.

Some scientists suspect that reports of the Mongolian death worm may be based on misinterpretation or exaggeration. They argue that familiar animals such as snakes or large worms could easily be mistaken for a mythical creature in the harsh conditions of the Gobi Desert.

In summary, the legends of the Mongolian Death Worm are an exciting mix of fear, mysticism, and adventure.

6.8. The Legend of the Mothman

The legend of the Mothman in West Virginia is another of the most mysterious stories in modern folklore. This strange creature, described as a large, humanoid being with enormous wings and glowing red eyes, was first sighted in the small town of Point Pleasant in the 1960s. Accounts of the Mothman and the events surrounding it have left a deep cultural mark and have been the subject of numerous books, films, and documentaries.

The first documented sighting of the Mothman occurred on November 12, 1966, when five men working at a cemetery in Clendenin, West Virginia, reported seeing a large, human-like creature with wings.
Just three days later, on November 15, two young couples from Point Pleasant reported seeing a similar creature. Roger and Linda Scarberry and Steve and Mary Mallette reported to police that they were followed by a large, gray creature with glowing red eyes while driving along a remote road near the former TNT factory. The TNT factory, a relic from World War II, is located about six miles north of Point Pleasant and was a popular hangout for teenagers.

In the following months, there were numerous reports of Mothman sightings in and around Point Pleasant. Witnesses described the creature as being about 2 meters tall with wings that had a span of 3 to 4 meters. The bright red eyes, glowing in the darkness, were considered particularly disturbing. Many witnesses reported a feeling of fear and anxiety when they saw the creature. Some reports also described strange noises made by the Mothman, similar to the screech of a large bird or the sound of the wind.

A particularly tragic event often associated with the legend of the Mothman is the collapse of the Silver Bridge on December 15, 1967.

The suspension bridge connecting Point Pleasant to Gallipolis, Ohio, collapsed during rush hour, killing 46 people. Many Point Pleasant residents believed the Mothman sightings were a premonition of this disaster, and some reports claim the creature was seen near the bridge shortly before it collapsed.
The exact number of victims directly linked to the Mothman is difficult to determine. While the sightings themselves did not cause any direct deaths, the Mothman is often associated with the Silver Bridge disaster, in which 46 people died.

This connection between the sightings and the bridge collapse has helped solidify the Mothman legend, giving it a dark, prophetic character.

After the bridge collapse, sightings of the Mothman decreased rapidly, and the legend began to develop into a kind of modern mythology.

In addition to the reports and books, numerous documentaries and television programs about the Mothman have been produced, keeping interest in the creature alive. Every September, Point Pleasant celebrates the Mothman Festival, which attracts visitors from all over the world. The festival includes lectures, tours of major sighting sites, and a variety of activities centered around the legend. A life-size statue of the Mothman was even erected in downtown Point Pleasant in 2003 and has become a popular tourist attraction.

Various theories have been proposed to explain Mothman sightings. Some researchers suggest the creature may be a large owl or sandhill crane, whose unusual appearance and behavior in the dark have been mistakenly interpreted as a supernatural being. However, the exact causes of the sightings remain a mystery, and the legend of the Mothman remains a mystery.

The reports about the mysterious creature, the tragic Silver Bridge disaster, and the numerous books and films (e.g., from 2002: "The Mothman Prophecy") have created a living legend that continues to captivate many people and invites them to reflect on the inexplicable.

6.9 The Legend of the Goatman

The legend of the Goatman is one of the most disturbing stories in modern American folklore. This mysterious creature, described as half-human and half-goat, has reportedly been sighted in various parts of the United States, particularly in Maryland, Texas, and Kentucky. Reports of the Goatman encompass a multitude of encounters and sightings spanning several decades.

The most well-known version of the Goatman legend comes from the state of Maryland, particularly the region around Prince George's County.

The first reports of the Goatman appeared in the 1950s, but the legend gained wider notoriety in the 1970s. According to the most popular version of the story, the Goatman is a former scientist who was involved in a secret experiment at the Beltsville Agricultural Research Center.

The experiment went wrong, and the scientist transformed into a monstrous creature with the body of a human and the head and legs of a goat. This creature is said to now roam the forests and along the roads in the area, taking revenge on humans.

Another widely reported sighting of the Goatman in Maryland occurred in November 1971, when several teenagers reported being stalked by a creature with glowing red eyes and a terrifying howl while picnicking near the drawbridge on Governor Bridge Road. This bridge, also known as "Crybaby Bridge," has since become a popular spot for paranormal investigations and nighttime visits from curious locals. Reports of the sighting were picked up by local newspapers, further spreading the legend.

In the 1980s, further sightings of the Goatman were reported in Maryland. A group of Boy Scouts camping near Bowie, Maryland, claimed they were attacked by a large, goat-like creature. Although no one was injured, the group described the encounter as deeply frightening and convincing. These reports reinforced belief in the Goatman's existence and made him a staple of local folklore.

Another location associated with the Goatman legend is the Old Alton Bridge, also known as "Goatman's Bridge," in Denton County, Texas. Originally built in the 19th century, the bridge is now a popular spot for ghost hunters and paranormal researchers.

According to legend, the Goatman was an African-American goat farmer who was lynched at the bridge by racist vigilantes in the 1930s. Since then, his ghost is said to haunt the bridge, and there are numerous reports of strange noises, apparitions, and unexplained phenomena in the area surrounding the bridge.

In Kentucky, particularly in the Louisville area, there are also reports of a similar creature known as the "Pope Lick Monster." This creature is said to live near the railroad bridge over Pope Lick Creek and is often described as a hybrid of a human and a goat or sheep.

Legend has it that the Pope Lick Monster hypnotizes or scares people into luring them onto the tracks, where they are then hit by trains. Although there are no confirmed reports of casualties directly attributable to the monster, there have been several fatal accidents on the bridge, further fueling the legend.

The number of victims who can be directly linked to the Goatman is difficult to determine.

The legends and stories told about the Goatman have often been passed down from generation to generation and may be exaggerated or distorted. Nevertheless, reports of encounters with the Goatman have both frightened and captivated many people.
The scientific community remains skeptical of reports of the Goatman. There is no physical evidence for the existence of such a creature, and many scientists and researchers suspect that the legends originated as urban myths based on deeply held fears and cultural narratives.

The stories and encounters with the Goatman invite us to reflect on the inexplicable and explore the boundaries between reality and myth.

6.10. Sightings of humanoids in Brazil

Reports of humanoid sightings in Brazil represent an interesting chapter in modern UFO and cryptozoology history. These reports include encounters with beings that exhibit human-like (humanoid) characteristics, but differ significantly from known human appearances. Humanoids are described as beings that have a human body structure—that is, a head, two arms, and two legs—but often exhibit other striking features such as unusual skin color, oversized eyes, or alien anatomy.

Brazil has a long history of reports of such encounters, ranging from the dense rainforests of the Amazon to bustling urban areas.

One of the most famous humanoid encounters in Brazil occurred in 1957 and is known as the "Antonio Villas Boas Case." Antonio Villas Boas was a Brazilian farmer working in his field on the night of October 16, 1957, when he noticed a strange red light in the sky. The light approached him and revealed an egg-shaped object that landed on three legs.

Boas reported that he was abducted by small, humanoid beings with pale skin and large, blue eyes. These beings allegedly took him to their ship and subjected him to medical examinations before finally releasing him.

The case attracted international attention and is often considered one of the first well-documented accounts of abduction by extraterrestrial humanoids.

Another notable sighting occurred on January 19, 1996, in the city of Varginha, Minas Gerais State. The "Varginha Incident" is one of the most famous UFO incidents in Brazil and is often compared to the Roswell Incident in the United States.

On that day, several witnesses, including three young women, reported seeing a strange, small creature with large red eyes and brown, oil-stained skin.

The women described the creature as being about 1.5 meters tall, with a large head and prominent veins. Military and police forces were also reportedly called to the area, and there were rumors that the Brazilian military had captured the creature and taken it to a secret facility. Although officials deny the events, the Varginha incident remains a mystery in Brazilian UFO research.

There are also numerous reports of encounters with humanoids in the Amazon region. In the dense rainforests and remote villages, locals often tell stories of strange, humanoid beings emerging from the forest and then silently retreating.

One such encounter was reported in 1977 in the city of Colares, in the state of Pará. During this incident, numerous residents reported being attacked by flying objects emitting light beams. These beams allegedly caused burns and other injuries to the victims.

The case, known as "Operation Prato," was investigated by the Brazilian Air Force, which documented numerous sightings and reports over several months. Although the official investigations failed to provide a definitive explanation, the incident remains a disturbing example of reported humanoid encounters in Brazil.

In 2004, another case of humanoid sighting was reported in the city of São Paulo. A man named Ricardo Antonio, walking home from work late one night, reported seeing a luminous object in the sky rapidly approaching and landing over a nearby park.

Several humanoid beings with silver skin and large, black eyes emerged from the object. Antonio claimed the beings communicated with him telepathically, sending him reassuring messages before reboarding their craft and flying away. This case received considerable media attention and was investigated by several UFO research organizations.

The number of victims in these incidents is difficult to determine, as many reports of injuries or psychological trauma remain vague and unconfirmed. In the Colares case, several people were injured, and at least two deaths have been indirectly linked to the alleged attacks. However, the exact nature of these injuries and their causes remain controversial and are the subject of ongoing debate.

However, the scientific community remains skeptical about reports of humanoid encounters in Brazil. There is no physical evidence.

In summary, reports of humanoid sightings in Brazil represent a complex and interesting phenomenon.

6.11 The Lizard Man

The legend of the Lizard Man, a mysterious, reptilian creature sighted in the swamps of South Carolina, is another story from modern American folklore. Humanoids, to which the Lizard Man belongs, are beings that possess human-like characteristics but also exhibit unusual or alien features. Reports of the Lizard Man include encounters from various locations, particularly in the area around Bishopville in Lee County, South Carolina.

The first documented sighting of the Lizard Man occurred in the summer of 1988. On June 29, Christopher Davis, a 17-year-old resident of Bishopville, reported being attacked by a strange creature. Davis told police that his car had a flat tire on a remote road near the Scape Ore Swamp.

While changing the tire, he heard a strange noise and suddenly saw a green, scaly creature with glowing red eyes, about 2 meters tall, approaching him. Davis reported that the creature had sharp claws and tried to reach the car, while he quickly got in and drove away. The creature reportedly jumped onto the roof of the car and left scratch marks.

Police took Davis' report seriously and examined the scratches and damaged side mirror on his car.
In the following weeks and months, several other Lee County residents reported seeing a similar creature or noticing unusual tracks and noises near their homes. The reports described the creature as large, muscular, and with reptilian features such as scaly skin and a long tail.

A particularly notable sighting occurred in July 1988, when a couple from Brown Town, also near the Scape Ore Swamp, reported that their car had been severely damaged overnight. The body showed deep scratches, and parts of the car had been chewed to pieces. Police found unusual footprints near the scene, which were three-toed and approximately 35 centimeters long. These prints were examined by experts, but no definitive explanation could be provided.

In August 1988, Tom and Mary Way reported seeing the creature on their property. They described the creature as about 2 meters tall, with greenish-brown skin and glowing eyes. They reportedly heard the creature emit a deep, roaring sound before disappearing into the swamp. Similar footprints were found in this sighting as well.

Reports of the Lizard Man quickly attracted media attention, and the small town of Bishopville became the center of intense coverage and speculation. Local authorities and Lee County Sheriff Liston Truesdale conducted a comprehensive investigation to determine what was behind the reports. Despite numerous sightings and traces found, no definitive explanation for the creature's existence could be found.
Over the years, reports of the Lizard Man surfaced repeatedly. In 2008, exactly 20 years after the first sightings, residents again reported unusual occurrences and encounters with a similar creature.

Bob Rawson and his wife Madeline of Bishopville reported finding deep scratches and bite marks on their car, similar to the 1988 reports. They also claimed to have heard strange, deep noises coming from the nearby swamp.

Most reports on this topic include sightings, damage to vehicles or property, and experiences of fear or discomfort as a result of the encounters.

Many scientists and researchers suspect that the reports may be based on misinterpretations of familiar animals, such as alligators or large lizards native to the swamps of South Carolina. Others speculate that they are deliberate deceptions or psychological phenomena.

6.12 The Green Children of Woolpit

In 12th-century England, a time when legends, religious ideas, and folk beliefs shaped everyday life, an event occurred in a small village that deeply unsettled the people of the time and continues to provide fodder for speculation today. The village of Woolpit in the county of Suffolk was an unassuming place, a place where farmers plowed their fields and traders traveled along dusty roads. But one day, two children were discovered there who seemed so unusual that they were difficult to identify.

It was during the harvest that farmers near old wolf dens encountered two strange figures: a boy and a girl who seemed completely bewildered. Their clothing was made of a fabric unknown to anyone in the area, and they spoke a language no one understood. Most striking, however, was their skin color, which had a greenish tinge, as if affected by some illness or spell.

The villagers brought the two to Woolpit. There, they tried to give them food, but they refused to touch the local bread, vegetables, and meat. Only when raw beans were served did they begin to eat. For medieval people, who explained everything within the framework of their religious world, this was a sign that these children must have come from another, alien world.

After some time, the girl began to recover. She got used to the food, learned English, and integrated into village life. Gradually, her skin lost its greenish hue until she finally looked like the others. Her brother, however, remained weak, fell ill, and died a few weeks after their arrival. The girl grew up, became an adult, and eventually married. But she told a story that forever linked her life to the mystery of Woolpit.

According to her, she and her brother came from a land where the sun never shone. There, a kind of twilight reigned, everything was filled with a green glow, and the people lived in a kind of eternal twilight world. They entered this human world through an underground passage. They saw a bright light, followed it, and suddenly emerged in the middle of the fields near Woolpit.

The story was recorded by chroniclers, including Ralph of Coggeshall and William of Newburgh. Both independently reported on the green children, their strange language, and their origin story. For the scholars of the time, the event was not a curiosity, but rather an indication of the unfathomable ways of God or a warning to be brought to the attention of believers.

Today, there are various explanations. Some historians suggest that they were orphans from a neighboring region who had developed greenish skin due to malnutrition and iron deficiency. A disease such as chlorosis, also known as "green sickness," may have caused the hue. Their unusual speech may have been an unknown dialect that the people of Woolpit didn't understand. When the girl regained her strength and ate normal food, the strange skin color disappeared.

Other interpretations go further. Some see in the story a reference to children who came from underground caves or mines, isolated from the world of light. Its description of a land without sun could hint at a life in darkness, where plants and humans took on a different appearance. Still others connect the tale with ideas of parallel worlds or even encounters with extraterrestrial beings who stepped through the gate of another reality.

Regardless of which theory you prefer, the case of the green children remains a piece of tradition that shows how people in the Middle Ages dealt with the inexplicable. Where modern readers seek scientific explanations, people then turned to myths, religious interpretations, or legends. Thus, two lost children with strange skin color became figures whose story has endured for centuries.

The girl who survived eventually became part of the village community, but her tale of a distant, lightless land remained in the chronicles. Today, the legend lives on in Woolpit. Street names and inns commemorate the Green Children, and visitors from all over the world travel to learn more about these enigmatic figures.

Whether the two actually existed or whether the chroniclers wrote down a fairy tale based on rumors is uncertain. But the story conveys a sense of how the Middle Ages dealt with the unfamiliar. It tells of how easily something unusual could become the stuff of myth, and how such myths were in turn passed down through generations. Two children with greenish skin, discovered in a field, thus made the leap from village chronicle to world literature and, to this day, are part of those stories that cannot be fully explained and, precisely for this reason, are continually retold.

Chapter 7: Happy coincidences and inventions

This chapter shows how many significant inventions and discoveries have come about through happy coincidences and unexpected events. These stories illustrate that innovation often emerges from the most unpredictable situations and that chance and creativity can work hand in hand to change the world. Stay open to life's unexpected moments, for they could be the source of the next great idea.

7.1 The discovery of penicillin

Sometimes it's not meticulously planned experiments or research programs prepared years in advance that change the world, but a simple coincidence coupled with a keen eye. This was the case in 1928, when Scottish bacteriologist Alexander Fleming made a discovery that catapulted medicine into a new era. His discovery of penicillin marked the beginning of the antibiotic era—and has since saved millions of lives.

The story begins uneventfully in a London laboratory at St. Mary's Hospital. Fleming, already known at the time for his work on antibacterial substances, had left Petri dishes containing staphylococcus cultures. Upon returning from a short vacation, he noticed that one of the dishes was contaminated with mold. Normally, this would have been considered just an annoying lab error, something to be disposed of immediately. But Fleming did the opposite: He took a closer look.

What he saw was remarkable. Around the greenish-blue mold, which was later identified as *A marked pencil* identified, there was a clear zone. In this area, the bacteria were killed or at least severely inhibited in their growth. Fleming matter-of-factly noted that the fungus apparently released a substance that rendered bacteria harmless. A laboratory accident had provided him with a clue – and Fleming was observant enough not to miss it.

He initially named the substance "penicillin" and began systematically investigating its effects. He discovered that penicillin was particularly effective against gram-positive bacteria, including pathogens that caused serious illnesses such as scarlet fever, pneumonia, and blood poisoning. Even though Fleming was unable to isolate penicillin in a pure, stable form at the time—the substance decomposed too quickly—he had laid the crucial foundation for the discovery. The real medical revolution didn't come until a decade later. In the late 1930s, researchers at Oxford University resumed Fleming's work. Howard Florey, Ernst Boris Chain, and their colleagues developed methods to extract and stabilize penicillin in larger quantities. They initially tested it on mice and found that even fatal infections could be treated with penicillin. Human trials soon followed, with spectacular success.

With the outbreak of World War II, research gained even greater urgency. Infections were one of the leading causes of death among wounded soldiers, and a drug that could effectively combat bacteria was invaluable. The United States and Great Britain therefore launched massive production programs. By 1944, the year of the Normandy landings, penicillin was already available in sufficient quantities to save tens of thousands of wounded. Some called it "the Allies' secret weapon" at the time.

From this point on, medicine changed fundamentally. Until then, infections from even minor injuries or everyday illnesses were potentially fatal. A simple case of pneumonia could end a young person's life within days. With penicillin, the picture changed dramatically: diseases that had previously been almost impossible to treat could suddenly be cured.

The story also has its ironic side. Fleming himself was by no means a pedantic researcher. Contemporaries described his laboratory as messy, sometimes even chaotic. It was precisely this lack of "laboratory perfectionism" that likely contributed to a Petri dish being left open long enough for the mold to penetrate. Had Fleming been more orderly, he might have disposed of the fungus immediately—and the discovery might have been delayed or left to another researcher.

Fun fact: When Fleming received the Nobel Prize in Medicine in 1945, along with Florey and Chain, he suddenly became a world-famous figure. In interviews, he often stated that he himself had discovered penicillin by chance. He downplayed his own achievement. Chance alone wouldn't have been enough – what was crucial was that Fleming recognized the significance of his observation and pursued it further.

The discovery of penicillin is still considered one of the greatest medical revolutions. Millions of lives have been saved since then, life expectancy has increased dramatically, and diseases such as syphilis, scarlet fever, and streptococcal infections have lost their terror. At the same time, it marked the beginning of a new era in research: In the decades that followed, ever new variants of antibiotics were developed.

But here, too, another, less pleasant side of the story emerges. Fleming himself warned early on about a problem that is now one of the most pressing issues in medicine: the development of resistance. In his 1945 Nobel Prize speech, he predicted that bacteria could develop resistance if penicillin was used improperly or too sparingly. His words proved prophetic – today, physicians around the world are battling multi-resistant germs that render antibiotics largely ineffective.

Despite this dark side, the discovery of penicillin remains a prime example of the power of chance and the importance of scientific curiosity. An inconspicuous patch of mold in a London laboratory changed the course of human history—and continues to demonstrate that sometimes the greatest revolutions begin where you least expect them.

7.2. How Velcro was invented by a dog

Sometimes the greatest inventions literally lie by the roadside—or in a dog's fur. The Swiss engineer George de Mestral probably wouldn't have imagined that a harmless walk with his four-legged friend in 1941 would lead to a technological revolution. But that's exactly what happened when he returned home after a trip through woods and meadows and discovered that countless tiny burrs had stubbornly clung to his dog's fur and his clothing.

Most people would have been annoyed and simply plucked out the pesky plant seeds. De Mestral, however, was a man with an inquisitive eye. He was impressed by how reliably and firmly the burrs clung. They held so tightly that they couldn't simply be shaken off, yet at the same time they could be detached again without causing any damage. A perfect, reusable "seal" that nature had used for millions of years to disperse its seeds.

De Mestral took some of these burrs home and curiously examined them under a microscope. What he saw was ingenious in its simplicity: tiny, elastic hooks that anchored themselves in the loops of fabric or animal fur. It was a biological mechanism so effective that the burrs could easily spread for miles by clinging to animals or humans.

This small discovery inspired de Mestral with an idea that he pursued with the meticulousness of an engineer. He began searching for a technical equivalent—a material consisting of one side with tiny hooks and another with matching loops. After years of experimentation, he finally found a practical solution: nylon. This synthetic material could be processed to form tiny, robust hooks and loops. Thus, the principle of Velcro was translated into technology—the hook-and-loop fastener was born.

Initially, however, the invention was met with skepticism. Many considered it a gimmick with no practical use. Zippers, buttons, and buckles had long been established, and few could imagine replacing these tried-and-tested methods with a "scratch tape." But de Mestral persisted. He filed a patent, improved the production technology, and searched for possible applications.

Hook and loop fasteners experienced their decisive breakthrough in the 1960s when NASA discovered them for their space programs. In weightless space, it's difficult to fasten things or quickly open and close them. Hook and loop fasteners proved almost ideal for securing tools, equipment, or even astronaut suits. This media attention ensured that hook and loop fasteners were suddenly considered high-tech—and from then on, they also became widespread in everyday life.

Today, it's an indispensable part of our lives. From shoes and children's clothing to medical applications and sports equipment – the Velcro fastener is ubiquitous. What's particularly exciting is that it's also extremely important in medicine. Prosthetics, bandages, and blood pressure cuffs all use its simple yet reliable principle. It's even used in aerospace to this day, in a direct lineage back to the time when a Swiss man took his dog for a walk.

George de Mestral's idea required not only patience but also a thick skin—in the truest sense of the word. Many manufacturers initially rejected him because they considered production too complex. Only when he developed a machine that could reliably cut the tiny hooks from nylon did the project become commercially viable. Today, he is considered a prime example of the power of bionics—the transfer of natural principles to technical applications.

7.3. The origins of Coca-Cola

Sometimes a global career begins quite modestly—with a sticky syrup in a small pharmacy in the American South. This was the case in 1886 in Atlanta, Georgia, when pharmacist John Stith Pemberton developed a recipe that wasn't originally intended as a soft drink. Pemberton, a former officer who had been severely wounded in the American Civil War and had suffered from chronic pain ever since, was looking for a remedy that would provide relief while also invigorating. His mixture consisted of an aromatic syrup in which coca leaves and cola nuts—rich in caffeine—were the main ingredients.
At a time when many pharmacies mixed their own tonics and elixirs, Pemberton's creation was nothing unusual. People hoped such concoctions would help with fatigue, headaches, or digestive problems. Originally, his syrup even contained wine and was sold under the name "Pemberton's French Wine Coca." Only when stricter Prohibition laws came into force in Atlanta did Pemberton have to remove the alcohol from his recipe. It was replaced with carbonated water—a happy coincidence that transformed a medicinal tonic into one of the world's most famous soft drinks.
The first sale of Coca-Cola took place on May 8, 1886, at Jacobs' Pharmacy in Atlanta. For five cents, one could enjoy a glass of the new beverage, which the pharmacist advertised as "delicious and refreshing." Initially, only nine glasses were sold daily—an inconspicuous start for a product that would later reach billions of people.
The real success story, however, didn't begin with Pemberton himself. The pharmacist was a gifted inventor, but not a good businessman. Shortly after the invention, he sold shares in his recipe, and when he died in 1888, it was an entrepreneur named Asa Griggs Candler who recognized the potential of Coca-Cola. Candler acquired the rights, invested in advertising, and thus laid the foundation for a brand that soon became known throughout America.
Candler was a marketing genius. He distributed free coupons, had Coca-Cola printed on fans, calendars, and thermometers, and made the drink an integral part of everyday American culture. At the same time, Coca-Cola transformed from a "medicine" to a pure soft drink. Soon, the distinctive bottles emerged, whose shape is now recognized worldwide.

The history of the ingredients is also interesting. In its early years, Coca-Cola actually contained small amounts of cocaine, as the coca leaf extracts were not fully purified. It wasn't until around 1904, as awareness of the dangers of cocaine grew, that the recipe was changed so that the leaves were used only for flavoring—without any intoxicating effect. The kola nut, however, remained as a natural source of caffeine, and together with sugar, it formed the energetic foundation of the drink.

In the 20th century, Coca-Cola became more than just a soft drink. During World War II, the company ensured that American soldiers overseas had access to Coca-Cola—often setting up a production facility specifically for this purpose. For the soldiers, the brown soda became a symbol of home, and for many countries, it was their first contact with the brand. Paradoxically, the war helped make Coca-Cola known globally.

Today, Coca-Cola is a symbol of the American way of life. No other beverage is so strongly linked to the idea of freedom, consumerism, and modernity. It appears in pop culture in countless films, songs, and works of art. Andy Warhol made the bottle iconic with his famous silkscreen prints, and the company's advertising—from Santa Claus in a red coat to the slogan "It's the real thing"—continues to shape generations.

Fun fact: It's often said that Coca-Cola invented the modern image of Santa Claus in red and white. This isn't entirely true—similar depictions existed before—but the Coca-Cola advertising campaigns of the 1930s made him popular worldwide. The fact that he was now dressed in the company's colors certainly helped to infuse the brand with even more positive emotions.

From an inconspicuous mixture in a pharmacy to a global phenomenon: Coca-Cola is a prime example of how chance, business acumen, and clever advertising can transform a simple idea into a symbol of modernity. To this day, the exact recipe remains a closely guarded secret.

7.4 The coincidence that led to Post-it Notes

Post-it Notes, the colorful, self-adhesive sticky notes, were invented by a happy accident and an innovative flash of inspiration. In 1968, 3M scientist Dr. Spencer Silver discovered an adhesive that adhered slightly but didn't form a permanent bond. Years later, his colleague Art Fry remembered this adhesive when he was looking for a way to attach bookmarks to his church choir hymnal that wouldn't slip. The resulting Post-it Notes are now an indispensable part of offices and homes around the world.

7.5. The history of potato chips

In 1968, chemist Spencer Silver was working at 3M to develop a particularly strong adhesive. Instead of a superglue, he got the exact opposite: a substance with very weak adhesion. It could be easily removed without leaving a trace and was anything but what his superiors had originally demanded. Many colleagues considered the result a dead end. But Silver was convinced that this "failed product" could one day prove useful.

For years, he tried to publicize his invention within the company. He called it "removable glue" and repeatedly presented it at internal seminars. But no one could quite imagine the use of an adhesive that barely held anything together permanently. It wasn't until years later that one of his colleagues, Art Fry, came up with the crucial application. Fry sang in the church choir in his free time and was regularly annoyed that the bookmarks in his hymnal would slip or fall out while he sang. Suddenly, he remembered Silver's glue—a material that would be perfect for securing small strips of paper in such a way that they would stay in place but could be removed again at any time.

Fry began to experiment. He applied the adhesive to small pieces of paper and tested them in his hymnal. The results were astonishing: The notes adhered reliably, but could be removed and reused as often as desired. He soon began using the notes in his office as well – and discovered they were a fantastic tool for attaching notes to documents, files, or walls without causing damage. His colleagues were enthusiastic, and the idea began to spread throughout the company.

But the path to a marketable product was by no means easy. In the 1970s, 3M management was skeptical. They were unsure whether there would even be a market for these "sticky notes." An initial test run in a few cities met with only moderate success. It wasn't until 1980, when a large-scale marketing campaign was launched, distributing Post-it Notes free of charge to offices and companies, that the breakthrough came. Within a very short time, users recognized their practical value – and never wanted to work without them again. Post-it Notes became a global phenomenon. The bright yellow notes—the color was also a coincidence, as the laboratory paper on which the first samples were produced happened to be available in yellow—found their way into offices, homes, schools, and universities all over the world. Today, they come in every imaginable shape, size, and color, but the principle has always remained the same: a simple, reusable sticky note that sticks exactly where you need it. Fun fact: Post-it notes have become not only a symbol of office organization, but also a cultural phenomenon. In the 1990s, entire works of art were created from colorful notes, and they appeared in films and TV series as a visual symbol of creativity, idea generation, and chaotic thinking. The story of two students in the USA who decorated the facade of an entire skyscraper with tens of thousands of Post-it notes became particularly legendary – proof that even small notes can have a big impact.

7.6 The discovery of vulcanized rubber

The discovery of vulcanized rubber by Charles Goodyear in the 1830s revolutionized the production and use of rubber and had a profound impact on numerous industries.

His groundbreaking innovation made it possible to produce durable and resilient rubber products.

Before the discovery of vulcanized rubber, natural rubber was the main ingredient in rubber products. Natural rubber, obtained from the sap of the rubber tree (Hevea brasiliensis), has significant disadvantages, however.
It was sticky and melted in warm temperatures, while it became brittle and cracked in cold weather.
This instability severely limited its usability.

In 1834, Charles Goodyear began intensively experimenting with rubber to improve its properties. His initial experiments were unsuccessful, and he suffered numerous setbacks. Despite financial difficulties and multiple imprisonment for debt, Goodyear persisted. He was convinced he could find a method to make rubber more durable and practical.
The breakthrough came in 1839 when Goodyear experimented in a small workshop in Woburn, Massachusetts.
According to legend, the discovery happened by chance when Goodyear accidentally dropped a mixture of rubber and sulfur onto a hot stove. The mixture began to foam and smoke, but when it cooled, Goodyear noticed that the rubber remained solid and elastic.

In 1844, Goodyear received a U.S. patent (Patent No. 3,633) for his vulcanization process. Although his invention was revolutionary, Goodyear faced numerous legal and financial challenges.
Charles Goodyear died in poverty in 1860, but his legacy lives on.

The Goodyear Tire & Rubber Company, named in honor of Charles Goodyear, was founded in 1898 and is now one of the world's largest tire manufacturers.
His name is still a household name for every motorist today.
From car tires to medical devices to sporting equipment, vulcanized rubber is ubiquitous today.

7.8 The discovery of the microwave

The discovery of the microwave has now become an integral part of many households.

We owe this technology to a chance experiment in the 1940s.

Percy Spencer, an engineer and researcher at the Raytheon Company, is the man behind the discovery of microwave technology. Spencer, born in 1894 in Howland, Maine, had a distinguished career in electronics and radar technology during World War II.

In 1945, Spencer was working on a magnetron, a device that generates microwaves and is used in radar systems.
During an experiment, he noticed something strange: a chocolate bar in his pocket had melted. Fascinated by this observation, Spencer began systematically investigating the effects of microwave radiation on food.

Spencer placed various foods near the magnetron. He observed that popcorn kernels popped quickly near the device and that an egg placed near the magnetron exploded.

Spencer recognized the enormous potential of this discovery and began developing a cooking appliance that could use microwaves to prepare meals. His employer, the Raytheon Company, recognized the commercial potential of the discovery and began developing a microwave oven. In 1946, Raytheon filed the first patent for a microwave oven.

The first commercial model, the Radarange, was launched in 1947. The Radarange was large, expensive, and primarily intended for use in restaurants and cafeterias.

The first Radarange was about 1.8 meters tall, weighed 340 kilograms, and cost around $5,000. Despite its size and cost, the device quickly found use in restaurants, train stations, and airplane kitchens, where its ability to heat food quickly was particularly appreciated.

In the decades that followed, engineers worked to miniaturize the technology and reduce costs to make microwave ovens affordable for home use. By the 1960s, they had succeeded in making the devices more compact and user-friendly.

The breakthrough for household use came in the 1970s, when the Japanese electronics company Sharp launched affordable, compact microwave ovens. These new models were significantly smaller, lighter, and more cost-effective than the first commercial microwave ovens. The price dropped to a few hundred dollars, and the microwave began to find its way into more and more households.

It enabled faster and more convenient meal preparation, and ready meals and microwave meals became popular, which also influenced the food industry.

Whether you're a fan of microwave meals or not, this discovery is undoubtedly remarkable.

7.9. The discovery of the color Prussian Blue

Sometimes an error in the laboratory leads to results that change the world more lastingly than any planned research ever could. This was the case in 1704 in Berlin, when the paint manufacturer Johann Jacob Diesbach wanted to produce a pigment and stumbled upon something that later became known as "Berlin Blue" or "Prussian Blue"—the first modern, synthetically produced color in history.

At the time, Diesbach was working in the workshop of the eccentric chemist Johann Konrad Dippel, a man known not only as a natural scientist, but also as an alchemist, philosopher, and occasionally even a charlatan. Diesbach was actually trying to produce a vibrant red pigment that would be of great value in painting and textile dyeing. He used potassium carbonate, as was common in such experiments. But what he didn't know was that the material was contaminated with animal blood. Blood contains iron compounds—and precisely this inconspicuous circumstance led to a chemical reaction that no one would have expected.

Instead of the desired shade of red, a deep, intense blue appeared in the mixture. Diesbach was initially surprised, perhaps even disappointed. But he quickly realized that he had stumbled upon something never seen before in this form. The newly formed compound, later chemically identified as iron(III) hexacyanoferrate(II), possessed extraordinary coloring power and unusual stability. It was a pigment that did not fade easily, that was strong and luminous—in short, a minor sensation.

The new color was soon dubbed "Berlin Blue," later "Prussian Blue," and quickly became a household name. Until then, a strong, durable blue had been difficult and expensive to obtain. Lapis lazuli, the gemstone pigment known as "ultramarine," had to be laboriously extracted from Afghan mines and transported to Europe at great expense. It was often unaffordable for artists. Berlin Blue, on the other hand, was comparatively inexpensive and could be produced in larger quantities. It thus democratized the color blue in art—and opened up entirely new possibilities.

In the 18th and 19th centuries, Prussian Blue became a favorite among painters. It can be found in numerous paintings of the period.

7.10 The invention of cornflakes

Sometimes the greatest inventions aren't the result of years of planning, but simply the product of mishap. This is what happened to two brothers from Michigan, USA, who, in the late 19th century, were simply trying to prepare a healthy meal for their patients and, in the process, created one of the most successful breakfast cereals in the world. We're talking about John Harvey Kellogg and his brother Will Keith, who made a discovery in a small town called Battle Creek that continues to give millions of people a crunchy start to their day.

John Harvey Kellogg was a physician, health advocate, and director of the Battle Creek Sanitarium, a hybrid of sanatorium, clinic, and health resort run strictly according to Seventh-day Adventist principles. He was convinced that a meat-free diet, plenty of exercise, hygiene, and abstinence were the foundation of a healthy life. He considered alcohol, tobacco, and even coffee dangerous poisons. Instead, he preached temperance, purity, and, above all, a simple, vegetarian diet that would keep body and mind pure. His patients, including celebrities and wealthy citizens from across America, were therefore given meals consisting of vegetables, fruit, nuts, and grains. But the doctor was looking for something special: a dish that was easily digestible, nutritious, and yet so unexciting that it wouldn't tempt anyone to indulge in "sinful cravings." Breakfast was to play a central role in this almost monastically strict dietary program.
And this is where chance comes into play. One day, John Harvey and his younger brother Will were experimenting with wheat dough. They wanted to make a kind of bread mash, but the result was anything but successful: The dough was sticky, difficult to roll out, and looked spoiled. Normally, it would have been thrown away – but the brothers were thrifty and curious. They rolled the dough in rollers, hoping to make it usable after all. Instead of a smooth sheet of dough, they produced thin flakes that became hard and crispy when baked.
When they tasted these flakes, they were surprised to find that they were not only edible, but even had a pleasant crunch. Topped with milk, they were easy to chew and digestible. A failed experiment had given rise to a completely new meal. The brothers later refined the process, first with wheat, then with corn – and thus the first cornflakes were born.

The irony of the story: What was intended as a healthy, unassuming diet food soon developed into one of the most successful industrial food products in the world. The brothers soon found themselves at odds. John Harvey, the physician and moral reformer, wanted to continue producing the cereals strictly according to his own vision—without sugar, without unnecessary flavor; after all, the product should promote virtue, not indulgence. Will Keith, however, who had business acumen and understood the market, saw the potential for a broader customer base. He experimented, adding sugar, and making the cornflakes sweeter, tastier, and thus suitable for mass consumption.

This difference in philosophy led to a rift. John Harvey stuck with the sanatorium and his vision of an ascetic diet. Will Keith, on the other hand, founded the "Kellogg Company" in 1906 and made cornflakes a global bestseller. Soon, the Kellogg name adorned the colorful boxes found in millions of kitchens. The brother who once only managed the sanatorium's cash registers became the breakfast king, while the strict doctor faded into the background.

But why were cornflakes such a hit? Their success lay in the combination of zeitgeist and practicality. America at the turn of the century was a country on the move. More and more people were moving to the cities, and the pace of life was accelerating. Nobody wanted to spend hours standing at the stove in the morning. Cornflakes offered the perfect solution: a quick, light meal that could be served without much effort. Simply pour milk over it, and breakfast was ready.

In addition, the flakes were considered modern and hygienic. In an era of fears of spoiled meat, unsanitary markets, and disease, the industrially packaged cornflakes seemed like a piece of the future: clean, safe, and convenient. And through clever advertising, Will Keith Kellogg succeeded in cementing the image of cornflakes as "healthy" and "energy-rich," even though the sugar content called this claim into question.

An amusing fun fact: John Harvey Kellogg originally intended cornflakes to help curb lewd thoughts and sexual desires. In his mind, the bland breakfast would curb passions and thus contribute to a morally pure life. That these same cornflakes were being advertised a few decades later with colorful cartoon characters like Tony the Tiger to sweeten children's mornings is one of those historical ironies that could hardly be invented.

Over time, cornflakes were further developed, refined, and flavored with all sorts of ingredients: fruits, nuts, honey, or chocolate. Other companies entered the market, and the "cereal," as it's called in the US, became an integral part of breakfast culture. Entire generations of children grew up with a bowl of cornflakes or similar cereals, while their parents appreciated the quick convenience.

It's almost forgotten that it all began with sticky dough that could have been thrown away. But this very coincidence shows how closely failure and success can be intertwined. If the Kellogg brothers had simply abandoned their failed experiment, there might not be cornflakes today—and breakfast tables around the world would look very different.

7.11 The invention of the tea bag

It's often coincidences or mistakes that change the course of everyday history. The story of the tea bag is just such a case. No one intended to develop this product. It wasn't the result of an inventor's ingenious plan, nor the result of a sophisticated strategy by a large corporation. Rather, it was a misunderstanding between a retailer and his customers that was the starting point. And yet, it gave rise to one of the most successful and everyday inventions in modern culinary culture.

By 1900, tea was already firmly established in many households. In Europe and America, it was no longer confined to high society but had established itself as an everyday beverage. Anyone who wanted to drink tea bought loose leaves, boiled water, put the pot on, and let the leaves steep. It was a ritual, sometimes almost a ceremony, but it also required patience and a few equipment such as strainers, pots, and special utensils.

During this time, a New York tea merchant named Thomas Sullivan came up with an unusual idea, which later turned out to be an unintentional innovation. Around 1908, he sent out samples of his tea. To reduce costs, he filled the leaves not into tins, but into small silk bags. He himself had a very pragmatic approach: customers would remove the leaves and brew them in a teapot as usual. But many of his customers understood the packaging differently. They dipped the bags directly into hot water and were surprised to find that it worked. The tea brewed, the water colored, and there were no crumbs in the drink.

Thus, a mere package had become a completely new product. The tea bag had been born without Sullivan's intention. Customers were thrilled because suddenly they didn't need a strainer or a teapot. Just put a tea bag in water, wait a few minutes, and a cup of tea was ready.

The first silk tea bags were expensive and unsuitable for mass production. But word of the idea spread, and soon other retailers began experimenting with cheaper materials like gauze or gauze. In the 1920s, the first rectangular paper bags that could be manufactured industrially appeared. This marked the beginning of the true triumph of tea bags.

While the US quickly embraced this practical way of drinking tea, it took a little longer in Europe. The British, in particular, for whom tea was more than just a beverage, clung to the traditional brewing in a teapot. In their eyes, the tea bag was a cheap trick, perhaps even an insult to the culture of tea drinking. But over time, convenience prevailed here too, at the latest after World War II, when practicality became more important than tradition.

An interesting side note: It wasn't until the 1950s that the Lipton company standardized the rectangular bag as we know it today. Before that, there were round or pyramid-shaped versions, which were attractive but more difficult to produce. With the machine-made production of the rectangular shape, actual mass production began, and from then on, there was no turning back.

The invention of the tea bag not only changed trade, but also drinking habits. Tea was no longer a beverage enjoyed only during breaks or in social gatherings. It could be prepared quickly and easily, even in the office or on the go. The tea bag made tea an everyday companion and democratized the beverage, which had previously often been associated with wealth and social status.

Of course, critics were inevitable. Connoisseurs emphasized that the tea bags usually contained only fragments and tea dust, which, while quickly releasing aroma, were less complex in flavor. Anyone who wanted truly good tea had to continue using loose leaves. But the majority of consumers decided otherwise. Practicality prevailed, and millions preferred the small tea bags to fussing with pots and strainers.

Over time, the tea bag evolved. Pyramid tea bags were introduced, offering more room for the leaves to expand, and tea bags made of biodegradable materials. Marketing also played a role: advertising portrayed the tea bag as a modern, clean, and practical product. This ensured its unrivaled success.

Today, the tea bag is so commonplace around the world that it's easy to forget how recent this invention is. As recently as the early 20th century, tea was almost exclusively drunk loose. This change was due to a misunderstanding. Had Thomas Sullivan sent his samples in small tins, history might have been very different.

But a simple commercial error led to an invention that fundamentally changed our drinking habits. The tea bag made tea accessible to the masses, brought it into cafeterias, offices, and living rooms, and gave the beverage a whole new meaning. What started as an improvised idea became a global product that billions of people use every day.

Chapter 8: Aliens, UFOs, Extraterrestrial?

> *This chapter compiles some events and sightings that may be related to UFOs and extraterrestrials. It is not a scientific discussion, merely a compilation of fascinating incidents. Everyone is welcome to make their own interpretations of this.*

8.1 The Roswell Incident

It all began inconspicuously in the summer of 1947, with a man who simply wanted to keep his ranch in order. William "Mac" Brazel, a simple sheep farmer, discovered debris on his expansive land in early July that caught his attention. Scattered across the fields were sheets of foil, rods, string, and strangely shiny pieces of metal so light even children could have carried them. Brazel later recalled that some pieces had a form stability he had never experienced before: You could bend them, and yet they would spring back immediately. For a rancher, it was clear that this was no ordinary junk—but then what?
Brazel brought some of the finds to Roswell, to Sheriff George Wilcox. Wilcox, an experienced man, was immediately irritated. He had seen many things, but nothing like this. Unsure what to do, he informed the nearby Roswell Army Air Field, home of the 509th Bomb Squadron, the unit that had just dropped the atomic bombs on Japan and operated in strict secrecy.
This ushered in Major Jesse Marcel, the base's intelligence officer. Marcel, along with soldiers, drove out to the ranch, collected the debris, and brought it back to the base. Later, decades after the event, Marcel would say he was convinced he had held something completely unknown in his hands. "It was out of this world," he explained in interviews. He described the material as indestructible, thin as cigarette paper, yet untearable. This statement, from the mouth of a veteran officer, became the centerpiece of many subsequent Roswell theories.

The July 8 press release, in which the 509th Bomb Squadron announced that it had recovered the remains of a "flying saucer," was likely a communications disaster. Within hours, the sensation spread worldwide. But the retraction came just as quickly. General Roger Ramey of Fort Worth, Texas, presented the alleged debris to the press: the remains of a weather balloon with a radar reflector. Photographs show Ramey standing next to Marcel as they unfolded the balloon. Decades later, Marcel claimed he had been coerced into participating in the deception, even though he knew it was not the footage he had seen at the ranch.

In addition to these high-profile statements, stories from civilians also circulated. The account of Glenn Dennis, a Roswell undertaker, is particularly well-known. Dennis recounted receiving a call from the military in the summer of 1947. They were asking for small, sealable children's coffins—an unusual request. Shortly afterward, he was at the military hospital, where a nurse tearfully told him about strange corpses: small bodies with large heads, strangely thin arms, and no hair. Years later, he drew a picture of these beings. Critics accused Dennis of embellishing his story, but it remains a core part of the legend to this day.

Others also reported strange sightings. Some residents claimed to have seen military convoys transporting large crates in the middle of the night. A rural doctor was reportedly called to help, only to be immediately turned away. A nurse, whose name could never be clearly established, told friends she had seen "non-human bodies"—shortly afterward, she was transferred.

Sheriff George Wilcox himself never made any public statements, but his wife is said to have later told friends that her husband had "stumbled upon things that were too dangerous to talk about."

This multitude of voices—from officers to nurses to civilians—made the case so elusive. No single statement constitutes conclusive proof, but together they formed a mosaic that fueled suspicions of a cover-up.

In the 1990s, the mystery deepened further when the Air Force released two official reports. The first explained the debris as being from the secret "Project Mogul," a balloon program to monitor Soviet nuclear tests. The second was intended to refute the rumors about corpses: the witnesses had presumably seen test dummies falling into the desert as part of parachute experiments. However, this explanation seemed to many like an afterthought to reassure the public. After all, several years had passed between the alleged dummy experiments and the summer of 1947.

Roswell became a projection screen for distrust of the government. During the Cold War, it was plausible that secret projects were being concealed. But the longer the silence persisted, the greater the scope for speculation became. Authors like Stanton Friedman collected eyewitness accounts and used them to form the basis of what we now know as the modern UFO myth.

Perhaps the most famous—and at the same time most infamous—artifact of the Roswell saga is the "alien autopsy video," which was broadcast worldwide on television in 1995. It showed doctors dissecting a small, humanoid body.

Millions of viewers believed they had finally seen the truth. The video was later exposed as a fake, but the damage—or rather, the impact—was there: Roswell finally became synonymous with UFOs and extraterrestrial mysteries.

Today, Roswell is not just a historical event, but a cultural phenomenon. The town thrives on its myth: museums, festivals, even street signs are decorated with little green men. What was once a misunderstanding, or perhaps a secret military operation, has transformed into a global symbol for the question: Are we alone in the universe?

8.2 The balloons in the sky of Los Angeles 1942

In the early morning hours of February 25, 1942, just months after the attack on Pearl Harbor, Los Angeles was struck by a strange and disturbing event that became known as the "Battle of Los Angeles." This event led to mass panic and left many unanswered questions.

Shortly after 2 a.m., an unidentified flying object was spotted over the skies of Los Angeles. At a time of heightened vigilance and fear of further Japanese attacks, the sighting triggered immediate alert. The city was plunged into darkness, and searchlights began scanning the skies.

The military reacted quickly, firing thousands of grenades and anti-aircraft missiles at the unidentified object, which reportedly moved slowly over the city. The sky was illuminated by an impressive light show, and the noise of the explosions was deafening. But despite the massive fireworks display, the object appeared to remain unharmed and eventually disappeared without a trace.
As dawn broke, there were numerous reports and eyewitness accounts, speaking of various sightings and speculations about the nature of the object. Some claimed it was enemy aircraft, others suggested it was a weather balloon or even an alien spacecraft.

The military later declared it a false alarm, triggered by a misidentified weather balloon. However, this explanation was questioned by many, as the massive military response and the multitude of eyewitness accounts did not seem consistent with a simple weather balloon.
Over the years, various theories have attempted to explain the event. Some believe it was actually an invasion by enemy aircraft that were cleverly disguised or more technologically advanced than previously thought. Others speculate that it was a secret military exercise or a test of new technologies.

There are also those who believe in an encounter with extraterrestrial visitors. The "Battle of Los Angeles" remains a mysterious event in history. It demonstrates how easily panic and misinformation can spread in times of great fear and uncertainty.

Despite official explanations, many questions remain, and the event continues to be investigated and debated by historians and UFO enthusiasts alike. It is a striking example of how unexplained events can capture the collective imagination and give rise to persistent legends and myths.

8.3 The "Foo Fighters" sightings during World War II

During World War II, Allied pilots frequently reported strange, unexplained light phenomena in the sky, which they called "foo fighters." These phenomena, which differed from known flying objects not only in their appearance but also in their movements, caused confusion and concern among both pilots and military strategists.

The first reports of the Foo Fighters came from American night fighters in Europe. Pilots described glowing spheres in various colors—often red, orange, or white—and moving at high speed.
These lights seemed to track the aircraft, making abrupt changes in direction, and then suddenly disappearing. Despite intensive attempts to capture or destroy them, no Allied weapon seemed to have any effect on these mysterious lights.

The sightings were not limited to the European theater of war. Pilots in the Pacific also reported similar phenomena. These unidentified flying objects did not appear to be attacking Allied aircraft, but their presence was so frequent and conspicuous that it caused concern among the crews.

At first it was thought that the Foo Fighters could be a secret weapon of the Axis powers,
Perhaps designed to confuse Allied pilots or disrupt their aircraft. However, this hypothesis was never confirmed, and the Axis forces themselves occasionally reported similar sightings, suggesting that they, too, were unaware of the nature of these lights.

The Allied and Axis militaries undertook numerous investigations to identify and understand the Foo Fighters. Intelligence reports and scientific studies were commissioned to find possible explanations. Some of these reports suggested that the lights might be attributable to natural phenomena such as electrical storms, ball lightning, or atmospheric reflections.

Other theories assumed that these were psychological effects caused by the extreme tension and fatigue of the pilots in the war zone.
Another hypothesis suggested that the Foo Fighters may have been the result of technical malfunctions or optical illusions caused by the new radar and navigation systems that were widely used during the war. Despite these numerous theories, no definitive explanation for the Foo Fighters has been found.

After the war, the sightings and reports of the Foo Fighters remained an unsolved mystery. They became a popular topic in UFO research, fueling speculation about extraterrestrial visits and secret military technologies. In the 1950s and 1960s, as interest in UFOs and extraterrestrial life grew worldwide, the Foo Fighters were often linked to other famous UFO sightings and encounters.

Today, the Foo Fighters are an example of unexplained wartime phenomena. They demonstrate how little we sometimes know about the nature and causes of certain phenomena and how such mysteries can capture the human imagination.

The Foo Fighters remain an important part of military and historical research, reminding us that there are still many mysteries in the world waiting to be solved.

8.4 The "Black Knight" satellites

The legend of the "Black Knight" satellites is a mysterious chapter in the history of modern space exploration. These mysterious objects, which have supposedly orbited Earth for centuries, have given rise to numerous speculations and theories, ranging from scientific explanations to extraterrestrial origins.

The story began in the 1950s, when the U.S. Army and the private company RCA (Radio Corporation of America) reportedly received strange radio signals during the first space expeditions. These signals appeared to be coming from an unknown object orbiting the Earth in a polar orbit.

Such an orbit was not used by either the Soviet Union or the United States at the time, which led to immediate speculation.

In the decades that followed, various alleged sightings and radar observations of the "Black Knight" satellite were reported. In 1960, the US military discovered an unknown object in orbit that was not among the known satellites of the superpowers.

The astronauts of the Apollo missions are also said to have seen the object and described it as an "unidentifiable flying object."

A particularly well-known photo of the alleged "Black Knight" satellite dates back to 1998, when the Space Shuttle Endeavour photographed a mysterious object in orbit during mission STS-88. The image shows a dark, irregularly shaped object that has since been the subject of intense discussion and analysis.

Theories about the origin of the "Black Knight" satellite are varied. Some believe it is an alien spacecraft that has been observing Earth for thousands of years. Others suspect it was a secret military project of the United States or the Soviet Union that was never officially recognized.
Still others believe it's space debris, possibly a lost piece of a previous satellite or a rocket stage cover. Despite numerous investigations and analyses, there is still no definitive explanation for the "Black Knight" satellite. Official explanations, identifying the object as space debris or a thermal blanket from a satellite launch, have failed to convince UFO enthusiasts and conspiracy theorists.

8.5 The unidentified flying objects over Belgium

In the late 1980s and early 1990s, Belgium became the scene of one of the most famous and well-documented UFO sightings in history. This series of events, known as the "Belgian UFO Wave," began in November 1989 and continued into the early 1990s, with hundreds of eyewitnesses, including police officers, military personnel, and civilians, reporting strange flying objects in the sky.

The first significant sighting occurred on November 29, 1989, when two police officers from Eupen, a town near the German border, observed a large, dark, triangular-shaped flying object with bright lights hovering silently over the countryside. The officers' description was detailed: a flat, triangular object with three large, white lights at the corners and a red light in the center.

In the following months and years, numerous other eyewitnesses reported similar objects. These reports came from various parts of the country and often described large, triangular flying objects moving silently and with a speed and maneuverability far beyond what could be expected from known aircraft.

The phenomenon reached its peak on the night of March 30-31, 1990, when the Belgian military decided to deploy two F-16 fighter jets to intercept the unidentified flying objects detected on radar. The F-16 pilots reported that the objects were moving in an unusual manner, reaching extreme speeds and abruptly changing direction—maneuvers that no known aircraft could have performed at that time.

Radar recordings from the Belgian Air Force confirmed the pilots' statements. The UFOs were detected by various radar systems, and the data showed that they were capable of accelerating from a stationary state to very high speeds within seconds and suddenly changing direction. These maneuvers were so extraordinary that they attracted considerable attention and speculation.

Another notable element of the Belgian UFO wave was a photograph of a triangular UFO taken by an anonymous photographer. This image was circulated worldwide and is still considered one of the best visual evidences of UFO sightings. Despite numerous analyses and investigations, the authenticity of the photo has never been completely refuted.

The Belgian government and the Air Force took the incidents seriously and worked closely with civilian UFO researchers and scientists to investigate the events. However, a comprehensive explanation was never found. While some skeptics suggested that the sightings could have been due to military tests or secret aircraft, these hypotheses were never confirmed.

The "Belgian UFO Wave" remains one of the best-documented and most intensively studied UFO phenomena in history. It has had a lasting impact on public perceptions of UFOs and remains a fascinating mystery.

8.6 The unidentified flying objects over Phoenix

On the evening of March 13, 1997, one of the most famous and widely documented UFO events in modern history occurred in Phoenix, Arizona. Thousands of people reported sightings of massive, unidentified flying objects in the sky, now known as the "Phoenix Lights." These sightings sparked a wave of speculation, investigation, and controversy that continues to this day.

The events began around 7:30 p.m. local time, when residents in the city of Henderson, Nevada, reported a large, V-shaped object in the sky, silently and slowly moving southeast. Throughout the evening, sightings spread across hundreds of kilometers, from Nevada through Arizona to northern Mexico.

Witnesses' descriptions were remarkably consistent: a large, wedge-shaped or V-shaped object with several bright lights on the bottom, seemingly gliding silently through the air.
The sightings in and around Phoenix were particularly spectacular. Around 8:00 p.m., many residents of the city reported seeing a huge, triangular object so large it appeared to obscure the sky. It moved slowly and majestically over the city before disappearing to the south. Witnesses described the object as dark and massive, with five to seven bright lights along its leading edge. Some also reported a faint, buzzing sound accompanying it.

These sightings were documented by a wide range of people, including police officers, pilots, and military personnel. Many witnesses took photos and videos of the lights, which were later analyzed in detail. The images showed a series of bright lights moving across the sky in a V formation, contributing to the credibility of the reports.

The official reaction to the "Phoenix Lights" was initially hesitant. The military and government made only sparse statements and appeared to have little interest in a comprehensive investigation. A few days after the sightings, the military stated that the lights were the result of training flights and flares dropped by A-10 fighter jets of the Arizona Air National Guard during an exercise over the Barry Goldwater Range. However, this explanation was considered inadequate and contradictory by many witnesses and UFO researchers.

The "Phoenix Lights" sparked intense debate and raised many questions. Why were the lights visible in the sky for so long? Why did they move so synchronously and silently? Why was there no official statement or investigation that comprehensively explained all the observations and reports? These questions remain largely unanswered to this day.

In 2007, a decade after the original events, Fife Symington, then-Governor of Arizona, publicly admitted that he too had seen the lights and could not identify them. He described the object as "eerie" and "otherworldly," further fueling speculation.

8.7. The unidentified flying objects over Nellis Air Force Base

Nellis Air Force Base in Nevada, one of the most famous and best-secured military installations in the United States, has been a center for air force exercises and test flights for decades. But in addition to its official activities, the base has also been the scene of numerous UFO sightings that continue to puzzle and fuel speculation. Particularly noteworthy are the sightings of unidentified flying objects that caused a sensation in the 1990s.

One of the most famous sightings over Nellis Air Force Base occurred in 1994. A video taken from the base itself shows an unidentified flying object moving at high speed and with remarkable maneuverability.

The video, which was later released to the public, was recorded by the base's air traffic control systems and shows an object flying in a manner that far exceeded the known capabilities of the aircraft at the time.
The object seen in the video displays no recognizable shape consistent with known aircraft. It exhibits sudden changes in direction and accelerations that no known propulsion technologies can explain. The operators at the base monitoring the object expressed visibly surprised and perplexed about the nature and origin of the object in the video.
This sighting wasn't the only one of its kind. In the 1990s, there were several reports of unidentified flying objects near Nellis Air Force Base. These objects were sighted by both military personnel and civilians. They often described luminous, fast-moving objects that seemingly defied the laws of physics.

The military's response to these sightings was reserved. Officials did not issue comprehensive statements and often avoided public comment on the reports. This attitude contributed to the emergence of numerous conspiracy theories and speculation. Some believe the sightings could be connected to secret military projects or experimental aircraft being tested at Nellis Air Force Base. Others suspect extraterrestrial origins and view the sightings as evidence of visits from advanced extraterrestrial civilizations.

Some UFO researchers and enthusiasts suspect that Nellis Air Force Base and the nearby Area 51 are centers for the research and testing of extraterrestrial technology. They argue that the unidentified flying objects may be alien spacecraft or prototypes based on extraterrestrial technology being studied and replicated by the U.S. government.

Despite numerous theories and speculations, the truth about the unidentified flying objects over Nellis Air Force Base remains a mystery. Official documents and detailed explanations are rare, and many questions remain unanswered. What these objects were, where they came from, and why they appeared over one of the most well-protected military bases in the world remains unknown.

8.8. The mysterious "Starchild Skull"

The discovery of the so-called "Starchild Skull" has puzzled and sparked controversy since its discovery in the 1930s. This unusual skull, found in a remote region of Mexico, differs significantly from normal human skulls in several aspects and has fueled speculation about its origin and nature.

The skull was discovered by an American teenager traveling in Mexico. He found it in a cave along with another normal human skull. The "Starchild Skull" was named because of its unusual features and speculation that it might not be fully human.

Unusual features of the Starchild Skull:
Shape and structure: The Starchild Skull has an unusually large, rounded shape with flat cheekbones and a greatly enlarged braincase. The skullcap is much thinner and lighter than that of a normal human skull, yet extremely strong.

Eye sockets: The eye sockets of the skull are flatter and wider than those of humans, giving the impression that the individual's eyes were much larger.

Bone structure: The composition of the bone indicates unusually high amounts of collagen, which makes the skull both light and strong. Studies have shown that the density and structure of the bone fibers deviate from the human norm.

Genetic anomalies: DNA analyses of the skull were performed multiple times to determine its origin. Initial tests revealed that the mitochondrial DNA material on the maternal side was human. However, later, more detailed analyses of the nuclear DNA material indicated significant differences, indicating a mixture of human and possibly non-human traits.

Theories and speculations:
*Genetic mutation or deformation:*Some scientists and skeptics believe the skull is the result of a genetic mutation or a congenital deformity. Conditions such as hydrocephalus or other rare diseases could explain the skull's unusual features.

*Hybridtheorie:*A popular but controversial theory claims that the "Starchild Skull" is the result of cross-breeding between a human and another, non-human species. Proponents of this theory point to the skull's genetic abnormalities and unusual physical properties as evidence.

Extraterrestrial origins: Another speculation, especially popular in UFO and extraterrestrial circles, is the hypothesis that the "Starchild Skull" belonged to an extraterrestrial being. The unusual features and unusual bone structure are interpreted as evidence of extraterrestrial origin.

The Starchild Skull has undergone numerous scientific examinations, including genetic testing, X-ray and CT scans, and microscopic analysis.

Despite numerous studies, the exact nature and origin of the skull remains unclear. The scientific community remains divided, with some researchers calling for further investigation and others viewing the case as an example of unusual but natural genetic variation.

8.9 The strange stories of alien abductions

Alien abduction stories are a frequently discussed and disturbing phenomenon that has made headlines around the world in recent decades. These accounts tell of people claiming to have been taken, examined, and sometimes altered by extraterrestrial beings against their will. These strange stories have sparked numerous theories and debates and remain a mysterious topic in modern culture and ufology.

Although the phenomenon of alien abductions only gained wider attention in the 20th century, there are reports of similar experiences dating back far into the past. These early stories were often placed in a religious or mythical context in which people were "abducted" by gods or supernatural beings.

However, the modern discourse on alien abductions began in the 1950s and 1960s, when the first documented cases became known in the United States.

Famous cases of alien abduction

Betty and Barney Hill (1961): One of the most famous cases is that of Betty and Barney Hill, a married couple from New Hampshire. They claimed to have been followed by a UFO during a nighttime car ride and eventually abducted aboard the spacecraft. Under hypnosis, they reported medical examinations and strange beings examining them. Their case is considered the first well-documented report of alien abduction and has been widely investigated and discussed..

Travis Walton (1975): Another famous case is that of Travis Walton, a forestry worker from Arizona. Walton claimed to have been abducted by a UFO after being struck by a beam of light. He was found five days later and, under hypnosis, was able to recall detailed examinations by extraterrestrial beings. His story was featured in the book "The Walton Experience" and the film "Fire in the Sky."

Whitley Strieber (1985): In his book "Communion," author Whitley Strieber reported repeated abductions by extraterrestrial beings. His detailed descriptions and the emotional depth of his accounts made his book a bestseller and sparked widespread debate about the phenomenon.

Many alien abduction reports share similar characteristics, leading to the hypothesis that it may be a real and recurring phenomenon. The most common characteristics include:

Loss of time: Abducted individuals often report having "disappeared" for a certain period of time and having no memory of that period. This "missing time" is sometimes restored through hypnosis sessions.

Medical examinations: Many abductees report undergoing medical examinations aboard UFOs. These examinations often include physical tests, taking tissue samples, and inserting devices into the body.

Communication with extraterrestrials: Some abductees report having contact with the extraterrestrial beings through telepathy or another form of non-verbal communication. These beings are often described as humanoid, but with significant differences, such as large heads and almond-shaped eyes.

Return to the place of origin: After abduction, most people are returned to the place from which they were abducted. They often have no immediate memory of the events, only vague feelings or nightmares.

Reports of alien abductions have given rise to a variety of theories and attempts at explanation:

*Psychological explanations:*Some psychologists and researchers suspect that abduction reports may be based on psychological phenomena such as sleep paralysis, false memories, or hallucinations. Traumatic experiences may also play a role, as the brain processes them in the form of abduction experiences.

*Cultural phenomena:*Another theory is that reports of alien abductions are the result of mass hysteria or cultural conditioning. The widespread prevalence of science fiction and media reports about UFOs may mislead people into interpreting their own experiences in a similar way.
Of course, there are also those who believe the reports are true and that extraterrestrial beings are indeed abducting and studying humans. This theory is supported by the ufology community, which continues to search for evidence of extraterrestrial life.

The strange stories of alien abductions remain a mysterious and controversial topic. Despite numerous reports and investigations, there is no definitive evidence for the existence of alien abductions.

8.10 Japan Airlines Flight 1628

On November 17, 1986, the crew of Japan Airlines Flight 1628 experienced a remarkable and still controversial event that received considerable attention in the history of aviation and UFO research.

The flight, a regular cargo service, departed from Paris and was en route to Anchorage, Alaska, with a cargo of French wine. The aircraft, a Boeing 747-200F, was piloted by Captain Kenju Terauchi, an experienced pilot with over 10,000 flight hours. He was joined on board by co-pilot Takanori Tamefuji and flight engineer Yoshio Tsukuba.

At approximately 5:11 p.m., while the aircraft was crossing the icy, clear skies over Alaska, Captain Terauchi suddenly noticed unusual lights in the sky. He reported that these lights initially appeared to be two small airplanes flying near the aircraft at high speed. The lights were maneuvering in a manner that alarmed the experienced pilot. They changed position abruptly and appeared to have intelligent control.

These strange objects remained near the aircraft for about 10 minutes before suddenly moving in front of the Boeing 747. At that moment, the entire crew witnessed a spectacular spectacle: A huge, cylindrical object, about twice the size of an aircraft carrier, appeared and appeared to be escorting the aircraft. Captain Terauchi described the object as metallic and equipped with rows of flashing lights.

Terauchi reported the incident to ground control in Anchorage. Air traffic controllers confirmed that they saw the objects on radar. Initially, the objects appeared to be present, then suddenly disappeared from the radar screens. Ground control asked a nearby military aircraft to confirm the sighting, but it was unable to report any visual contact.

During this unusual incident, Captain Terauchi attempted to elude his aircraft through various maneuvers, but the unknown object remained nearby, following the Boeing 747. Finally, after about 50 minutes, the objects disappeared as suddenly as they had appeared. The rest of the flight to Anchorage passed without further incident, and the aircraft landed safely.

The events of this flight were later investigated by the Federal Aviation Administration (FAA). Captain Terauchi was interviewed repeatedly and maintained his detailed description of the incidents. He even drew sketches of the objects observed. Despite his credibility and the confirmation of the radar observations, the case remained unsolved and was ultimately classified as "unidentified."

JAPAN AIRLINES FLUG 1628

This encounter sparked worldwide interest and speculation. UFO researchers considered it one of the most convincing cases of UFO sightings, while skeptics pointed to the possibility of optical illusions or natural phenomena. Regardless of the final explanation, the sighting of Japan Airlines Flight 1628 remains a curious chapter in the history of aviation and the exploration of the unknown.

To this day, it remains one of the best documented and most questioned cases in the history of UFO sightings.

8.11. The Encounter at Ariel School

The Ariel School encounter, which occurred on September 13, 1994, is another example of remarkable and best-documented events in the history of UFO sightings.

The encounter took place in Ruwa, a rural area about 20 kilometers southeast of the Zimbabwean capital, Harare. That morning, during recess, 62 students aged 6 to 12 experienced something that would change their lives forever.

It was an ordinary school day at Ariel School, a private school attended by children of diverse ethnic backgrounds. The students were playing in the playground when suddenly a bright light appeared in the sky.

At first, some children thought it was a meteor or an airplane. But the light moved in a way they had never seen before. It seemed to float and abruptly change direction.
The students watched as the light approached and finally landed in a bush about 100 meters from the school grounds. A round, metallic object hovered above the ground, and from it emerged two small beings, about one meter tall. The beings had large, black, almond-shaped eyes, slender bodies, and wore shiny silver suits.

The children stood frozen, watching the scenes unfolding before their eyes. Some of the older students tried to calm the younger ones.

The beings didn't appear to pose a threat, but communicated in a non-verbal manner that the children described as a kind of telepathic message. They spoke of feelings and impressions sent into their minds, particularly about the need to protect the environment and be wary of the dangers of technological progress.

The encounter lasted about 10 to 15 minutes before the beings returned to their vehicle, which shot into the sky at high speed. The students ran to the teachers to report their experiences. The teachers, initially skeptical, were soon convinced when they noticed the sincerity in the children's reports.

None of the children deviated from their story, and all described the events and creatures in a similar way.

In the following days, the school was visited by researchers and media representatives.

Dr. John E. Mack, a renowned psychiatrist and Harvard professor, studied the children's reports in depth.

He conducted numerous interviews and found that the children showed no signs of delusion or hallucinations.

The children's reports were not only detailed but also consistent, meaning that the descriptions largely agreed.

They had no previous experience or knowledge of UFOs or extraterrestrial beings.
The Ariel School encounter is a mystery. There is no clear explanation for what the children saw and experienced. The students' detailed and consistent accounts, coupled with the skeptics' inability to provide a convincing alternative explanation, make this event a well-documented UFO sighting.

To this day, many of the students from that time, now adults, talk about the encounter and cling to their stories. The Ariel School encounter remains a remarkable example of a collective UFO sighting and continues to raise questions about the nature of such phenomena and the possibility of extraterrestrial life.

8.12. The USS Nimitz Encounter (2004) / Tic-Tac Event

The USS Nimitz encounter in 2004 is a well-documented UFO sighting of modern times.

This incident, which gained worldwide attention through the release of Pentagon videos, raises significant questions about the nature and origin of unidentified flying objects.

In November 2004, the USS Nimitz Carrier Strike Group was operating about 100 miles southwest of San Diego, California, on a routine training exercise.

The strike group consisted of the USS Nimitz, a nuclear-powered aircraft carrier, and several escort ships, including the guided-missile cruiser USS Princeton.

During the exercises, the USS Princeton's radar systems began detecting unidentified flying objects performing unusual flight maneuvers.

These unidentified flying objects, described by the crews as "Tic Tacs" due to their shape, moved at astonishing speeds and seemed to defy the laws of physics. The objects were first detected at an altitude of 80,000 feet (about 24,000 meters) before descending to sea level in an extremely rapid dive and then abruptly stopping.

On November 14, 2004, two Boeing F/A-18F Super Hornet fighter aircraft, piloted by Commander David Fravor and Lieutenant Commander Jim Slaight, were dispatched from the USS Nimitz to identify the objects.

Upon approaching the unidentified flying objects, Commander Fravor reported that one of the objects was moving directly toward him. He described the object as approximately 40 feet (12 meters) long, with no visible wings or propulsion jets, and moving rapidly and unpredictably.

Commander Fravor tried to move toward the object, but it evaded his movements.
The object then suddenly accelerated and disappeared from view within seconds.

The F/A-18F Super Hornets returned to the USS Nimitz, and another team of fighter jets, equipped with more advanced infrared sensors, was dispatched to further investigate the phenomenon. This second encounter was recorded by the aircraft's infrared sensors and later released as one of the famous Pentagon videos.

These videos, known as FLIR1 (Forward Looking Infrared), show the "Tic Tac" object moving at high speed, seemingly without any means of propulsion or visible wings.

The radar data from the USS Princeton and the visual confirmation from the pilots of the F/A-18F Super Hornets agreed, making the USS Nimitz encounter a well-documented UFO incident.

After the aircraft returned and the collected data was analyzed, the reports and videos were forwarded to the Pentagon. The incident became part of a comprehensive investigation by the Advanced Aerospace Threat Identification Program (AATIP), a secret Pentagon program established in 2007 to investigate UFO sightings and other unidentified aerial phenomena.

In 2017, the "FLIR1" videos were published along with other UFO videos by the New York Times and the To The Stars Academy of Arts & Science, sparking worldwide attention and renewed discussion about the existence of UFOs and their possible extraterrestrial origins. These publications led to official confirmation by the Pentagon that the videos are authentic and that the phenomena they depict remain unexplained.

The extraordinary maneuvers performed by the "Tic Tac" objects and the extensive documentation of the incident by military radar and camera systems make this case a crucial point in the debate about UFOs and their possible origins. To this day, the question remains unanswered as to what exactly the crew of the USS Nimitz and the pilots of the F/A-18F Super Hornets saw in November 2004.

8.13 The USS Omaha Encounter (2019)

The USS Omaha's encounter with unidentified flying objects in July 2019 is another notable recent event in modern UFO research.

This incident attracted widespread attention when video footage and military reports were released showing a mysterious object disappearing into the Pacific Ocean.

In July 2019, the USS Omaha, a U.S. Navy Independence-class littoral combat ship, operated off the coast of California in international waters. The USS Omaha is known for its advanced radar systems and its ability to monitor and engage a wide range of threats.

During a routine surveillance mission, the crew members suddenly spotted an unidentified flying object moving unusually fast and maneuverably through the airspace.

The object was detected and tracked by the USS Omaha's advanced radar systems. The crew determined that the object had no discernible wings or known propulsion systems, which are typically found on aircraft.

The unidentified object moved at high speed and performed maneuvers that were beyond its known technological capabilities.

One of the most remarkable features of the object's maneuvers was its abrupt changes of direction. The object altered its trajectory at extreme angles and appeared to show no signs of inertia or drag, which one would expect from traditional aircraft.
These maneuvers would place enormous structural stresses on conventional aircraft, which they would likely not be able to withstand.

The object underwent rapid and significant altitude changes. It was first sighted at high altitude, but then quickly descended to sea level. These altitude changes were performed in a very short time and demonstrated maneuverability far beyond the capabilities of known aircraft. Such rapid altitude changes would result in massive G-forces in conventional aircraft, which would be dangerous to the aircraft's structure and occupants.

The most extraordinary phase of the encounter occurred as the object approached the water surface.

Before submerging, the object hovered briefly above the water's surface. This ability to stop and hover at high speed suggests a type of propulsion system currently unknown to us. The object's stability and control during hovering were remarkable.

The object submerged itself seamlessly into the water, without any sign of resistance or deceleration. This is particularly remarkable, as the transition from air to water would result in significant damage or destruction to known flying vehicles. The ability to submerge and potentially operate underwater suggests a technology that functions both in the air and underwater.

This behavior, captured in the released video footage, suggests that the object may have been able to operate both in the air and underwater, making it a so-called USO (Unidentified Submerged Object).
The object disappeared into the ocean without leaving any trace or signs of wreckage or crash.

The US Navy released video footage in May 2021 showing the spherical object moving at high speed and submerging in the water.

The images were taken by the crew of the USS Omaha using a FLIR (Forward Looking Infrared) camera system that records thermal images.

The videos and associated radar data support the crew's reports of the object's extraordinary flight and diving maneuvers.

Following the encounter, the US Navy launched an investigation to determine the nature and origin of the object. The Navy confirmed the authenticity of the video footage and classified the phenomenon as "unidentified."

This classification means that the observations and collected data do not allow for a conventional explanation. The phenomenon remains unexplained because it does not fit into the familiar categories of aircraft, drones, or natural phenomena.

The release of the videos and the confirmation by the US Navy have revived the discussion about UFOs and USOs. The US Department of Defense has emphasized that it continues to seriously investigate unidentified aerial phenomena to identify potential threats to national security.

8.14 The Rendlesham Forest Event: the British Roswell

It was the night after Christmas 1980 when something happened in Rendlesham Forest in the English county of Suffolk that remains one of Europe's most mysterious stories. The winter air was bitterly cold, wisps of fog hung over the fields, and the forests surrounding the American air bases of Woodbridge and Bentwaters were silent. There, in the midst of the Cold War, nuclear weapons were stored in top secret, even though they officially didn't exist. Any irregularity could pose a security threat, and so the guards were especially vigilant. In this tense atmosphere, guards suddenly reported unusual lights flashing between the trees.

At first, it was thought that a crashed plane had crashed. Three men were dispatched to investigate. Equipped with flashlights and radios, they made their way through the dense undergrowth. They expected to find smoke, debris, and perhaps injured pilots, but instead they encountered something that defied rational explanation. Hovering between the trees was a bright object, triangular in shape, barely larger than a small car, with a metallic-looking surface that glowed in the changing light. A red light blinked at its tip, and bluish rays flickered at its sides. One of the men, Sergeant Jim Penniston, later reported getting so close he touched the surface. He saw symbols on it that reminded him of hieroglyphs and felt a surge of energy run through his hand. Seconds or minutes passed before the object rose silently and disappeared among the treetops. When the soldiers returned to the site, they found three circular impressions in the ground, arranged symmetrically, as if something heavy had been standing there.

The story could have ended there, but two nights later there were further sightings. This time the base's deputy commander, Lieutenant Colonel Charles Halt, was himself with a group of men to check out what was happening. He carried a tape recorder, and the recordings, later known as the "Halt tape," have survived to this day. In the darkness, you can hear the men's voices excitedly reporting on lights flashing between the trees, moving, and suddenly disintegrating into several objects. At one point, Halt describes how a red light sends a beam downwards to the ground. His voice sounds controlled, but you can hear the tension in every word. At the same time, the measuring devices near the prints registered slightly elevated radiation levels, higher than in the surrounding area.

These recordings made the incident unique, as such direct documentation of a military incident was rare. While many UFO stories are based on vague memories, this is a contemporaneous recording from a high-ranking officer. Combined with the accounts of several witnesses, the imprints in the ground, and the measurements, a picture emerged that many people found difficult to argue away.

But of course, there were attempts to find a rational explanation. Skeptics pointed to the Orford Ness lighthouse, located a few kilometers away. Its powerful light rotated at intervals and, through the forest, could create the impression that a bright object was floating among the trees. Bright stars like Sirius, which were unusually prominent in the sky that winter night, could also have played a role. Atmospheric effects and the play of light and shadow were cited as explanations for other observations. Under stress, in icy darkness, and in an environment where any irregularity could be interpreted as a danger, misinterpretations were easily possible.

But these explanations didn't answer all the questions. What were the symmetrical marks in the ground about? Why did several men independently report seeing a triangular object in close proximity? And how should Penniston's account of touching the aircraft be assessed? Furthermore, the incident took place in a military context, where discipline and observation skills should be taken for granted.

The British Ministry of Defence later declared that the incident posed no threat to national security and closed the matter. However, in the 2000s, files were released showing that the events were indeed recorded and investigated, albeit without a clear conclusion. Critics suspected that the government downplayed the significance to avoid drawing attention to the fact that nuclear weapons were stored at the bases. For many observers, this behavior itself was suspect and reinforced suspicions that there was more to the story than was officially admitted.

In the years following the incident, Rendlesham became a focal point in UFO literature. Books, documentaries, and articles took up the story; witnesses gave interviews, some of whom stuck to their stories well into old age. Others later qualified their memories or explained that they themselves were unsettled by the situation. For the Rendlesham region, the event became part of the local identity. Today, a hiking trail, the "UFO Trail," leads visitors to the sites where the sightings allegedly occurred. What was once a restricted military area is now a tourist attraction.

The Rendlesham event differs from many other UFO sightings in its diversity of elements. There are not just vague eyewitness accounts, but an entire chain of observations spanning several nights. There are ground impressions, measurements, tape recordings, and official reports. All of this together creates a picture that has never been fully resolved. For skeptics, it remains a case of optical illusions, nervousness, and group dynamics. For believers, it is one of the best pieces of evidence that Earth has received a visit from space. For historians, in turn, it is a reflection of its time, an event in the shadow of the Cold War that encapsulates the fears, secrets, and longings of that era.

Today, decades later, the case remains unsolved. No one has been able to prove conclusively that extraterrestrial visitors landed in Rendlesham Forest. But equally, not all the details have been conclusively explained. And that's precisely what makes it so fascinating: The story remains open, sufficiently documented to be taken seriously, yet mysterious enough to defy any definitive interpretation. So it lives on, in books, television programs, and in the stories of those who were there at the time.

So it's no wonder that the event is still called the "British Roswell." Not because it provided definitive proof of extraterrestrial life, but because it defies simple explanation and thus remains mystical.

Chapter 9: Other Curiosities

This chapter is a loose collection of other curiosities that did not fit into any of the previous chapters, but still deserve to be included in this work.

9.1 The Voynich Manuscript

The Voynich Manuscript is one of the most intensively studied manuscripts in the world. This medieval book, named after its discoverer, Wilfrid Voynich, has been an unsolvable mystery for historians, linguists, and cryptographers alike since its rediscovery in 1912.

The manuscript, dated to the late 15th or early 16th century, consists of approximately 240 pages filled with an unknown script and strange illustrations. The text is written in a still-undeciphered language or code that cannot be found in any other known script or language. Despite numerous attempts, the text of the Voynich Manuscript has not yet been read or translated, leading to a variety of theories about its origin and purpose.

The illustrations in the manuscript are as enigmatic as the text. They depict strange plants not found in any botanical collection, mysterious figures in baths and pools, astrological diagrams, and strange apparatus. These images have led to speculation that the manuscript could be an alchemical, astrological, or medical work, possibly with occult or esoteric content.

There are several main theories about the origin and purpose of the Voynich Manuscript:
A coded scientific or medical work: Some researchers believe the manuscript is an encrypted manual on medical or scientific topics. The strange plants and diagrams could contain references to remedies, medical procedures, or scientific experiments.

A complex forgery: Another theory is that the manuscript is a deliberate forgery created in the Middle Ages to impress or deceive a wealthy patron. However, this theory has been challenged by the elaborate and detailed illustrations and systematic text.

An incomprehensible work of art or a fantasy language: Some experts speculate that the manuscript is the work of a brilliant artist or writer who created a fantasy language and imaginary plants and scenes. This theory is supported by the unusual and creative illustrations.

An esoteric or occult book: Due to the mysterious nature of the manuscript and its often strange illustrations, some believe it to be an occult or esoteric work containing secret knowledge or rituals understandable only to initiates.

Despite numerous theories, the Voynich Manuscript remains an unsolved mystery. Modern techniques such as computer analysis and artificial intelligence have been applied to decipher the text, but so far without success. The manuscript's secrets remain hidden, and it remains unclear whether they will ever be fully revealed.
The Voynich Manuscript is now housed in the Yale University Library and continues to attract the attention of researchers and enthusiasts.

9.2. The "Kryptos" artwork at CIA headquarters

At the heart of CIA headquarters in Langley, Virginia, stands a work of art that has puzzled cryptologists, amateur codebreakers, and intelligence officers alike since its unveiling in 1990. This work of art, known as "Kryptos," is a sculpture by American artist Jim Sanborn consisting of four encrypted messages engraved on a large, coiled copper plate.

"Kryptos" was designed with the specific purpose of being a mysterious puzzle waiting to be solved. The name "Kryptos" comes from the Greek word for "hidden" or "secret." Since the sculpture's installation, many have attempted to decipher the encrypted texts, with three of the four sections successfully cracked over the years. The fourth section, considered the most difficult puzzle, remains unsolved to this day.

The first three sections of the "Kryptos" sculpture reveal mysterious messages when deciphered:

First section: The first section was deciphered in 1999 by a team led by computer scientist Jim Gillogly. The text contained a cryptic message about the slow revelation of secrets:

Original:
„EMUFPHZLRFAXYUSDJKZLDKRNSHGNFIVJYQTQUXQBQVYUVLLTREVJYQTMKYRDMFD"

When decoded, this results in the sentence:

" Between subtle shading and the absence of light lies the nuance of illusion.

The second section is considerably longer and reads like a mini-spy novel. It is encoded on the record:

Original:
„VFPJUDEEHZWETZYVGWHKKQETGFQJNCEGGWHKK?DQMCPF QZDQMMIAGPFXHQRLG TIMVMZJANQLVKQEDAGDVFRPJUNGEUNAQZGZLECGYUXUEE NJTBJLBQCRTBJDFHRR YIZETKZEMVDUFKSJHKFWHKUWQLSZFTIHHDDDUVH?DWKBFU FPWNTDFIYCUQZEREEV LDKFEZMOQQJLTTUGSYQFPEUNLAVIDXFLGGTEZ?FKZBSFDQV GOGIPUFXHHDRKF

FHQNTGPUAECNUVPDJMQCLQUMUNEDFQELZZVRRGKFFVOEE
XBDMVPNFQXEZLGRE
DNQFMPNZGLFLPMRJQYALMGNUVPDXVKPQNVEENQHTTMTMZ
FPKWGDKZXTJCDIGKUH
UAUEKCAR"

When decoded, this results in the message:
"It was totally invisible. How's that possible? They used the Earth's magnetic field.
The information was gathered and transmitted underground to an unknown location.
Does Langley know about this? They should. It's buried out there somewhere. Who knows the exact location? Only W.W. This was his last message. 38°57'6.5"N 77°8'44"W.

The third section, solved in 1999, contains a passage that makes a reference to Howard Carter and the discovery of Tutankhamun's tomb:

Original:
„ENDYAHROHNLSRHEOCPTEOIBIDYSHNAIACHTINCHSALEEYTK
LUQET
TETWZDQCEWKVKUIRALBNYRENMNEAQCWDNHUPVRIBIXMML
E
WEDXWGJCVVGIYGEPNFFMEKVIJNUCVUVUVMQNANQMNEQY
QQTTREYWEIFGS"

When decoded, this results in the message:

"Slowly, desperately slowly, the rubble blocking the lower part of the passage was removed. With trembling hands, I made a small opening, inserted a candle, and peered inside. The hot air caused the flame to flicker, but gradually details of the room emerged from the fog. – 'Can you see anything?' – 'Yes, wonderful things.'"

The fourth section of "Kryptos" remains the ultimate mystery. Despite intensive efforts by professional cryptologists and amateur codebreakers, this part of the text has not yet been deciphered.
The fourth section contains only 97 characters. It reads:

OBKRUOXOGHULBSOLIFBBWFLRVQQPRNGKSSOTWTQSJQSSEKZ
ZWATJKLUDIAWINFBNYP
VTTMZFPKWGDKZXTJCDIGKUHUAUEKCAR

Despite intensive efforts by amateur cryptologists, mathematicians, the NSA, and even CIA employees, the solution remains unknown. However, artist Jim Sanborn has offered three clues:

- The sequence of letters **"NYPVTT"** In plain text the word „**BERLIN**".
- He later revealed that the words „**CLOCK**" ("clock") and „**NORTHEAST**" ("Northeast") are included in the text.

But what do these words mean? Is it a location in Berlin? A time or a date? Or perhaps a reference to a physical hiding place somewhere on the CIA's premises? Some suspect that Sanborn intentionally incorporated a double encryption, making the puzzle extremely difficult, perhaps even unsolvable.

Three parts have been solved, one part remains hidden – and that's precisely what makes Kryptos so exciting. It's a work of art that simultaneously represents an eternal mystery. The fact that it stands on the premises of the world's most powerful secret service makes it even more intriguing.
Jim Sanborn himself once said, "There is no art without mystery." And so, to this day, Kryptos remains a monument to the power of encryption—and a silent reminder that even the CIA cannot reveal every secret.

9.3 The Lost City of Atlantis

The legend of Atlantis, a highly developed and powerful city that supposedly sank beneath the sea thousands of years ago, has captured the imagination of humans since ancient times. This mystical city is first mentioned in the writings of the Greek philosopher Plato, who describes Atlantis as a utopian island destroyed by a natural disaster within a single day and night.

The story of Atlantis is one of the most famous and controversial legends in world history and has inspired generations of explorers and adventurers to search for its lost location.

Plato's story
Plato described Atlantis in two of his dialogues, "Timaeus" and "Critias," written around 360 BC. According to Plato, Atlantis lay beyond the "Pillars of Heracles" (now known as the Strait of Gibraltar) and was larger than Libya and Asia combined. The island was a center of wealth, culture, and advanced technology, and was ruled by a powerful king. However, because of its greed and corruption, Atlantis fell out of favor with the gods, who eventually destroyed the island with an earthquake and catastrophic flood.

Theories and speculations
Since Plato's time, numerous theories about the location and existence of Atlantis have circulated. Here are some of the most prominent:

Santorin (Thera): One of the most widely discussed theories is that Atlantis was actually the Minoan island of Santorini (Thera), destroyed by a massive volcanic eruption around 1600 BC. The Minoans were a highly advanced civilization, and the destruction of Santorini may have formed the basis for the legend of Atlantis.

Crete: Some researchers believe that the Minoan civilization on Crete, which was also affected by a volcanic eruption and subsequent tsunamis, was the inspiration for the Atlantis story.

The Azores: Another theory proposes that the Azores, an archipelago in the Atlantic, could be the remains of Atlantis. Supporters of this theory argue that the geographic location and underwater formations indicate a submerged landmass.

Andalusia: Some historians and archaeologists have proposed that Atlantis may have been located in what is now Andalusia, Spain. This theory is based on archaeological finds and ancient texts that indicate an advanced civilization in this area.

Antarctica: A less common theory suggests that Atlantis was located in present-day Antarctica, which may once have been ice-free. However, this hypothesis is controversial and rejected by most scientists.

Despite numerous expeditions and research, the exact location of Atlantis has not yet been determined. Modern scientific methods such as underwater archaeology and satellite imaging have made some interesting discoveries but have not provided conclusive evidence.

The story of Atlantis therefore remains in the realm of legend and myth.

9.4 The Story of the Flying Dutchman

The legend of the Flying Dutchman is one of the most famous and mysterious seafaring tales of all time. This eerie and mystical tale has inspired sailors, writers, and filmmakers for centuries. The story tells of a ghost ship cursed to sail the oceans forever, never calling at a port.

The legend of the Flying Dutchman has its origins in the 17th century, a time of intense maritime trade and dangerous voyages. There are several versions of the story, but the most common tells of a Dutch sea captain named Hendrik van der Decken, who encountered a severe storm while sailing from Amsterdam to the East Indies.

Despite his crew's desperate pleas to turn the ship around, the captain vowed that he would circumnavigate the stormy Cape Peninsula, even if it took him until the Day of Judgment. His blasphemy and defiance were subsequently punished by divine power, and he and his crew were condemned to sail the seas for eternity, never reaching port or finding rest.

Sightings of the Flying Dutchman
Since the legend was first mentioned, there have been numerous reports from sailors claiming to have seen the Flying Dutchman. These sightings are often accompanied by dark and eerie circumstances. The ghost ship is said to appear luminous or ghostly, often surrounded by an unnatural light. Eyewitnesses report seeing the ship suddenly appear, only to disappear just as suddenly.

One famous account comes from British King George V, who allegedly saw the ghost ship as a naval cadet in 1881. According to his diary entry, the Flying Dutchman appeared in the midst of a storm and then quickly disappeared. Other famous sailors and explorers have also documented similar sightings.

Cultural
The legend of the Flying Dutchman has found its way into literature, opera, and cinema. It has been taken up by writers such as Washington Irving, Edgar Allan Poe, and Frederick Marryat. Richard Wagner transformed the story into his famous opera "The Flying Dutchman," which premiered in 1843 and dramatically depicts the tragedy and fate of the cursed captain.
In the 20th and 21st centuries, the legend of the Flying Dutchman has continued to inspire pop culture, appearing in numerous films, television shows, and books, including the popular "Pirates of the Caribbean" film series, in which the ghost ship plays a central role.

As with many legends, there are rational attempts to explain the story of the Flying Dutchman. One possible explanation is the phenomenon of the Fata Morgana, a complex form of atmospheric refraction that can cause ships to appear floating or ghostly under certain conditions.

Other theories suggest that the legend may have originated from actual historical events in which ships and their crews mysteriously disappeared or were struck by storms and misfortunes. These events may have been embellished and mythologized over time.

9.5 The Nazca Lines

The Nazca Lines, a network of giant geoglyphs stretching across Peru's arid coastal plain, are one of the world's greatest archaeological mysteries.

These impressive line patterns, created by the Nazca culture some 1,500 to 2,000 years ago, fascinate scientists and visitors alike and raise numerous questions about their origin and purpose.
The Nazca Lines were first discovered in the 1920s by Peruvian archaeologists and later by pilots flying over the region.
The geoglyphs are only fully visible from the air, which significantly influenced their discovery and investigation.

These huge geoglyphs cover an area of about 500 square kilometers and include hundreds of figures, including lines, geometric patterns, and depictions of animals and plants.

The Nazca Lines were created by removing the top layer of dark pebbles, exposing the lighter soil beneath. This technique produced clear and lasting contrasts that have persisted over the centuries.

The geoglyphs vary greatly in size: some lines extend for several kilometers, while the animal and plant motifs, such as the famous hummingbird, spider, monkey, and whale, reach lengths of up to 300 meters. They are impressive in their size and precision.

The exact purpose of the Nazca Lines remains unknown, but there are several theories that attempt to explain their formation and use:

Astronomical calendar markers A popular theory is that the Nazca Lines served as astronomical markers or calendars. Some geoglyphs may have alignments to specific star constellations or solar and lunar events, which may have helped the Nazca determine agricultural cycles.

Ritual paths and ceremonies: Other researchers believe the lines were created for ritual or ceremonial purposes. The Nazca may have used the lines as sacred paths, walked during religious processions to honor their gods or to pray for fertility and rain.

Water sources and cultures: It is also thought that some geoglyphs indicate water sources or are associated with water worship rituals. In the arid desert, water was a vital resource, and the lines could represent a symbolic connection to underground water streams or springs.

Landmarks and area markers: A more pragmatic theory suggests that the Nazca Lines served as territorial markers or signposts that helped inhabitants orient themselves in the vast, flat landscape.

Modern technologies such as satellite images and drones have significantly advanced the study of the Nazca Lines. Archaeologists use these tools to discover new geoglyphs and conduct detailed analyses. Despite these advances, the mystery of the Nazca Lines remains largely unsolved.

The geoglyphs were declared a World Heritage Site by UNESCO in 1994.

9.6. The unidentified flares of Marfa

In the remote desert area near the town of Marfa in West Texas, mysterious luminous orbs known as the "Marfa Lights" or "Marfa Flares" have appeared in the night sky for over a century.

These unidentified flares have impressed researchers, tourists, and locals alike, spawning numerous theories and speculations.

The Marfa Lights usually appear on clear, dark nights east of Marfa, near the Chinati Mountains. Observers describe the lights as bright, floating spheres glowing in various colors—often white, yellow, red, or orange. The lights move in seemingly random paths, flickering, disappearing, and reappearing. Sometimes they appear to split or merge, and they can hover in the air or appear to hover just above the ground.

The first documented sightings of the Marfa Lights date back to the 1880s. Ranchers and settlers reported strange, unexplained lights on the horizon, which they often mistook for Apache campfires.

These early reports show that the lights existed long before the introduction of modern technology, which rules out some of the later attempts at explanation.

Several scientific teams and researchers have attempted to investigate and explain the Marfa Lights. Despite efforts to capture and analyze the phenomenon, the exact nature of the lights remains unclear. Some of the main theories include:

Atmospheric phenomena: A common theory is that the lights could be caused by atmospheric conditions such as temperature inversions or the refraction of light. These phenomena can bend and distort light from distant car headlights, streetlights, or other light sources, making them appear like floating lights.

Piezoelectric effect: Another theory suggests that the piezoelectric effect, in which certain crystals like quartz generate electricity under mechanical stress, could cause the lights. There are geological formations in the Marfa region that could promote such effects.

Bioluminescence: It has also been speculated that bioluminescent organisms, such as certain types of fungi or insects, could cause the lights. However, this theory is less popular because the intensity and behavior of the Marfa lights are not typical of known bioluminescent phenomena.

Exotic explanations: In addition to scientific explanations, there are also more exotic theories, ranging from extraterrestrial activity to secret military experiments. These theories are particularly popular in popular media and among UFO enthusiasts, but are not scientifically proven.

The Marfa Lights have become a tourist attraction. Every year, thousands of visitors travel to Marfa to see the mysterious lights with their own eyes. The city has even built a special observation deck that offers visitors an optimal view of the area where the lights most frequently appear.

The Marfa Lights phenomenon has also entered pop culture, with mentions in films, television shows, and books.

Despite numerous investigations, the exact nature and cause of the lights remains unclear, making them one of nature's great unsolved mysteries.

9.7. The metallic spheres of Klerksdorp

The Klerksdorp metallic spheres, discovered in a pyrophyllite mining area near the South African town of Klerksdorp, have caused a stir and controversy since their discovery in the 1970s. These small, perfectly formed objects raise questions about their origin and purpose and have spawned both scientific and speculative theories.

The Klerksdorp spheres are small, metallic objects measuring between 2.5 and 10 centimeters in diameter. They consist of a hard, almost perfectly round core surrounded by a narrow, disc-shaped rim or groove. The surface of the spheres is smooth and features parallel grooves or ridges, making the objects even more unusual.

The spheres were discovered in rock layers dated to approximately 2.8 billion years ago. This discovery caused a great stir, as the rock in which the spheres were embedded dates back to a time long before the emergence of human life on Earth.

Initial investigations revealed that the spheres were made of an unknown metallic material with high hardness and density. These properties made them difficult to cut through or analyze, leading to further speculation about their origin.

Scientists have proposed several theories about the formation and origin of the Klerksdorp spheres:

Natural phenomenon: A widely held theory is that the spheres are the result of natural geological processes. These processes may have created the spherical structures through the slow deposition of minerals in subterranean cavities or layers.

Meteorite fragments: Another theory suggests that the spheres could be the remains of meteorites that fell to Earth billions of years ago. These fragments could have been formed by erosion and other geological processes, explaining their unusual shape and structure.

Early life forms: It has also been speculated that the spheres may have biological origins, possibly as fossilized remains of microorganisms or other primitive life forms. However, this theory is considered unlikely by most scientists, as there is no direct evidence of biological structures.

In addition to scientific explanations, the Klerksdorp spheres have also given rise to a number of speculative and controversial theories:

Some proponents of the pre-astronautics theory, which states that extraterrestrial civilizations visited Earth in the past, view the spheres as possible artifacts of extraterrestrial origin. They argue that the spheres' perfect shape and precise grooves could indicate advanced technology.

Another speculative theory suggests that the spheres are relics of an ancient, advanced civilization that existed on Earth billions of years ago.

However, this theory is highly controversial and is largely rejected by the scientific community.

Despite extensive investigations and analyses, the exact origin and creation of these objects remains unclear.

9.8. The Treasure of Oak Island

Oak Island, a small island off the coast of Nova Scotia, Canada, has been the scene of one of history's greatest treasure-hunting mysteries for over two centuries. The legend of the Oak Island crypto hoard has attracted numerous adventurers, historians, and researchers, all attempting to solve the mystery of the supposedly buried treasure.

The story began in 1795, when a young man named Daniel McGinnis discovered a mysterious, round depression in the ground on Oak Island. He and his friends began digging and encountered a layer of stones about a meter below the surface. This piqued their curiosity, and they continued digging, periodically encountering further layers of wooden planks and other materials.

Over the years, the hole, which became known as the "Money Pit," was further excavated by various groups of treasure hunters. In ever deeper layers, they found clues such as coconut fibers pointing to tropical origins and marked stones with enigmatic inscriptions.

The Money Pit's structure is unique and complex. At regular intervals of approximately 3 meters, excavations encountered horizontal oak platforms separated by layers of clay or coal. These carefully constructed layers led to the assumption that the pit is connected to a system of flood tunnels, which were activated during further excavations and quickly filled the pit with water.

Many theories surround who buried the treasure and what it might contain. Here are some of the most prominent:
Pirates: A widespread theory states that the treasure was buried by famous pirates such as Captain Kidd or Blackbeard. This theory is supported by the island's proximity to known pirate routes.

Temples: Another popular theory suggests that the Knights Templar may have buried the treasure, possibly the legendary treasure of the Templar Order, including religious relics such as the Holy Grail or the Ark of the Covenant.

Spanish conquistadors: It is also believed that the treasure came from Spanish conquistadors who brought back gold and other treasures from the New World during their conquests.

Freemasons: Given the Money Pit's complex architecture and mysterious inscriptions, there are also theories that suggest a connection to the Freemasons and their secret rituals and treasures.

During the 20th and 21st centuries, numerous expeditions and technical surveys have been conducted on Oak Island to unravel the mystery of the Money Pit. These modern efforts have led to significant discoveries, including ancient tools, wooden structures, and human remains, further substantiating the legend.

One particularly notable project is the TV documentary series "The Curse of Oak Island," which has aired since 2014. The series follows brothers Rick and Marty Lagina and their team in their attempts to solve the island's mystery. They have used various advanced techniques, including ground-penetrating radar, drilling, and diving in the flood tunnels, to find further clues.

Despite numerous expeditions and discoveries, the exact nature and contents of the treasure remain a mystery.

9.9 The Secret of the Crystal Skulls

Crystal skulls are archaeological mysteries of modern times. These quartz skulls, discovered in various parts of the world, have attracted researchers, historians, and esotericists alike, spawning numerous theories and speculations about their origins and purpose.

The crystal skulls are carved from clear or smoky quartz crystals and vary in size and detail. Some skulls are life-size and extremely detailed, while others are smaller and more stylized. The most famous crystal skulls are the "Mitchell-Hedges Skull," the "British Museum Skull," and the "Paris Skull," each of which is housed in various collections and museums.

Crystal skulls first received significant attention in the early 20th century, when British adventurer and explorer Frederick Albert Mitchell-Hedges claimed to have discovered a crystal skull in the ruins of Lubaantun, an ancient Mayan city in Belize, in 1924. The skull, known as the Mitchell-Hedges Skull, is considered one of the most impressive and best-crafted crystal skulls.
Other significant skulls were discovered or brought to public attention in the following decades, including the British Museum Skull and the Paris Skull, both housed in Europe. However, their exact origin and age are disputed.

There are numerous theories about the origin and purpose of crystal skulls:

Pre-Columbian artifacts: One theory suggests that the skulls belong to pre-Columbian cultures such as the Maya or Aztecs and were used as religious or ceremonial objects. However, this theory is disputed by many scholars due to a lack of archaeological evidence and stylistic differences.

Modern forgeries: Research has shown that some of the crystal skulls were likely made in the 19th or 20th century using modern tools. These findings have given rise to the theory that most or all of the skulls are fakes, created by skilled artisans to deceive collectors and museums.

Extraterrestrial origins: A popular but controversial theory claims that crystal skulls originate from extraterrestrial civilizations. Supporters of this theory believe the skulls were either left on Earth by extraterrestrial visitors or were created using advanced technology unavailable to ancient civilizations.

Many esoteric and spiritual groups believe that crystal skulls possess mystical powers. They are said to have healing properties, store information, or serve as a means of communication with higher dimensions or extraterrestrial civilizations. This theory is supported by numerous New Age literature and speculations.

Modern scientific research has attempted to unravel the mystery of the crystal skulls. Using methods such as electron microscopy and X-ray crystallography, researchers have analyzed the manufacturing techniques and the age of the skulls. Most results indicate that many of the crystal skulls were made using modern tools, supporting the theory of modern forgeries.
Nevertheless, some skulls, such as the Mitchell-Hedges skull, remain enigmatic because their precision and detail are difficult to explain. However, these studies have not provided definitive evidence of pre-Columbian or extraterrestrial origins.

9.10. The strange noises in the catacombs of Paris

The Catacombs of Paris are a network of labyrinthine underground tunnels and chambers stretching more than 300 kilometers beneath the French capital. Originally used as stone quarries, the catacombs were used in the late 18th century to store the remains of overflowing Parisian cemeteries. The remains of over six million people are stored there. In addition to their dark history and the eerie sight of stacked bones and skulls, the catacombs are also known for a number of strange and unexplained sounds, which are repeatedly reported by visitors and researchers.

Visitors and researchers of the catacombs have reported various strange and often disturbing noises over the years. Among the most common reports are:

Whispers and voices: Many people report hearing whispers and indistinct voices in the deep tunnels, even though they are in a seemingly empty part of the catacombs. These voices often sound as if they are coming from a distance or standing right next to you, even though no one is visible.

Steps: Footsteps are another common sound heard in the catacombs. These footsteps can be heavy and muffled or light and quick, and sometimes seem to be following or approaching the listener.

Knocking and scratching: Some reports speak of repeated knocking or scratching noises on the walls or from the deeper, darker parts of the catacombs. These sounds are particularly eerie, as they give the impression that someone or something is trying to escape from the vault.

Lamentations and Music: Rare, but particularly eerie, reports describe hearing dirges or eerie music echoing through the tunnels. These sounds are difficult to locate and seem to come from different directions simultaneously.

There are several theories that attempt to explain the strange noises in the catacombs:

A natural explanation could be the special acoustics of the catacombs. The winding tunnels and chambers can reflect and amplify sound in unusual ways, resulting in echoes and acoustic illusions. Sounds from the surface or other parts of the catacombs could reverberate through the tunnels and be distorted.

Another explanation could be air currents. The catacombs are known for their complex air circulation patterns. Air currents flowing through the tunnels could produce unusual noises that could sound like whistling, murmuring, or knocking.

However, the gloomy atmosphere and history of the catacombs could also affect visitors' senses, making them more susceptible to auditory hallucinations. The expectation of experiencing something sinister could lead to ordinary sounds being interpreted as supernatural.

Some people, however, believe the sounds are due to paranormal activity. Given the millions of dead whose remains lie in the catacombs, it is speculated that the souls of the deceased may still linger there, attempting to communicate with the world of the living.

The strange noises in the catacombs of Paris remain a fascinating and eerie mystery. While there may be natural explanations for many of these phenomena, the fact that so many people have independently experienced similar things remains remarkable. Whether they are acoustic illusions, psychological effects, or something supernatural, the sounds contribute to the catacombs' dark and mysterious aura.

9.11 The enigmatic faces of Belmez

These strange apparitions first appeared in the 1970s in the small Spanish village of Belmez de la Moraleda. Since then, the faces of Belmez have attracted researchers, skeptics, and curious observers from all over the world, seeking to unravel the secrets behind these mysterious images.

The story of the faces of Belmez began in August 1971, when María Gómez Cámara discovered a strange stain pattern on the kitchen floor of her house. Upon closer inspection, it became apparent that the pattern appeared to depict a human face. The family initially attempted to remove the face by picking at the concrete floor and replastering it. But to their astonishment, the face reappeared after a short time, and soon other faces followed.
The faces in Belmez vary in size, expression, and detail. Some are clearly recognizable, while others appear more blurred. The images depict both male and female faces of various ages. The faces also appear to change over time, with new faces appearing and old ones disappearing or fading.

Many believe that the faces of Belmez are a paranormal phenomenon, possibly ghostly apparitions or manifestations of energies from the afterlife. This theory is supported by the fact that human remains were found beneath María Gómez Cámara's house, possibly from an ancient cemetery.

Skeptics have suggested that the faces are the result of chemical reactions in the concrete floor. They suspect that certain minerals and moisture in the soil interact to form the spots that resemble faces. However, this theory has not been confirmed by numerous analyses and tests.

Another theory is that the faces were intentionally created by humans, possibly through the use of chemicals or pigments. This theory has been supported by some tests that found traces of zinc, lead, and chromium in the concrete floor. However, there is no conclusive evidence to definitively confirm this claim.

A psychological phenomenon known as pareidolia may also play a role. Pareidolia is the human brain's tendency to recognize patterns in random or unclear images, such as faces in clouds or rocks. This could explain why the faces appear so distinct to some people.

Over the years, numerous scientific investigations have been conducted to shed light on the origin of the Belmez faces. Researchers have taken soil samples, conducted chemical analyses, and examined the images under various lighting conditions. Despite these efforts, the exact cause of the faces remains unsolved.

The faces of Belmez have fascinated not only the scientific community but also the general public. María Gómez Cámara's house has become a tourist attraction, and the phenomenon has been covered in documentaries, books, and television programs.

While some plausible explanations have been suggested, there is no definitive answer to the question of how and why these faces appear.

9.12. The Marree Man-Geoglyph in Australia

The Marree Man geoglyph was discovered in June 1998 by a charter pilot named Trevor Wright, who was flying over the desert region near the small town of Marree, South Australia. Wright noticed the giant figure in the red sand.

The geoglyph, also known as Stuart's Giant, is one of the largest and most enigmatic works of art in the world. This gigantic depiction of a human outline, drawn into the desert landscape of South Australia, is approximately 4.2 kilometers long and covers an area of approximately 2.6 square kilometers. The figure's outline is about 35 centimeters deep and up to 30 meters wide, making the geoglyph clearly visible from the air.

It depicts the stylized figure of a man who appears to be holding a throwing stick or boomerang in his hand.

The origin of the Marree Man geoglyph remains unclear to this day. Despite extensive research and speculation, there is no definitive answer as to who created the image and for what reason.

One theory is that it was created by modern artists or a group of individuals who wanted to keep their identities secret. However, there is no concrete evidence or known individuals who have claimed responsibility for this act.

It has been speculated that the geoglyph could be a modern homage to the art of Australia's Indigenous peoples. The depicted man and throwing stick may indicate traditional hunting practices important to the Aboriginal people.

Some believe the geoglyph was created as a public relations stunt or advertising gimmick to attract attention and potentially generate economic benefits for the region. Again, there is a lack of concrete evidence or accountability.

9.13 The mysterious underwater "pyramids"

The discovery of mysterious underwater pyramid-like structures has caused a worldwide sensation in recent decades. These submarine formations, reminiscent of the monumental structures of ancient civilizations, have become a spectacular puzzle for scientists, archaeologists, and adventurers. From Japan to the Bahamas, these "pyramids" raise questions about their origins, their purpose, and the possibility of past, advanced civilizations.

The Pyramids of Yonaguni, Japan

The pyramids of Yonaguni, Japan, are among the archaeological mysteries of recent times. In 1986, Japanese diver Kihachiro Aratake accidentally stumbled upon an underwater structure that left him speechless. Off the coast of the small island of Yonaguni, on the southwestern edge of the Japanese archipelago, at a depth of approximately 25 meters, lay a massive, rectangular rock formation that, at first glance, appeared to be man-made. Giant steps, platforms, and seemingly symmetrical surfaces lined up like monumental structures, quickly giving rise to the name "Pyramids of Yonaguni."

Since this discovery, researchers have debated whether this is a purely geological phenomenon or the remains of an ancient, unknown civilization. At first glance, the massive terraces appear to be man-made structures. Right angles, flat platforms, and column-like structures are reminiscent of temples, altars, or pyramids. Particularly impressive is a kind of monumental staircase that appears to be carved into the rock. Those who see these images for the first time inevitably think of the ruins of great civilizations—only underwater.

However, geologists point out that the region around Yonaguni is known for its tectonic activity and regular earthquakes. The rock from which the structure is composed is highly layered and tends to form straight edges and step-like shapes when fractured. From this perspective, the Yonaguni formations are nothing more than the result of natural erosion, amplified by the power of the sea, which has eroded the stones over millennia.

But other scientists disagree. In particular, Japanese professor Masaaki Kimura of the University of Ryukyus was convinced that the precision and interplay of the formations could explain more than just natural forces. Kimura spent decades studying the structures and interpreted them as the remains of a sunken city. He believed he could identify walls, streets, and even carved figures. For him, the pyramids were evidence of a highly developed culture that may have existed more than 10,000 years ago and was engulfed by the rising sea levels after the last ice age.

This theory fits perfectly with legends that tell of sunken continents like Atlantis or Mu—mythical civilizations supposedly swallowed by the tides of the world's oceans. Proponents of this view see Yonaguni as proof that human history may be far older and more complex than we previously assumed.

There is also a mediating hypothesis that assumes a combination of nature and culture. According to this hypothesis, nature could have created the basic forms through tectonic fractures and erosion, which were then further modified by humans. Thus, originally natural structures could have evolved into cult sites, meeting places, or even buildings.

What makes the discussion even more fascinating is the lack of conclusive archaeological finds. Neither tools nor pottery nor other artifacts that would conclusively prove human activity have been discovered so far. This makes it difficult to settle the question. Proponents of the civilization theory argue that traces of humans have long since been washed away by ocean currents. Critics counter that there is no known case of large structures without accompanying artifacts – and that geology provides the most plausible explanation.

Regardless, Yonaguni remains a fascinating place. Divers from all over the world travel there to see the massive steps and platforms with their own eyes. Some report an almost awe-inspiring feeling as they float through the stone alleys, which resemble the remains of an ancient city. It's as if witnessing a meeting of nature and myth.

Fun fact: Some researchers have even seen patterns in the structures that they interpreted as carved animals or faces—including a supposed "turtle" and a "human mask." Whether these are genuine carvings or simply the work of nature remains unclear to this day.

The pyramids of Yonaguni are therefore more than just a geological curiosity.

Die „Bimini Road", Bahamas

The "Bimini Road" in the Bahamas is one of the most famous and controversial underwater structures in the world. Its discovery in 1968 marked the beginning of a debate that continues to this day: Is it a purely natural phenomenon or the remains of a long-lost civilization?

Off the coast of North Bimini, just a few meters below the water's surface, lies a formation of massive limestone blocks. It lies about 5.5 meters below the water's surface and extends for about 800 meters. The formation consists of large limestone blocks arranged in a nearly straight line. Each block measures about 3 to 4 meters long and 2 to 3 meters wide, with a thickness of about one meter. Some blocks are rectangular, others have more irregular shapes. Together, they form an almost perfectly straight line stretching for some 800 meters, like a road leading directly into the depths of the ocean. This arrangement inevitably evokes associations with human construction—a road, a wall, perhaps even the remains of an ancient harbor.

Speculation began shortly after the discovery, and it wasn't long before the Bimini Road was linked to the legend of Atlantis. The American prophet Edgar Cayce had already prophesied in the 1930s that the remains of Atlantis would rise in the Bahamas. When divers actually discovered a stone "road" just a few decades later, many saw this as confirmation of his words. The media enthusiastically seized on the story, and soon the Bimini Road was considered one of the hottest leads to Plato's sunken continent.

Archaeologists and geologists, however, reacted more soberly. They pointed out that limestone in the region occurs in large layers, which can break up and form edges due to tectonic processes, ocean currents, and erosion. These natural processes regularly create cuboid-shaped slabs of rock reminiscent of human paving stones. Undersea currents can then further expose them and arrange them into formations that appear artificial. From this perspective, the Bimini Road is nothing more than a freak of nature—fascinating, yes, but not man-made.

But the proponents of the Atlantis theory are not so easily convinced. They point to the regularity of the blocks, their seemingly planned arrangement, and the way some of them lie on top of each other, almost like an ancient wall. Some see the structure as the remains of an ancient harbor, built several thousand years ago, when sea levels were lower and large parts of the Bahamas were habitable. Radiocarbon dating of shells and corals attached to the stones has revealed ages of between 2,000 and 4,000 years ago—a period in which advanced civilizations were already flourishing in the Mediterranean. Could it be, then, that peoples also lived in the Atlantic whose buildings are now swallowed up by the sea?

In addition, the formation is not alone. Divers report seeing smaller, parallel structures nearby that appear like additional roads or walls. Some speak of rectangular platforms that give the impression of foundations. These observations, Atlantis proponents argue, can hardly be explained by geology alone.

The Bimini Road therefore remains a point of contention between two worlds: sober science, which recognizes geological processes in the stone blocks, and speculative archaeology, which sees them as the remains of a lost civilization. The tension between these two perspectives is what makes this place so fascinating.

Today, the Bimini Road is a popular destination for divers and snorkelers. Those who descend there swim over enormous slabs of stone that appear to have been built by a forgotten culture, while colorful fish swim among the boulders. Many report that the sight evokes a sense of awe—even if they're convinced it's "just" geology.

The legend of the Bimini Road has also entered pop culture. Numerous documentaries, novels, and even computer games portray the stone road as the gateway to Atlantis. Some see it not just a road, but part of a massive structure still hidden beneath the sand and mud.

Whether the Bimini Road is a geological wonder or the last visible evidence of an ancient culture may never be definitively determined. But that's precisely what makes it so fascinating.

The Pyramids of Cuba

In 2001, a discovery off the coast of Cuba made headlines and continues to captivate explorers and adventurers alike. A Canadian research team led by marine engineer Paulina Zelitsky and her husband Paul Weinzweig, using modern sonar technology to examine the seafloor off the Guanahacabibes Peninsula, came across what appeared to be the remains of a gigantic, sunken city. At depths of over 600 meters, the sonar revealed monumental structures. In addition to the pyramids, there are several rectangular structures that could look like buildings or temples. These objects are arranged symmetrically, indicating a complex and planned construction.

The sonar images also show evidence of roads or platforms connecting the various structures.

Particularly striking were two massive, pyramid-shaped structures, which at first glance bore striking similarities to the well-known structures of Egypt. Their clearly recognizable edges and symmetrical shapes cast doubt on whether they could be merely a natural phenomenon. Alongside them were rectangular structures that resembled the foundations of buildings, as well as platforms and linear formations that some researchers interpreted as streets. The overall picture was reminiscent of the ruins of an ancient city—except that it lay deep beneath the water's surface.

The discovery immediately sparked speculation. Some saw the Cuban pyramids as evidence of a previously unknown advanced civilization that may have existed more than 10,000 years ago, at a time when sea levels rose dramatically after the end of the last ice age. This rise would have flooded entire landmasses and swallowed civilizations, whose traces may now lie hidden at the bottom of the ocean. Parallels to legends like Atlantis or Mu were quickly drawn, and some media outlets even referred to them as the "Atlantis of the Caribbean."

But the scientific community quickly dampened the euphoria. Critics pointed out that geological processes such as volcanic activity, tectonic shifts, and erosion can also produce regular, rectangular, and step-like structures. Such formations could have occurred naturally, particularly in the Caribbean region, which is characterized by complex plate tectonics. The fact that the discovery was located at a depth of over 600 meters also made it difficult to explore: Normal diving is impossible in these zones, and even remotely operated underwater vehicles quickly reach their limits.

Zelitsky and Weinzweig published sonar images and short video recordings that were indeed impressive: huge, regular blocks reminiscent of monumental structures. But without systematic excavations and physical samples, the interpretation remained uncertain. While the researchers themselves remained cautious, emphasizing that "it is not yet known whether these are natural formations or man-made structures," the media and mystery writers quickly adopted the more spectacular version—a sunken civilization in the Caribbean.

Since then, myths and legends have surrounded the so-called Pyramids of Cuba. Some theories see them as the remains of an ancient culture, far older than the Maya or Aztecs, whose knowledge was lost at sea. Others link the discovery to the hypothesis of "primordial civilizations" that are said to have existed 12,000 years ago, before the floods following the Ice Age engulfed large parts of the coastal regions.

The scientific community, however, is demanding more data. Without extensive expeditions, which would cost millions, it remains difficult to definitively determine the nature of these structures. Added to this is the political situation: Cuba was not easily accessible in the early 2000s, and international research projects were difficult to implement.

To date, research on the Cuban pyramids has made little progress. There are neither published large-scale studies nor archaeological finds that could prove their construction by humans. Yet the silence surrounding the structures only makes them more mysterious. For many adventurers and conspiracy theorists, the Caribbean Sea thus represents another chapter in the long history of sunken worlds, reminding us that the oceans may conceal more than we imagine.

And so the question remains: Are the Pyramids of Cuba a natural wonder, formed by the forces of geology? Or, deep in the darkness of the ocean, do they actually lie the remains of an ancient city forgotten by history? The only thing that is certain is that the sea has kept its secrets well.

9.14 The Bat Bomb

The bat bomb, one of the most curious weapons developments of World War II, was a project that would take shape in the United States.

In the laboratories of Lytle Adams, an American scientist with a penchant for unusual solutions, the idea of using millions of Mexican free-tailed bats as biological bombs was developed.
The plan: The bats would be dropped over Japan in special bombs. Once they reached their target, they would hide in Japan's numerous wooden buildings and detonate small incendiary bombs attached to their bodies.
The hope was that the many small fires would quickly spread into a major blaze and thus cause massive damage to Japanese infrastructure.
The Mexican free-tailed bat was chosen based on several factors:
It was large enough to carry a small incendiary bomb, it occurred in large swarms and was easy to catch, and this bat had the habit of staying in confined spaces such as caves or even buildings.
Initially, millions of bats were to be captured in the southwestern United States. They were then to be packed into special bombs supplied with oxygen to ensure the animals' survival during transport.
The bomb-laden planes would fly over Japan and drop the bat bombs at high altitude. The sudden change in pressure during the drop would activate the bombs and release the bats.
The bats were supposed to disperse throughout the cities and seek shelter in wooden buildings. There, the small incendiary bombs attached to their bodies were supposed to be ignited by body heat or a special mechanism.
The period in which the project was actively pursued was from 1942 to 1945. Although the project seemed promising and several successful test runs were conducted, it was never deployed. There were many reasons for this:
With the impending defeat of Germany and the atomic attacks on Hiroshima and Nagasaki, the project lost its urgency.
Organizing such an attack involving millions of animals would also have been logistically extremely complex and would have required enormous resources.

Even if the bats were to be recaptured after the operation, there were concerns about animal welfare and the possible ecological consequences.

In conclusion, it remains a curious chapter in military history, although military conflicts never had and never have the reputation of contributing to happiness, joy and a better state of the common good.

The Gate to Hell

In the middle of the Karakum Desert, one of the driest regions on earth, a fire has been burning for more than fifty years, attracting and frightening people in equal measure. The Darwaza Gas Crater, better known as the "Gate to Hell," is a gigantic hole approximately seventy meters in diameter, inside which flames blaze incessantly. It acts like a window into the underworld—and yet is the result of a very earthly problem: the Soviet search for natural gas.

The formation of the crater is closely linked to Turkmenistan's history. The region boasts enormous gas reserves and remains one of the world's largest natural gas exporters. As early as the 1960s and 70s, the Soviet Union was committed to systematically exploiting these mineral resources to supply its economy and secure its energy dependence. The Karakum Desert was a promising, albeit inaccessible, area for geologists.

In 1971, Soviet engineers drilled near the village of Darwaza to tap into a new gas source. However, the subsoil proved unstable. During drilling, the ground collapsed beneath the machines, creating a massive crater. Methane—an invisible, highly flammable gas—flowed uncontrollably from the hole. This was a dangerous situation: on the one hand, the methane threatened to escape into the atmosphere, where it is a potent greenhouse gas, and on the other, there was a risk of explosion for people and animals in the surrounding area.

The engineers therefore opted for a solution that seemed obvious at the time, albeit risky: They deliberately ignited the gas. It was expected that the gas reserves would burn out within a few days and the fire would extinguish itself. But the geological layers beneath the desert apparently contained significantly more gas than expected. Days turned into weeks, weeks into years – and now the "Gate to Hell" has been burning continuously for over five decades.

The question of whether the fire could be extinguished repeatedly arose. Theoretically, it would be possible to fill the crater with sand, earth, or concrete to cut off the oxygen supply. In practice, such plans have so far failed due to the sheer size and depth of the hole. Moreover, the gas is escaping not only from isolated sources, but from a widespread network of underground reservoirs. Even if the crater were sealed, there would be a risk that the gas would escape elsewhere and spark new fires. So, the efforts remained mere political announcements: The Turkmen government repeatedly declared its intention to extinguish the fire, but these efforts were never implemented.

The "Gate to Hell" is unique today, but not entirely without comparison. Underground coal or gas fires burn for decades or even centuries in other countries as well. In India, for example, an underground fire has been smoldering in the Jharia coalfield for over a hundred years, threatening entire villages. In the USA, an underground coal fire has existed in Centralia, Pennsylvania, since 1962, turning a small town into a ghost town. The Darwaza Crater differs, however, in one respect: While most of these fires rage invisibly underground, it is an open spectacle of flames and heat – a "Gate to Hell" that can be seen with one's own eyes.

Today, the crater has become a curious attraction. Adventurous tourists travel in jeeps through the Karakum Desert to stand on the edge of the pit and gaze into the blazing depths. The heat is so intense that it can be felt from several meters away. For Turkmenistan, the "Gate to Hell" is both a symbol and a warning: a metaphor for the country's vast energy reserves – and for the uncontrollable consequences when humans believe they have nature under control.

9.15 The Turkish Chess Automaton

The Chess Turk, also known as "The Turkish Chess Automaton" or simply "The Chess Automaton", is one of the mysterious deceptions and inventions of the 18th century.

This device, disguised as a chess-playing automaton, was constructed by Wolfgang von Kempelen in 1770 and played chess games against human opponents, giving the impression that it was an independently operating machine. In fact, the Chess Turk was a clever illusion that used a hidden human chess master to control the machine's moves.

The Chess Turk consisted of a large chess table equipped with chess pieces, upon which sat a life-size figure in Turkish clothing. The apparatus was designed to challenge a human opponent to a game of chess. The Turk figure, complete with turban and oriental garb, sat behind the chess table and moved the chess pieces at the command of the hidden operator.

The illusion was made possible by the careful construction of the cabinet beneath the chess table. Before the game, the cabinet was opened to reveal that it was filled with complex mechanical devices. However, these devices were largely dummies. In reality, the cabinet was designed to conceal a human chess player who controlled the game through an ingenious system of levers and gears.

The chess automaton was demonstrated in many European courts and caused a great sensation. The machine defeated many prominent figures of its time, including Napoleon Bonaparte and Benjamin Franklin. People were amazed by the machine's apparent intelligence, and the secrecy surrounding its mechanism only added to its mystification.

One of the most impressive performances of the Chess Turk took place in 1809, when it played against Napoleon Bonaparte. Fascinated by the machine, Napoleon attempted to outsmart the Chess Turk by making illegal moves. The Chess Turk responded by returning the pieces to their original positions and continuing the game, arousing Napoleon's astonishment and admiration.

The truth about the Chess Turk remained a well-kept secret for a long time.

It wasn't until the 1820s that the writer Edgar Allan Poe published a detailed analysis debunking the deception. Poe's article "Maelzel's Chess-Player" revealed that a human player inside the cabinet controlled the machine's moves. Despite this revelation, the Chess Turk remained a popular attraction and continued to be performed.

Although the automaton was an illusion, it demonstrated people's enthusiasm for the idea of machines that could mimic human behavior. The Chess Turk remains a significant example of the combination of mechanics, illusion, and human ingenuity.

In summary, it was one of the most remarkable deceptions of the 18th century.

Closing words

I encourage you to share what you've read with friends and family. Discuss the curious facts and amazing stories you've discovered here. There's nothing more beautiful than sharing knowledge and enthusiasm and marveling together.

*A heartfelt thank you to everyone who has read this book. Your interest and curiosity are what make this book come alive.
Stay curious and open to the wonders of the world. There's still so much to discover!*

For interested readers, there is more to discover here:

https://www.amazon.com/stores/Michael-Arrow/author/B0DQDN3L2C?language=de&ref=ap_rdr&isDramIntegrated=true&shoppingPortalEnabled=true

imprint

Texte & Cover: © Copyright by Michael Arrow

All rights reserved.
This book or parts thereof may not be reproduced, duplicated, or distributed in any form without the written permission of the author.

Disclaimer
The information in this book has been compiled with the utmost care. However, the author assumes no liability for the accuracy, completeness, or timeliness of the content. Use of the content is at your own risk..

Photo credits
All illustrations in this book were generated using artificial intelligence (ChatGPT/DALL·E, OpenAI).

Printed in Dunstable, United Kingdom